COMING TO KNOW

D1630632

N 0029874 3

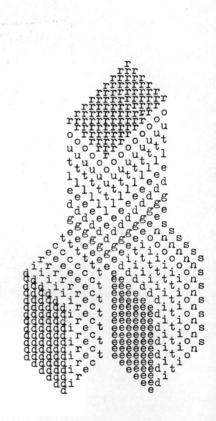

COMING TO KNOW

Edited by
PHILLIDA SALMON
Institute of Education
University of London

ROUTLEDGE & KEGAN PAUL
London, Boston and Henley

First published in 1980
by Routledge & Kegan Paul Ltd
39 Store Street,
London WC1E 7DD,
9 Park Street
Boston, Mass. 02108, USA and
Broadway House,
Newtown Road,
Henley-on-Thames,
Oxon RG9 1EN
Printed in Great Britain by
Redwood Burn Ltd Trowbridge & Esher

British Library Cataloguing in Publication Data

Coming to know
    1. Learning, Psychology of
    I. Salmon, Phillida
    153.1'5   BF318   80-40087

ISBN 0 7100 0455 9

CONTENTS

NOTES ON CONTRIBUTORS

MARY C. BAUR BA (Sussex) is Residential Child Care Officer in an independent school for maladjusted boys.

NICHOLAS P. EMLER BSc (Soton) PhD (London) is Lecturer in Psychology (Developmental and Social) in the Department of Psychology at the University of Dundee.

KAY FROST MA Hons, Dip. Clin. Psychol. is Senior Clinical Psychologist at the Royal Free Hospital.

JAGDISH S. GUNDARA BA, MA, PhD is Co-ordinator of the Centre for Multiracial Education at the Institute of Education, University of London.

NICK HEATHER BA, MSc, PhD is Senior Research Fellow in the Department of Psychiatry at the University of Dundee.

MILLER MAIR PhD is Psychologist at Crichton Royal, Dumfries.

ALAN RADLEY BTech. (Brunel), PhD (London) is Lecturer in Social Psychology in the Department of Social Sciences at Loughborough University.

HAROLD ROSEN BA, PhD is Professor and Head of the Department of the Teaching of English (Mother Tongue) at the Institute of Education, University of London.

PHILLIDA SALMON MA, PhD is Senior Lecturer in Child Development at the Institute of Education, University of London.

DAVID J. SMAIL BA, PhD is Area Psychologist, Notts Area Psychology Service, and Special Professor of Clinical Psychology at the University of Nottingham.

MARGARET SPENCER MA is Senior Lecturer in the Department of English at the Institute of Education, University of London.

INTRODUCTION
Phillida Salmon

When I think about myself in relation to what I have come to know,
several episodes in my life seem to stand out as particularly
important. One of these goes back to quite early childhood. Between the age of 7 and 10, I was not able to master the telephone.
I couldn't tell which end was which, and so it was always a matter
of chance which end I put to my mouth and which to my ear. As I
had to use the telephone at home about once a week to arrange a
lesson with a local violin-teacher, I regularly experienced the
shame of my very visible incompetence being witnessed by the five
other children in my family, whose scorn, disbelief or kindly rescue
were the usual sequel to my attempts at telephoning. In those days,
the earpiece and mouthpiece of telephones were more clearly differentiated than they are nowadays. There was certainly nothing wrong
with my eyesight; I was good at jigsaw puzzles, and I had a collection of very small china animals whose tiny details I often
dwelt on. And there must have been very many times when my aunt,
with patience and love, tried to help me connect the different
shapes of the receiver with where I should put them - as well as the
frequent, often exasperated instructions of the other children.
Yet, despite my adequate perceptual equipment and the teaching I
received, I could not, over several years, acquire this piece of
learning. (I stopped having violin lessons at 10, so this particular skill ceased to be needed then.)
    I now think the reason I could not learn to use the telephone
properly was that what I already knew about myself completely ruled
out the possibility of learning it. When it came to sports, physical or practical skills, finding your way about places, or knowing
where things were kept - in all these areas I was stupid and incompetent. I knew I was stupid, and I was known to be stupid. Because of this, nothing that could have increased my competence was
able to register with me. I don't think I really saw the telephone
receiver clearly, or actually heard the helpful things people said.
I just experienced, time after time, the same sickening, miserable
anticipation that yet again I was going to show myself up - and
that is what always happened.
    Some years later, when I was about 15, I had begun really to
enjoy playing the piano. My school music-teacher decided one day

1

that I should learn a piece by Beethoven. The piece she chose was
a bagatelle, which technically was easier than some of the other
pieces I had learned to play. But when I tried to learn it, I
seemed unable to master it; I couldn't get the notes or the rhythm
quite right, and I had a sense that I wasn't able, somehow, to
interpret the music. My teacher endorsed these feelings by eventually declaring that I had better drop the attempt to learn the
piece, and adding that perhaps, after all, Beethoven 'wasn't my
composer'.

   This judgment made me rather sad, but it didn't really surprise
me. I was familiar with several Beethoven symphonies, and loved
them. I also knew and liked some of Beethoven's piano music; but
this was almost entirely through hearing it played by my cousin
Stephen, who played virtually no other composer. Somehow this made
Beethoven piano music his. The sonatas and bagatelles belonged to
Stephen, and that meant I had no right to the music. There was no
question of his objecting to my learning something by Beethoven;
yet I knew that I was not entitled to make it my own. In one sense,
I suppose, I had the knowledge, the capacity, to play Beethoven;
but I was not free to draw upon that knowledge, because I could not
feel it to be mine. This had to do with family boundaries of
personal identity, which defined what kinds of orientations and
understandings one could and could not claim for oneself.

   At that time in my life I had been at a boarding school for three
years. I don't think I looked back much, then, to the period when I
had been a new girl at school. But in those early days I was
constantly being brought up against my own ignorance about how
things were and what one had to do. It seemed that I knew absolutely nothing. There were so many bewildering references to events
and experiences that I could not make out at all. What were comic
cuts, what did it mean to go over the way, or to be sent to report?
The daily routine was equally mysterious. The other girls seemed to
be as surprised as I was that I did not know that pupils never used
the front staircase, that you did not go up to the dormitories
before 5 o'clock, or that the bottom sheet went to the wash and the
top sheet went to the bottom when you changed the bed for the
laundry. Going in to tea on the first day of term, I was met by
amazed looks; somehow I had failed to know what everyone else knew,
that you changed out of your school tunic before tea. About the
other people there, my ignorance was equally vast. How was I ever
going to distinguish between so many faces, let alone learn all
their names? There was so much that I did not understand, either,
in the talk I heard. It was not that I did not know the terms; but
I could not grasp the meaning of those significant looks, or sudden
giggles, or anxious expressions, or weary sighs. It seemed to me
then that there was a whole world of knowledge that I was not in on,
and where nothing that I did know was of any use to me. Sometimes I
used to despair of ever being able to learn all that needed to be
known ... and yet, three years later, there I was, a part of my
school world, at home in its daily routines, taking its mode of
life completely for granted, and experiencing the present from
within its familiar framework. How on earth had I come to know so
much? No one had instructed me. I seemed simply to have absorbed
it all by some mysterious osmosis.

When I was well into adult life, and working in a hospital setting, I carried out some collaborative research with a psychiatrist who was interested in alcoholism. In doing this research, I came to experience another aspect of the complex process of knowing. The central question in the project was how alcoholics see themselves, and whether there are certain common themes in their self-perceptions that are not shared by other people. To try to answer this question I became involved, over about a year, in individual testing sessions with a large number of men. The task I asked them to do was of judging people from their photographs. Making inferences as well as they could from appearance alone, they ranked in order ten photographs of men, on such characteristics as sociability and strength of character, and on their apparent similarity or dissimilarity to themselves as people, as well as to their personal ideal.

The purpose of this task was to assess whether alcoholics see themselves as the conventional wisdom portrays them - as weak, lonely, very different from how they would like to be, and so on. However, I gradually became preoccupied with something at a tangent to that question - with the way that people seem to define their ideal self. Early on in the research, I noticed something rather odd about the choices people made for this judgment. They nearly always seemed to choose, for the person they would prefer to be, the face which was most similar to their own. This did not happen when they were choosing the person who seemed closest to how they actually were. Their perceived real self did not generally look like them; their perceived ideal self almost always did. In case I was merely imagining this, I started to record in advance the photograph that I expected my subjects would choose for their ideal self - the face that I thought looked most like their own. Sure enough, that would typically be the one they picked. And this tendency was not confined to alcoholics; it was no less characteristic of the other psychiatric patients and the male nurses who served as our comparison groups.

The more I brooded over what this phenomenon might possibly mean, the more it seemed to tie in with aspects of my own relationship with myself of which I was dimly aware. My test results suggested that when people make comparisons between themselves and others, they tend to distance themselves from that part of their experience which is directional, striving, evaluative. At least, they distance themselves from it to the extent that the perceived ideal self is usually very different from the perceived actual self. But paradoxically they also express the closest possible identity with it by clothing it in the nearest approximation to their own physical image, that is by choosing the face most like their own. One feature of this situation is that others would more easily recognize a person in his/her ideal self aspect than as his/her 'real' self; and yet, probably it is the other way round for the person himself/herself. This seemed to me to be a matter of knowing and yet not knowing - of experiencing a large part of oneself as not really one's self. As I thought about it, I realized that my own experience of myself was very much like that. The person who was really me lived in constant awareness of another sort of person, who was always there with me, but was not me. That person continually made comments on me and my life, often being critical and sometimes inspiring. In this inner relationship, however, I was always subservient. The peculiar findings I had noticed in my research enabled me, for the first time in my life, to question this situation. I began to see that my values, my moral strictures, my hopes for myself, were every bit as much me as - the rest of me. It occurred to me too that in my experience of people whom I knew well, their personal imperatives featured just as strongly as other things about them. The same must be true of the way other people experienced me; the person they knew encompassed the ideal self who to me had been a kind of separate person living with me. This realization was very liberating. It became possible to feel a personal ownership of things that had always seemed outside and beyond me. It also enabled me to think about and question some of my values, which till then had always seemed beyond the possibility of question.

A few years ago I decided to start taking piano lessons again. I was fortunate enough, for a year, to have a teacher from whom I was able to learn a great deal. When I try to define what exactly I did learn, and how I learnt it, quite a lot seems to be involved. Some of this has to do with a general enlargement of what playing the piano means. The dimensions of loudness, speed and lightness now form part of the choices I am able to make. Of course I already knew the meaning of these terms, and I had been able to play both loudly and softly, quickly and slowly, and lightly and heavily before I started having these particular lessons. What is different now is that I have deliberately experienced varying my playing of particular pieces and phrases in terms of these and other dimensions. This has meant, for instance, rattling through a slow passage at a vastly speeded-up pace, putting the full weight of one's arm into the playing of a light staccato phrase, or playing a particular section in a new rhythm. By choosing, in a sense, to play things wrongly, I now know more fully than I could otherwise have done what it means to play them correctly. The quietness of a particular passage has more meaning for me because I know how it would sound if it were loud. Creating these variations has also brought a greater sense of control; more possibilities are open to me than were available before, and I am aware of having options in playing where previously I did not really feel in charge of what I was doing.

A quite different aspect of what I seem to have learnt concerns the level at which I experience playing. I used to think of my playing the piano as being a matter of the movements of my fingers, and to a lesser extent of the position of my hands and arms. I do not now experience playing as being located anywhere exactly in my body; it seems instead to consist in my feeling and thinking, which somehow express themselves - without my knowing quite how - in what my body does. No doubt this would not occur to the extent that it does if I did not also frequently practise making particular finger movements and attending closely to what is happening as I try to produce them. But the fact is that when I actually come to play a piece of music my awareness dwells not in my finger movements but in the kind of evocation that the music has for me; and I have come to trust that that awareness will translate itself into what I do, without my being consciously responsible for the way in which it happens.

How did this learning come about? It must have been partly a
matter of the way in which my piano-teacher himself experienced
music, and his own playing. Certainly the deliberate variation of
ways of playing particular passages was, so he said, a basic part
of his practising technique. But this in turn was, I think, one
aspect of a personal assimilation of music into himself. It seemed
to be this assimilation that gave him the freedom to experiment with
different modes of interpretation, rather than being tied to a
single way of playing any particular passage. The same sense of
being part of the music he played seemed to underlie his readiness
to talk about it at the level of feelings and ideas. But for me,
coming to experience and to know these things for myself was only
possible because of my teacher's attitude towards me. In everything
he suggested there was the assumption that I would be able to understand and to use what he said. No doubt seemed to exist about my
ability to play any kind of music. This is not to say that there
was any implication that music could be quickly or easily grasped,
or that some pieces were not a long way beyond my current level of
technical skill. What never seemed to be in question was that I had
it in me, if I was prepared to work, to play anything I felt drawn
to.

All these personal experiences seem to me to have something to do
with knowing and coming to know. Yet, when I look to the psychology
that is current about how people learn, I find that it does not have
much to say to me about my own experience. This is partly because
the definition of learning by psychologists is so very limited. The
name of learning is usually granted only to what is formally taught,
only to what is expressed in verbal or other symbols, only to what
officially goes on in educational institutions. This seems to me
to leave out so much. It leaves out all the learning that takes
place in families, among friends and intimates, at work, and
generally going about living. It leaves out, too, such a lot of
learning that takes place alongside, or even instead of, the formal
educational material that is supposed to represent its real content.
It is because I should like to extend greatly the boundaries of the
whole area that I want to talk about it in terms of knowing and
coming to know. These terms, I think, cover an altogether larger
conceptual sphere, and one that seems better to encompass the
experiences which people actually have in enlarging and trying to
enlarge their understandings.

The psychology of learning also seems to me to fail to help
because it denies the personal character of coming to know. Its
account is couched in terms of generalities that cut across personal
context, personal significance and personal relationships. Yet for
me, the personal nature of knowledge is its most fundamental aspect.
What one knows, in a final sense, one knows about oneself. Who one
is, is inextricably bound up with who one is known to be. Still
other features of the personal nature of knowing are the facts that
people learn through relationships with other people, that knowledge
is never independent of personal meanings and values, and that it is
embedded in social structures and groupings.

It seems to me, therefore, that it is time for a new view of how
people come to know what they do know. This book is an attempt to
formulate some of the perspectives that such a view might take.

In trying to extend our understanding of how people learn, perhaps
it would be useful to examine more in psychology than the aspects
which officially deal with learning. This would mean considering
some of the long-standing and deeply rooted dichotomies in psychology. Of these, perhaps the most significant is the distinction
between thought and feeling. Nowhere is this dichotomy more evident
than in the quite separate psychologies that have been developed to
cover learning and education, on the one hand, and personal crises
and psychotherapy on the other. In its overwhelming emphasis on
thinking, remembering and the acquisition of skill, educational psychology leaves out of account all the emotional aspects that
permeate every learning situation. Clinical psychology, conversely,
concentrates so heavily on the power of feelings as to have the
greatest difficulty in making room for the ideas which people involved in crises bring with them, or for the thinking which they do
while trying to work through these crises. The result of this dichotomy, I want to suggest, is an impoverishment of both areas in
psychology. And the dichotomy that these differentiated psychologies support is not merely an academic matter. It has resulted in
a polarization of people as learners and as sufferers, supposedly
requiring two very different kinds of social institution, with all
that this implies for the separation of some people from others, and
of some aspects from other aspects of ourselves.

The distinction between thinking and feeling so permeates our
language that it is probably impossible to escape it as long as we
use the conventional terms. Perhaps by adopting the concept of
knowing, which, more than most concepts in psychology, blurs the
edges between cognition and affect, we may be enabled to pay some
attention to aspects of people that are common to both educational
and clinical situations. It may be that it will be fruitful, for
our psychology of both situations, to view the things that people
know, and the ways in which they come to know what they know, as
absolutely central to an understanding of them. This would mean
looking at individuals in both educational and psychiatric settings
as people who already possess a great deal of knowledge and who, in
their engagements in these settings, are essentially involved in
coming to know, or failing to come to know, other things. Such a
view would be very different from what is mostly current now.

In different ways, both educational and clinical psychology
neglect the question of what people know, and of all the implications of that knowledge. The psychology of learning and instruction is essentially an impersonal and generalized psychology.
It takes no account of the biography, personal relationships or
social context of the learner; yet, in so far as these features
affect both what people already know, and the modes through which
they are able to learn, they are far from irrelevant. The accepted
principles of human learning also give no importance to the vast
range of tacit knowledge that learners bring with them, that they
assimilate in their learning context, and that that context,
knowingly or unknowingly, conveys. The failure to attend to
personal knowledge also leads to a denial of the socially constructed nature of explicit knowledge. All these features in the
official expertise about education are, of course, implemented in
the ways in which educational institutions are run. The separation

of educational content from personal experience, the authoritarian
relationships, the passive role of the learner, the neglect of
feeling, the non-acknowledgment of alternative views - all these
much-criticized aspects of schools and other places of learning can
be seen to derive from the conventional psychology of how people
learn.

In clinical psychology, the neglect of personal knowledge is
probably part of the heritage of a discipline originally framed in
terms of medical concepts. Among such concepts the key one of
mental illness, by definition, rules out of court all the activities
in which a mind engages. The ideas, thoughts, interpretations and
understandings that a 'mentally ill' person possesses are automatically classed as invalid - if one takes the term literally, at
least. In any case, idiosyncratic features of people, such as their
personal knowledge, are seen as essentially irrelevant to the
generalized condition of an illness. Of course for some time now,
clinical psychologists have been struggling to free themselves from
the medical model in which they have been entrammelled. But since
the very setting in which they function - the hospital - is one
which is derived from medical conceptualizations, it may be very
difficult for them to achieve a view that is genuinely free of these
conceptualizations. Certainly it is easy to see features in
clinical psychological thinking which perpetuate the devaluing of
what psychiatric patients know. The whole psychoanalytic tradition,
still so influential in psychotherapy, tends to deny the significance of all that adults, as adults, know. The very different,
behaviourist, school of thought, in the essentially mechanistic
model underlying it, incorporates a fundamental disrespect for
thought. One of the many consequences of this disrespect is a
translation of the struggle of people against what they know to be
social constraints into a personal failure to adjust. In this way,
a disregard of the importance of personal knowledge leads to an
automatic upholding of the status quo. More generally, the way that
psychotherapy is viewed in clinical psychology shows a basic lack of
attention to the personal knowledge of those involved. This applies
not just to the client at the receiving end, whose idiosyncratic
knowledge is typically omitted from accounts of the psychotherapeutic process; it is just as evident in the formulations of the
training, and the functioning, of the therapist. As a result, many
psychotherapists express a sense of discontinuity and confusion
about the relation between themselves as people and themselves as
therapists.

Taking seriously the idea of people as knowers would mean being
concerned about the kind of knowledge that individuals bring to any
situation - whether educational or clinical. This would certainly
entail some consideration of the childhood setting that a person had
experienced. For most people, this would involve the context of the
family. It is probably difficult to over-estimate the importance of
this setting, for the kinds of things that a person comes to know,
as well as the modes through which he/she learns and the philosophy
he/she holds about knowing. It is through their family lives - via
the complex and inexplicit negotiations that Berger and Luckmann
(1966) have called 'primary socialization' - that children acquire
their taken-for-granted reality. This means coming to know both

'how things are' and 'how things are done'. Such knowledge represents, during the childhood years at least, the unquestioned framework within which life is experienced - that is, within which other things come to be known. Later, through the various kinds of secondary socialization that adult life may involve, it is possible to rework many aspects of the reality-ground of one's experience. But as the first, the long-unchallenged, the extensively lived-in and intimately shared social reality, the initial family context must be tremendously significant in facilitating, or limiting, what a person can come to know.

At their most fundamental, the assumptions that make up the social reality of any family group have to do, perhaps, with the very acquisition of human identity. In the earliest encounters, it seems to be the crediting of young infants, by most mothers, fathers and siblings, with agency, reciprocity and communicative intent, which brings into being those very potentialities. That at least is the conclusion of those who, like Shotter (1975), have closely studied interactions between very young babies and their caretakers. But it is more than a common humanity that gets attributed to new family members. Somehow a specific, idiosyncratic identity is negotiated, through being experienced, conveyed, modified, elaborated and lived out. This distinctive family identity may be enriching or imprisoning; probably it is always partly both. In extreme situations, such as those documented by Laing and Esterson (1964), personal identity as experienced in families may be mystifying and alienating. In other situations family personalities may be set up as highly competitive, polarized or mutually exclusive; the heritage of what may be known will then be diminished for all those involved. Or if the personal identity is a static one, then what may be experienced will stop short at knowledge that would require an altered perspective.

Of course personalities in family groups do become renegotiated. Adolescence is a time when many people make strenuous efforts to establish fresh identities. The fact that this is usually so difficult is perhaps an indication of the strength of childhood family roles, and their influence upon what one may later achieve in the way of personal knowledge. For adolescents, it is certainly a struggle to break out of a previous identity. To act 'out of character', to cease to 'be oneself', among those with whom one's personal identity is firmly lodged, centrally important, and played out in countless large and small ways - to do this is threatening not only to those others, but also to one's own sense of stability and reality. What one is 'supposed' to be and do - a word that typically has a prescriptive meaning when children use it - constitutes a powerful compulsion as to the things one may and may not experience and therefore come to know.

In families, children come to know not just who they, as unique individuals, seem to be; they also find they have a group identity shared by others in the family and by 'our kind of people'. The importance of this group identity is probably a major one. It could perhaps be said to represent the hidden curriculum of the home in relation to a huge range of knowledge and experience. Part of this has to do with ways in which 'we' are set against 'them'. These ways define what possibilities are available, and what are precluded, in terms of social roles, modes of experience and life style. But in a still more general sense, this group identity seems to involve basic assumptions about whether or not things can be expected to make sense, and whether most things can or cannot come to be known and understood. Perhaps sometimes the assumption may be a more complicated one; one may in childhood absorb the sense that the way certain things are is accessible to under-standing, but not to 'the likes of us'.

Certain other very fundamental stances towards knowing also seem likely to be acquired quite early on within the family context. Here the concepts offered by Bakan (1966) as a way of looking at differences between men and women, and between Eastern and Western philosophies, may provide a perspective on two aspects of people's orientations towards knowledge. These concepts are the ones that Bakan calls 'agency and communion'. Agency is about doing. If one compares family groups in terms of the emphasis that they place upon doing, there seem to be large differences. Some families have a strong sense that what people do is likely to alter the way things are; they also believe that people have the right to action across a very wide sphere. There is a belief in both the effectiveness and the legitimacy of agency. In other family cultures there is little belief in human agency. Socio-economic factors may have a lot to do with this. There are now many writers who have documented the frus-tration, helplessness and alienation of the socially powerless. But a low emphasis on agency is also found in other kinds of family. A philosophical acceptance of the way things are is part of the outlook of many people who are not socially disadvantaged. The kind of assumption that a person makes about personal agency - and which is perhaps acquired very early on as part of the air one breathes - must have major implications for what and how that person comes to know. Attitudes towards agency imply distinctive ways of enlarging personal knowledge. They also define the kinds of thing it is and is not possible to know. Attitudes of this kind consti-tute, too, an active or a passive stance towards knowing as well as governing the extent to which knowledge is felt to be fixed or open to change.

Bakan's concept of communion also seems to encompass some centrally important aspects of the way that people approach knowledge - aspects that, again, are probably acquired through early family experience though perhaps modified later, just as may be the case for assumptions about agency. Certainly orientations towards communion - sharing - must be greatly affected by family life. Some families - implicitly of course - teach children to share a great deal of their experience and to expect that others, including adults, will share experience with them. Other families convey the expectation that most experience will remain private, and that the right to such privacy is basic. Probably most families have different assumptions and expectations for different aspects of experience, with some areas being highly open while others are totally taboo. Closed and open attitudes towards knowledge must influence how one learns - or how one teaches, or conducts psycho-therapy, come to that. People obviously differ in the extent to which they feel it is appropriate, and comfortable, to share their experience and to invite or accept personal disclosures from others.

And people evidently differentiate between areas of knowing, modes
of sharing, and the kinds of individual with whom it would be possible and impossible to share particular aspects of their experience.

What people know, the ways in which they come to know, and the
orientation that they bring towards knowing - all things that are
relevant to their engagement in educational and clinical settings -
seem likely to have at least some relation to themes in their
childhood family experience. But even children have experiences
beyond the family, in the course of which they come to further
knowledge; and this is obviously the case with adults whose participation in a variety of groups and projects leads to a huge range
of possible kinds and modes of knowing.

In our own society, much knowledge is differentiated by gender
identity. Put in the usual terms, this means that instrumental
kinds of knowledge are ascribed to males and expressive kinds of
knowledge to females. Questions of the justifiability of such
differentiations, as well as questions about the content involved
in them, are of course currently much at issue. But for most of us,
in our everyday lives, there are probably strong internal constraints upon what we should and should not know - constraints de-
riving from current sex-role stereotypes. For this whole question,
an experiment carried out by Hargreaves (1977) suggests the possibility of a rather unusual perspective. Hargreaves asked boys and
girls of junior-school age to perform a picture completion task.
They did this twice; first in the ordinary way, and then pretending
that they belonged to the opposite sex. Judged on quite subtle
classifying criteria, the second kind of drawing accurately reflected the content of the gender role involved. In a sense, this
shows that girls know how to be boys, and boys know how to be girls.

It seems important here to make the distinction between knowing
how to do something and actually doing it. Where psychological
concepts are concerned, this distinction is very explicitly made
with respect to 'intelligence', where 'competence' is not equated
with 'performance'; a person is viewed as having a potential that
is always greater than his/her test performance indicates. However,
this distinction is typically not made when it comes to sex-differ-
entiated behaviour. It is not generally thought that women and
girls have the potential to think analytically or to understand
machinery, but prefer to function in other modes. On the contrary,
it is widely assumed that females are incapable of these powers,
simply by virtue of being female, just as it is widely assumed that
males, through being male, are incapable of most of the caring and
tender roles, especially towards young children, in which women are
characteristically involved. And just because these assumptions are
so widely held most of us are probably not free to acknowledge as
our own, and therefore to be able to draw upon, the kinds of orientations and understandings that 'belong' to the opposite gender.

General assumptions about gender role are part of the air we all
breathe through our membership of society. But as well as such
general assumptions we encounter particular kinds of beliefs and
attitudes through becoming members of smaller social groups. Occupational groups, political ones, trade unions, clubs, special interest associations of any kind - all these social groups embody their
own kind of knowledge. Through belonging to such a group a person

comes not only to experience that knowledge but also to represent
it. Again, the knowledge is likely to involve both 'knowing that'
and 'knowing how to'. The fact that much of all this knowledge
characteristically remains implicit does not make it any the less
significant. Most of us are members of multiple social groupings;
the different kinds of knowledge that we acquire through such
groupings may be hard to integrate or even to reconcile. Perhaps
this is one reason why many people seem to experience discontinui-
ties and incompatibilities in what they know.

It may be that where educational and psychiatric institutions
fail people is precisely in not taking into account all these kinds
of personal knowledge. Superficially, this might seem more likely
to be the case for educational contexts since they, at any rate, are
explicitly concerned with learning and knowing. Yet perhaps psychiatric clinics and hospitals should be seen as equally bound up with
the things that people know. How would personal difficulties and
crises look if we were to view them as to do with personal
knowledge?

To take such a view would be to define knowing as absolutely
central to the relationships between people. And perhaps what
people know, and how they stand towards others, are indeed inextri-
cable. Certainly there is a lot of evidence that knowledge which
has been worked out and shared with others in close and personally
important relationships is very fundamental knowledge. The well-
documented resistance of Jehovah's Witnesses who have been subjected
to brainwashing is one instance of this; the ability to withstand
social ridicule and apparently clear contrary evidence for their
predictions on the part of the Messianic sect studied by Festinger
and his colleagues (1956) is another example. Social identity, if
it is lodged in a closely knit group with absent or hostile relations with the wider society, seems to guarantee the adherence to
its particular kinds of knowledge even in the face of the greatest
pressure.

Yet knowledge can also separate people. Nothing can be more
lonely or more terrifying than the awareness that one's experience
is alien and incomprehensible to other people and that ordinary,
firm knowledge, once shared with others, now seems dubious and unre-
liable. Perhaps it is out of this sense of becoming cut off from
what other people know that schizophrenics feel such panic and
bewilderment, and try such desperate manoeuvres to re-establish a
grasp on social reality. Knowledge can also, of course, divide
those involved in close personal relationships. Some people choose
to be constrained by a relationship rather than venture into
projects that they feel drawn to; this is because they sense that
such projects might involve coming to know kinds of things that
would in some way threaten the shared knowledge on which the relationship rests. And knowledge can, in fact, be very costly; established personal relationships may become untenable for precisely
this reason. Either solution to this dilemma may, however, involve
personal difficulties. For those who choose not to risk the loss of
a centrally important relationship, with all the pain that kind of
loss entails, there may instead arise a chronic, nagging sense of
restlessness and personal waste. Both these kinds of circumstance,
characteristic of many psychiatric problems, seem to have to do with

the tension between personal knowledge and personal relationships.
In other kinds of problem, the knowledge involved seems to concern
the deepest level of all - the knowledge of who one is.   Personal
identity is dependent upon the confirmation of others;   one cannot
feel an identity unless it is acknowledged by someone else.   As
Franz Fanon (1968), put it, Self is dependent on Other.   For some
people who come to be psychiatric patients, the social support for
their personal identity has been suddenly removed or else gradually
eroded through bereavement, children moving away, retirement, or
changes in setting or social role.   There are still others ending up
in psychiatric contexts whose problem is simply the diminishing and
degrading identity which our society grants them.   For many people
dragging out the years in the geriatric wards of psychiatric hospitals, and for many people passing their lives in the confines of
subnormality hospitals, their situation is that of living out the
personally contemptible status accorded to them by the society in
which they exist.

Both psychiatric and educational institutions seek to involve
people in some kind of change.   But it may be that not taking into
account the complex and idiosyncratic knowledge that each person
brings with him/her to any context leads to an inability to engage
adequately with that person.   At any rate, many attempts at teaching, and many kinds of therapeutic effort, do seem to achieve much
less than those carrying them out had hoped for.   It seems that
failure is of two kinds: either the educational or therapeutic
approaches made to individuals bypass their crucial personal
knowledge, or else they do violence to it.

It is probably not difficult to think of examples of irrelevance
both in learning and in psychotherapeutic situations.   The personal
meaninglessness of much of the school curriculum, its failure to
mesh in with pupils' own experience, is by now a familiar criticism.
Nor are learning situations that do not 'take' confined to schools.
Those undergoing higher education of any kind may find that they
have learned successfully how to pass written examinations - and
nothing lese.   When it comes to psychotherapy, some people merely
come to be able to talk about their problems;   the ability to do
anything about them remains as far away as ever.   And sometimes
people seem to experience psychiatric interludes as offering a new
kind of understanding, but this understanding is somehow quite
divorced from the everyday lives within which their dilemmas exist,
and to which they will return.

Perhaps, though, the situation is sometimes worse even than this.
What many people seem to learn in both educational and psychiatric
contexts is something unhappy and disabling.   In school, children
can learn that they are incompetent people, failures;   the writings
of John Holt provide an eloquent testimony of this kind of learning.
For some children - for example those in minorities - what school
may teach is that their personal knowledge is not acceptable as
knowledge, and that it precludes acquiring other kinds of knowledge
highly valued in school.   This may involve the sense that knowledge
shared with significant people and groups is somehow discounted by
others as invalid.   In some educational situations the knowledge
offered can be experienced as leading in directions that are totally
repugnant to what one most deeply believes.   This is because all

knowledge arises out of particular kinds of purposes and interests. Even the most 'neutral' and 'objective' knowledge is arrived at in this way. Different areas of knowledge are vested in different social groups. To adopt a particular kind of knowledge is to commit oneself to the assumptions contained in it, and to the lines of action implied by those assumptions. This means that arriving at any kind of understanding is far from being a detached process. On the contrary, coming to know anything involves highly personal matters. Another way of saying this is that in any field of knowledge there are always ramifications, in terms of social inter- ests, values and assumptions. Although these ramifications are seldom made explicit, it is they which in the end enable a person to make any kind of knowledge fully his/her own, which keep him/her from it, or which produce a sense of personal schism in what he/she knows. To know a thing is to take a certain stance towards the world, to adopt certain values and beliefs; if these run counter to centrally held understandings, or to one's own social identity, such knowledge is assimilated only at a heavy personal cost.

These considerations seem to be particularly important where what is learned is psychology. Of all kinds of knowledge, surely it is here that the greatest possible sensitivity to, and respect for, the personal knowledge of the learner is called for. Yet questions of the outlook and identity of the psychology student are character- istically left out of account. The result, perhaps, is that violence is often done to learners - and possibly to teachers too. One way through which this violence can come about is that much of the official expertise about people - embodied in academic psycholo- gy but also in political and social institutions - contains within it assumptions degrading to particular groups of people. The ascription of intellectual inferiority to black races would be an obvious example, as would the deficit theory of social-class differ- ences. At a more subtle level, the psychology of ageing is built upon its own form of deficit theory, while many concepts in clinical psychology entail assumptions of moral and human deficiency in those undergoing personal crises. Where social deviance is concerned, the official psychology underlying social policy towards crime involving women is based, as Carol Smart (1977) has shown, on a model of female personality as fundamentally primitive and amoral.

What those who become involved as patients in psychiatric settings are likely to learn is also psychology, and there the implications of that psychology for themselves are usually made more explicit. But the psychological knowledge that becomes assimi- lated in such settings goes beyond what is put over in explanations by psychiatrists, reassurances and advice from nurses, and what is said in psychotherapeutic encounters. Beside such official knowledge stands a huge body of unofficial and typically implicit knowledge, which is conveyed, for example, in communications between patients, and through the ways that psychiatric institutions are run. What comes to be known, in all this, for a person in the role of a psychiatric patient, may be something profoundly wretched and inhibiting. Some people learn a deep mistrust of all that they have previously known. Others come to acquire, as a permanent basis from which they live, an identity that is stigmatizing and shameful.

Paying attention to personal knowledge would involve looking

rather more carefully than is usual to the ways through which people
come to know what they do. The fact that reality is socially constructed means that the modes through which one learns are social
too. Knowledge is in people, it cannot exist without them; and it
is through people that understanding is mediated. Social interaction and social consensus seem to be vital in mediating knowledge
at every level. Even ideas and discoveries that emerge in private
solitude do not seem to be fully one's own until in some way they
have been shared with someone else. The engaging by the reader
through books with their authors, is also an essentially social
experience; in reading one is encountering the person who, conversely, has framed his/her message to an audience of persons. Of
course, much more is communicated through the medium of most written
texts than the explicit message itself. It is often the sense,
given off by the words, of the ramifications that the material holds
for the writer which can determine whether or not the content of the
book is assimilated.

As for direct interchanges with others in learning, these seem to
be significant in both obvious and quite subtle ways. At one level,
the opportunity to communicate with someone who knows more than
oneself about some area enables one to test out tentative ideas
against another's greater understanding and so to gain immediate
and explicit confirmation or disconfirmation of particular views.
But someone who has developed a high level of understanding in any
area also serves to exemplify what it means to have that kind of
knowledge. This, anyway, is one way of looking at the three qualities which it has been said a good teacher needs - competence,
integrity and commitment. These three things can be seen as
defining three major ways in which knowledge has personal meaning.
Competence involves a mastery of the implications contained in any
sphere of knowledge, a familiarity with the possibilities that it
opens up - being at home in the field rather than merely knowing it
in an empty, academic way. Integrity is perhaps a matter of the
degree to which that knowledge, in a person, is not implicitly
denied by other sorts of knowledge that he/she holds. And commitment seems to define the extent to which, for him/her, that
knowledge represents a rich theme in his/her life, because it links
up with what he/she most deeply knows. In the sense that these
aspects define very fundamental things about a person, it can
perhaps be said that in learning from someone one is learning
something about his/her 'way of being in the world'.

Learning from someone therefore seems to be very much a matter of
relating personally to him/her. In informal kinds of learning,
people probably absorb most from those with whom they are most
closely involved. Certainly where children are concerned it is
typically from parents, who are loved and therefore closely studied,
that a vast amount of knowledge is assimilated. But relationships
are two-way. Knowledge is imparted through communication; and what
is implicit in communication is the sense that the other person can
understand and make use of what is being said. Where this sense is
absent, what is ostensibly being offered is unlikely to be assimilated. It is surely because of the crucial importance of the attitude of the 'teacher' towards the 'learner' that certain kinds of
teaching relationship seem to work so much better than others. Re-

lationships that are purely authoritarian, which allow no mutuality of response, are generally ineffective in enabling meaningful personal learning to take place.   Those that acknowledge the particular reality of the learner, and which endorse his/her potential competence, are characteristically facilitating.

Ultimately, perhaps, we all learn and develop through experiencing jointly with others the possibility that we could develop. It may be that the phenomenon described by Shotter whereby mothers somehow enable in their babies the very potentialities which they see in them, is one that underlies all learning.   If this is so, then in a sense faith is the mechanism of learning, and the only limits to the extension of personal understanding are those of vision and imagination.

REFERENCES

Bakan, D. (1966), 'The Duality of Human Existence', Rand McNally, Chicago.
Berger, P.L. and Luckmann, T. (1966), 'The Social Construction of Reality', Penguin, Harmondsworth.
Fanon, F. (1968), 'The Wretched of the Earth', trans. C.Farrington, MacGibbon & Kee, London.
Festinger, L., Riecken, H.W. and Schachter, S. (1956), 'When Prophesy Fails', University of Minnesota Press, Minneapolis.
Hargreaves, D.J. (1977), Sex roles in divergent thinking, British Journal of Educational Psychology, vol.47, pp.25-33.
Laing, R.D. and Esterson, A. (1964), 'Sanity, Madness and the Family', Tavistock Publications, London.
Shotter, J. (1975), 'Images of Man in Psychological Research', Methuen, London.
Smart, C. (1977), 'Women, Crime and Criminology: A Feminist Critique', Routledge & Kegan Paul, London.

PART ONE

The first three chapters in this book are concerned with contexts that explicitly and officially involve learning. Mary Baur looks at the situation of pupils in the classroom of a junior school. Alan Radley considers educational practice in higher education - the university context. Finally, Margaret Spencer questions some widespread but unexamined assumptions about the acquisition of literacy. In considering how far 'learners' in these contexts do learn, and what it is they are likely to assimilate, all three writers take a critical look at the ways in which educational situations are typically run.

In most schools and colleges, knowledge is treated as an entity to be transferred from knower to learner. Learning is seen as the acquiring of knowledge; teaching is the handing over of what is to be known. It is this approach that, implicitly, each writer in this section is concerned to question from an examination of its effects in particular contexts. As they show, an approach to learning that treats knowledge as static, as disembodied, and as product rather than process, carries serious negative consequences for learners. At best it is likely to inhibit the full potential of people in educational contexts; at worst, it can alienate people from the material they are trying to grasp, or even from the whole situation of being a learner. The points at which each writer in this section takes issue with the transmission model of learning are distinctive, and relate to the particular context in question. Three broad aspects of the approach come under attack here: its impersonality, its individualism, and the passivity it attributes to learners.

One feature of the impersonal approach to learning is that it may leave the learner feeling that he/she has no place in the learning situation. This is a feature stressed by Baur and Spencer. In the 'stress and boredom' that characterize school life for many children, it may be the lack of personal acknowledgment that is responsible, as Baur suggests. In most classrooms, she argues, there is typically a failure to recognize the wide diversity of outlook, background and concerns among the children there. For some pupils this is because 'what they are good at does not rate in the classroom'. For others, the failure of adults ever to take their perspective can result in their becoming the sort of classroom

casualty that Baur documents. Yet to acknowledge and respect individual differences would, she suggests, enable children to take a
much fuller and more positive part in classroom life.

A similar point is made by Spencer in her discussion of children
learning to read. As she argues, unless the teacher can somehow
come to 'stand behind the child's head', no amount of expert
teaching is likely to work. And yet in teacher-training and
teaching research, the terms of reference are consistently taken
from the teacher's, not the learner's, standpoint - the implicit
assumption being that the child must orient to the perspective of
his/her instructor. As Spencer shows, reading itself is a fundamentally personal activity. But its personal nature is characteristically denied by the ways in which children in our society are
introduced to reading. The fact that children, like adults, read
for personal meaning - through stories to enlarge their experience
of themselves and their lives - this obvious fact is typically over-
looked. So when explanations are sought for the failure of particular children to learn to read, the personal meaning that literacy
has for them is seldom considered. Nor is it generally thought
important that the content of books for children should relate to
their personal contexts and experience. For many children, Spencer
suggests, the 'formal passage into literacy' offers nothing in the
way of personal meaning; it consists of 'a set of limp-covered
reading books, written in no one's language, called a reading scheme
... which asks questions like "Where is the red balloon?"'. The
same failure to incorporate the need for personal significance in
introducing reading is evident in the terms on which books themselves are offered to children. Typically, children have to use
books that belong to school, or to the often alien and perhaps
intimidating context of libraries; the relationship with a book
that such a use entails is very different from the feeling of
personal ownership that comes from having 'your own paperback,
fitting snugly into your back pocket'.

The impersonal view of learning, and the educational practice
that results from it, is also strongly challenged by Radley in his
discussion of the university context. His argument is that in the
end it is personal involvement on the part of a student that enables
him/her to grasp intellectual material. Through the interpene-
tration of ideas with one's own life experience, one achieves both
a freedom in relation to the discipline concerned, and a personal
commitment to the thinking in which one engages. Again, however,
as Radley shows, this crucial feature of learning is implicitly
denied by the ways in which teaching and learning are organized in
higher education. Essentially, the structure of learning in that
context divorces knowledge from those who are engaged in it, as
teachers and students. The underlying model is one of information
storage and retrieval; hence external assessment and a fixed syllabus. This way of organizing things necessarily removes the opportunity for personal creation of new content, and deprives the
student of the power of personal discrimination, since authority
towards the material is vested outside himself or herself. What
people are likely to learn in such situations is that academic
material can have no links with the problems that engage them
personally. Students - and teachers too - find themselves to be

separate from the academic context they inhabit; all too often,
this results in people who are 'estranged from the material on which
they are working'.

The second aspect of current educational practice that these
writers are concerned to challenge is its intrinsic individualism.
In all three accounts the essentially social nature of learning is
strongly emphasized. What Baur argues, in her portrayal of junior-
school classrooms, is that the classroom world is a fundamentally
interpersonal world, with potentially rich opportunities for social
learning that are, however, typically thrown away. The wide diversity of children who people any classroom offers much in the way
of mutual enlivenment and mutual enrichment; as Baur puts it,
pupils could come to know themselves in relation to a great variety
of other people. This would mean that children could grow as social
beings, developing mutual respect, consideration and responsibility.
But because classroom life is based on a model of the individual
learner, the regime is one which constrains and diminishes rather
than one that supports and develops the relationships between
pupils. Consequently, pupil interaction is reduced to 'surrep-
titious borrowing, fiddling around with things, and teasing each
other: children frittering away their energies to no one's satisfaction'. Baur also traces the development of the 'maladjusted
child' in the classroom to the failure to recognize the fact that
classroom events are interactions between people, not problems
within individuals. As she suggests, a recognition of this would
carry the understanding that to deal effectively with difficulties
involving any particular pupil necessitates looking at the behaviour
of others towards that pupil; when things go wrong it is the whole
interpersonal situation that needs examining.

Radley's emphasis on social aspects of learning in higher education is two-fold. On the one hand he argues that real personal
assimilation of academic material typically involves a relationship
between the student and the teacher. This relationship is not
something separate from the learning but is inextricably linked
with it. The process of grasping ideas draws together those
involved, since in formulating knowledge they achieve 'a shared
basis of understanding towards the problem which together they have
articulated'. But there is also another sense in which, as Radley
argues, learning in educational contexts is essentially a social
matter. Educational practice is of necessity the expression of a
social system. The way that learning is arranged in university
contexts reflects the functions that our society vests in universities, and the relationship which universities have with other social
institutions. This is the reason that to achieve any real change in
educational practice needs more than the isolated action of particular radical students and teachers; some fundamental assumptions,
hallowed in our society and embodied in other social institutions,
will have to be more widely re-thought.

Spencer's concern to stress that learning is essentially social
is also evident at several levels of her argument. Most basically,
she suggests, the activity of learning to read is itself a collaborative activity. It is the fact that teacher and child work
together on finding material in print, and that teacher conveys to
child the expectation of success, that enable the beginning reader

to approach the task with the confidence that is the most crucial
feature of being able to read. Reading, and learning to read, are
also inescapably social in their significance. As Spencer shows,
the social meaning of literacy necessarily changes as society does;
it does not have the same significance now, for instance, as it did
in Victorian times. As for the content of reading material, this
too is inevitably social; print 'informs social behaviour and
interprets society to itself'. Yet here too there is a failure to
recognize that learning to read is part of children's social experience. The dominance of a technical view of the area has resulted in
an 'industry of reading experts', with an intimidating armoury of
figures, charts and kits; the activity of reading has all too often
become divorced from the child's ordinary social life.

The last feature of the conventional organization of learning
that comes under attack in these chapters is the passivity it attributes to, and therefore imposes on, learners. This is a theme that
Radley and Spencer share. Both writers stress the necessity for the
active personal engagement of the learner with the task he/she is
involved in. Radley's argument is that, for real learning to occur,
the student needs to take the initiative; he/she must become a
'positive creator of enquiry'. Only through active involvement in
the task will he/she be able to create new understandings. And
creating what one learns is, as Radley shows, an appropriate way of
defining what takes place. In genuine learning, 'what emerges ...
is an interchange between student and teacher in which their
relating through the material is established in a form that was not
there before'. Yet, because of the way in which education is
organized in universities, it is very hard for this kind of thing
to happen. Since learners are not viewed as active agents in their
own learning, ideas are characteristically presented as 'the fixed
product of a discipline which exists quite apart from one's own
enquiries'. As a result, ideational material appears closed,
complete, a finished product, containing neither any clues as to
the doubts and struggles through which it came into being, nor any
invitation to the student to participate in working upon it.

In her consideration of children learning to read, Spencer
similarly emphasizes the key importance of engagement. As she
shows, reading is essentially an active process; it is necessary to
approach the material 'as if it made sense', to explore, try things
out, guess at meanings. And in the last resort, learning can happen
only if the learner takes the initiative; as Spencer puts it, we
learn to read 'only when we take the task in hand for ourselves,
rather than at the behest of others'.

Chapter 1

CHILDREN'S CLASSROOM ADJUSTMENT
Mary Baur

Whatever children's experiences are outside school - current or
past - they are nevertheless developing their perceptions and their
ways of relating to people in the context of their school. The
degree of adjustment that they show to their classroom situations
in their first years at school colours their life for a good few
years.

Before going any further I should say a few things about my position. First, I am not a teacher though I have done nearly a year
of supply teaching. Second, I am writing about schools with reference to certain traditionally-run primary schools that I have
visited for research purposes. Third, my idea of what children need
is probably coloured by what I believe I could have done with as a
child.

I am assuming that a key aspect of classroom experience is the
relationship that a child has with the teacher and with other
children. Both sets of relationships are, I believe, very much
influenced by the teacher. In class the teacher can use his/her
values relatively uncontested, and the criteria used by the children
in forming their self-images and in their perceptions of others at
school are often what they have picked up of these, and of the
standards that are otherwise upheld in school.

Taking an interview with a child (Francesca, 8 yrs 2 mths) to
illustrate this:

Question: What goes on between you and Hilary in class?
Answer: She talks about interesting things she can do reading.
Question: What do you talk about?
Answer: We talk about her.
Question: Why?
Answer: She's more interesting.

Interesting in the classroom context means for this child being good
at the tasks that are set there. Francesca was under a lot of
pressure from the teacher to try to do well. The teacher describes
her relationship with the child as 'Always trying to get her to
work'. Francesca's own description of the relationship was so
neutral that I felt, since she did not want to talk about it with

me, perhaps it was a bit fraught.

> Question: What goes on between Miss A and you?
> Answer: Every time I get my work right she ticks it; every time
> I get it wrong she puts a cross.

As an observer in her class I often saw Francesca being distracted
and it seemed that schoolwork was a real toil for her. Meanwhile,
in the rest of her interview, she described conversations she had
with other classmates about imaginary things and about things they
had seen on the news, and I felt that she was a lively minded,
curious child. Otherwise bright and spontaneous, faced with a task
in class she squirmed or got agitated - if she attempted it at all.
 For example: supposed to be reading her Reader, Francesca busily
dog-ears every single page of her book (crumpled, hastily-made dog-
ears). I felt for the book and wondered about her.... then she
slowly turns each page back to its rightful flatness and, smoothing
the book shut, she hisses to Sonia: 'I've did it'. Sonia, busy
reading, does not respond.
   Another day the task is writing sentences with words on the
board. One of the words is PART. Francesca, clutching a ruler in
her left hand, a pencil in her right, seems tense, moves jerkily.
She digs Paul in the side with her elbow: 'I have a PART of a
sweet. Does that make sense?' Why doesn't she know? Paul answers
(inaudible). Francesca writes. Teacher calls out 'There's a lot of
discussion going on at that table. What are you having to talk
about? Everyone else is managing without. If you are chattering
you are not working.'
   The enforcing of discipline occurs as to ways of carrying out
classwork as well as in questions of social behaviour. There seems
to be a very common belief amongst these pupils that there is a
right and a wrong way of proceeding, whatever the task.

> Teacher: I don't know you, so I think it would be a nice idea if
> you all wrote a story about yourselves. (A lot of
> noise: lots of the children start talking to each
> other.)
> Teacher: Quiet. What is the date?
> Most of the class: Thir-teenth-of-Oc-to-ber. (Chanted in
> unison.)
> Teacher: What is it going to be? (Meaning the story title.)
> (A girl calls out 'Winter' - following her own train of thought
> from the date to Winter?)
> Teacher: About myself. (She suggests they write about their
> family, hobbies, etc.)

In the next few minutes three boys came up to me, having written
their names, the date and the title. One asked: 'Shall I turn
over?' because he thought it was too untidy; the next: 'What shall
I write about?'; the third told me: 'I've done it wrong' (wrong
meant untidy, it transpired). Their dependency seemed depressing.
Anyway the nature of 'the right way' is to some extent determined by
the teacher that you happen to have. Teacher forbids the use of
rubbers for certain things.

Teacher: You know, Michael, if you do something wrong, you write
           it again.   You don't just rub a letter out;   don't be
           lazy.
Francesca to Observer: Will you help me with my sums?
Teacher: (trumpeting)   WHO said that?   Nobody is going to help
         you to do your sums.   If you need help you come here.
         (Then to another boy.)   Don't interrupt Robert.   Let him
         get on with his work.   (The two boys were in fact
         talking about how to do the sums.)

The priority was on getting on with the work quickly, quietly and
alone, rather than on getting on with people, or with the work with
people.

Teacher: Have you written that bit yet, Howard?
Howard: No.
Teacher: Then why are you chattering?

What happens outside class?   As far as I have seen there is nothing
as neat as one set of values for the classroom, one for the
playground, and one for home, but certainly something of such com-
partmentalizing for some children.   It is not just the teacher in
class who evaluates behaviour and children.   The children do this
to each other outside class as well, using somewhat different
criteria most of the time.   However it may not be until the later
years in primary school, or even sometimes until the early secondary-school years that children develop values opposing those of the
teacher or sub-group values such as, for example, Colin Lacey (1970)
identified at Hightown Grammar.   Is it possible meanwhile that young
primary-school children are more susceptible to the values of the
teacher and of the school?   Only a few, 'maladjusted', remaining
impervious, or standing opposed to the subtleties of value transmission, or to the attempted inculcation of certain behaviours and
attitudes?
     If one looks at casualties from the classroom - for example, the
'maladjusted' in special schools - the major task in helping them is
bringing them to be able to form relationships with other people.
In extreme cases the child has not even formed enough of a self to
begin to relate to others in any realistic way.
     In the schools that I visited I found that teachers quite readily
differentiated between children in their class in terms of their
adjustment to the situation.   Quite apart from the questionability
of 'good adjustment' to that strange situation being equatable with
normality, I found that the criteria for evaluating adjustment
varied from teacher to teacher.   I gained the impression that each
teacher was reaching for certain behaviours, some as desirable, some
undesirable, and that what these were varied from teacher to
teacher.
     Sometimes it would seem that it was the child rather than the
behaviours that determined the teacher's reaction.   This could mean
that the teacher was recognizing the different needs of individual
children, or that the teacher had some personal preferences that it
was difficult for him/her to conceal.
     My main concern is for children's personal growth, particularly

as facilitated and enriched in personal relationships. Somehow I
spent most of my school life as a good pupil, but being an outsider
- oscillating between feeling I could not care whether or not I was
liked and feeling that I was an impossible phenomenon and that it
was no wonder that I had no friends. Apparently I looked hostile
and unapproachable. That was, I think now, probably to frighten
people away in case they came close and then rejected me.

It would seem very important to me then for each child to have
the opportunity to know himself/herself in a wide variety of relationships, to feel free to come to know as many people as are
alive to him/her that he/she wants to know. School would seem to
have all the potential for providing such opportunity and yet, in
most formal classrooms, such are the constraints - fixed seating,
being urged to work on one's own, or quickly, or quietly - that
children can often not have much of the contact that they would
spontaneously choose to have with other children. Discipline,
rules, and so on, define and are often partly intended to minimize
the contact between pupils in class.

I think there is great scope for mutual enlivement and enrichment in the contact that children would have with each other in
class - as elsewhere - and that in trying to control their pupils'
relating in deference to curriculum goals, teachers sometimes con-
taminate what goes on between certain children. At worst relationships are reduced in expression, in the classroom, to surrep-
titious borrowing, fiddling around with things, and teasing each
other; children frittering away their energies to nobody's satisfaction. I am not suggesting that they might not sometimes like or
need to spend time in those ways, but that the regime in class might
encourage too much of it, while frustrating more straightforward,
constructive, creative interactions.

Obviously in a room of thirty-plus children who have to be taught
certain things by certain times, as far as is possible, some rules
have to be enforced as to what may or may not happen. After all,
probably few children would spontaneously choose, if given an alternative, to live a day like those that most traditionally-run
primary schools offer.

I should like to suggest that there would not be so many lost
children in schools if we understood more about their inner worlds
and their world outside school - and from there what their life in
school might mean to them - and if we made relationships in the
classroom as important as the children may need them to be. It
seems ridiculous that the workings of a child's psyche or inner
world are not really taken notice of until he/she breaks down in
some way and the psychologist is called in. I think we have handed
over too much to the psychologist and do not bring enough of the
child into our dealings with children in school. I'd like to
suggest also that there would not be so many children being naughty
or disruptive if we have a somewhat different attitude, notably a
more trusting one, towards children.

Are 'maladjusted' children more sensitive, more subtle in certain
ways than others? A depressed (lost, alienated) - desperate
(naughty, disruptive) continuum seems to have potential for disturbing the range of children that are seen as poorly adjusted and
for highlighting the differences between them in their classroom

behaviour and experience. There are those who have given up trying
to feed themselves into or from the classroom situation. There are
those who are desperately trying to fit in, by keeping up with the
work or in some other way. There are those who are being disruptive
through desperation.

The following are extracts of observations of a boy who appeared
depressed and alienated in class, and a girl who was desperately
trying to fit in by getting the work done.

A BOY WHO APPEARS TO BE DEPRESSED

Robin is a child who is hardly coping with the work at all and who
is spending a lot of his time in class daydreaming, or messing about
with certain other children.

Teacher, Mrs C, describes his behaviour when asked to describe
her relationship with Robin in class as 'Quiet, but naughty'.

Another boy in the class describes the same relationship: 'Robin
is a good fighter, so he fights everyone so Mrs C tells him off.'
What he is good at does not rate well in the classroom - on the
contrary. Observing him in class, Robin seemed to be mostly out of
it. For example, one day at 9.50 a.m. the class is story writing:

Robin has been to remedial reading and is now sitting and
staring. He has written 28 - the beginning of the date. He cuddles
and pats his shoe bag. He screws up one eye. He looks like an old
man who has nothing to do but sit and stare - my projection?
Suddenly he grabs a pencil and, looking across the class, he calls:
'John'. He points at Sammy, who, however, mouths something to John
about Robin. This makes John and Sammy laugh together about Robin,
who seems to suddenly switch off and wither - he turns to picking at
his shoe and staring at shadows and lights on the floor.

Patrick, another of his classmates, describes his relationship
with Robin:

    Patrick: We play in the playground together.
    Question: What about in class?
    Patrick: Just talk.
    Question: About anything special?
    Patrick: Robin sees flashes on the wall and I don't. He tells
              me to look and I don't see 'em.
    Question: Why do you think he sees them and you don't?
    Patrick: His eyes are bad.

It seemed that even in the social contacts that were not part of the
formal classroom set-up, Robin did not manage to hold his own very
well.

The classwork was a struggle that he did not always tackle:
 Sums - there is a queue of pupils about Mrs C's desk. She is
marking their work. Robin puts a block in his mouth; Kay at the
next table does the same. They make faces at each other, take the
Unipix blocks out, have a brief argument. Robin then goes back to
his blocks and starts making towers that topple over. Mouthing
words to himself, catching my eye, he stops. Kay knocks over his
tower. He does not react to her. Uses his next tower as a pretend

telescope. Looks at the clock through his other eye. 'Half an hour
left,' he says to Kay. He puts a block on the end of each of
several figures ... goes up ... uses two as glasses ... calls to
Leslie to look.

Another day - sums again; Mrs C tells Robin and Pat to do two
times, to write it out.

> Robin to Kay: What are two two's? (No response.) I think I can
> do this. (He seemed very enthusiastic and had
> what was for him an unusually childish voice. I
> felt he had been given a task that was at his
> level and he relaxed into it - but not for long;
> looks stuck a couple of minutes later.)
> Kay (coming back to her place past his): Two times two are four.
> Robin: Don't tell me. (Seeming pained. Then to himself) Three
> times three are six.

Kay asked me (O) if her table was right. Robin, not realizing that
Mrs C had told Kay and the other children at her table to do their
three times, says urgently, 'But she said do them ones'. He is
ignored. He scratches at a spot on his face until it bleeds. Break
time.

He does not seem to realize how much he is behind the others in
his work performance. His intense fighting might be his way of
using energy that cannot go into classroom life - because he is not
up to coping with the work. His visual peculiarities and preoccupations, meanwhile, might be a defence. Maybe he is taking flight
through them from the stress or boredom of being in class.

A GIRL WHO APPEARS TO BE DESPERATE

Sarah is a child who is desperately struggling to keep up in class.
Chatting to me in class she showed me her Reader. She said she made
mistakes all the time: 'It's called "The Old Man and the Magic
Clothes" and I go, "The - the - the - Old Man - and the the Magic
C c c clothes"' (very slowly, imitating herself read).

Her needs for help were enormous but she was trying to get it
from other children and not to show the teacher where she was at.
This seemed to be giving her, and some of her more able classmates,
who were meant to be getting on with their own work, a very uncomfortable time. For example, in the first lesson after lunch,
Sarah and some others are still doing some work Mr X gave them in
the morning - cutting up circles into halves, quarters, eighths and
sixteenths and doing some additions.

Sarah looked at the board puzzled. T, another girl, comes to sit
next to her; she has also got to finish sums. Meanwhile teacher
says there is a painting competition the children can enter. They
can paint anything in their town. She asks who wants to do it and
what they would choose to paint. Sarah says 'park', but she only
mouths it and goes back to her fractions looking fraught.

> Sarah: T, would you help me? (No response from T. Sarah
> puzzles alone.) T, would you fold this? (Circle that

> has already been folded into eight segments.   Sarah seems
> very unsure of herself.   T folds it for her.)

Another day, the second lesson in the morning, the task was to make
a card for Mother's Day.   Sarah asks W, another girl, to draw her a
flowerpot.   W does so.   Sarah hovers, watching, then goes back to
the table and draws a bit.

Sarah goes to W's table again, leans on it and says nothing.   N,
another girl at the table, reads out the rhyme W has written in her
card.   Sarah tries to mouth the words along with her but she does
not manage to read many of the words properly.

Sarah asks W a question (inaudible).   W answers.   Sarah goes back
to her table and draws some flowers in the pot drawn by W.   Sarah
says to herself, 'Right, done that'.   Seems really relieved.

However, after break Sarah starts another card because she
doesn't like what she has done.   She gets W to find her some gummed
paper.   She has difficulty first in trying to explain what paper she
means and flaps her arms in frustration.   Then she picks up her sum
card and mutters to herself: 'Did I do 39?'   Goes to the queue at
the teacher's desk, but gives up waiting, looking distracted.   Runs
after W:

> Sarah (to W):   How did you fold ...?
> W (to Sarah):   Don't ask me questions....   Have to do sums....
> Sarah: I just don't know how to do it.   (To herself.)
> W: Lost my pencil.   (To herself.)

Each seems very lonely and frustrated.   At the end of the lesson:

> Teacher (to class):   Team points for the tidiest table.   (Sarah
>   tries to hurry tidying.)
> Sarah: Yes, where does this go?   (No reaction.   Picks up bits of
>   paper on the floor very laboriously....   Sits down.
>   Tense and watchful....)

However it came about, it has suited us in our culture, at least for
a few centuries, to regard children as untrustable.   Once adult we
set about repressing the child in ourself and perhaps sometimes by
extension, through projection, the children outside as well.

Philippe Ariès (1973) quotes from the regulations for the
children at Port Royal:

> [This] constant supervision should be exercised gently and with
> a certain trustfulness calculated to make them think that one
> loves them and that it is only to enjoy their company that one
> is with them....   This makes them love this supervision rather
> than fear it.

And stifles all the undesirable behaviours they might indulge in if
left unsupervised?   Until eventually they have forgotten all their
extravagant needs and desires and are strong in their habits of hard
work and obedience?

Ariès explains, 'The object was to avoid the promiscuity of the
college which for a long time had a bad reputation, though not as

long in France, thanks to the Jesuits, as in England'.

Even if what goes on in most of our schools does not follow their recommendations very closely, it is interesting to note the attitude to social interaction in primary schools, and to the child's human development generally, in the Hadow Report (1931) and the Plowden Report (1967). There are substantial differences between the two but one still finds even in the Plowden Report something of the same view of children as that expressed in the passage on supervision in the regulations for the children of Port Royal, e.g.: 'If each child is valued for himself, he will have less reason to lie, whether from fear, idleness or the desire for self-aggrandisement.' This seems to say that it is necessary to treat the child strategically to get him/her to develop his/her good potential.

Discipline in the classroom that minimizes interpersonal relations amongst the pupils is difficult to phase out. Certainly, if immediately substituted by a more laissez-faire regime, problems arise.

John Holt (1974) describes and comments on a sequence of events of the sort often quoted by those who advocate strict discipline in the classroom and by those who oppose its use: 'In the most repressed classrooms children get so frustrated that of course what they do if left unsupervised is fight.' Holt writes: 'this appears to prove to teachers that children need to be controlled.' For me it illustrates the negative effect of a negative attitude to negativity. Aggression should be recognized as a healthy emotion for us to learn to express in restricted ways, or to control through concern or respect for others, if not love for them.

Through lack of trust, or through fear or for some other poor reason, we often unthinkingly control children. It seems very important that where rules are being enforced we are clear about their true function. If they are there for the immediate convenience of the teacher we should not lead the children to believe that they were invented for their benefit.

We have also to beware of our own projection when we are dealing with other people's behaviour. Some behaviours are difficult for us to relate to, for personal reasons, because they express aspects of ourselves with which we have difficulties, or because of past experiences of them in unsatisfactory relationships.

How we deal with the difficulty varies from person to person - and sometimes with our different states. Some of us have an unhealthy need to exercise control over others. This might come from a fear of loss of control over our own behaviours. If, for example, we feel the need to control a certain impulse in ourselves and then we see another person unashamedly expressing it, we may feel frightened, indignant or angry and we may protest and call on others to protest with us, sometimes in the name of some 'objective' value or standard. We may, however, vicariously enjoy its expression, or again we may ignore it as best we can. We each need sometimes to ignore certain things.

I am suggesting a more or less mild version of the evasion that David Bakan (1973) writes about in his study of the characteristics man has projected in the image of Satan:

One of the major problems associated with the attempts to compre-
hend evil is that our morality itself, our aversion to evil,
makes us tend to be aversive to looking at evil long enough to
understand it.... There is a sense in which it is the case that
evil inheres in the tendency not to look at evil, and the overcoming of evil inheres in the courage to look at it.

Children's negative feelings are, I think, often not sufficiently
acknowledged and not dealt with in school. I think this is just one
instance of a fairly widespread attitude in our society that anger
and even sadness are ugly aberrations from the normal, to be tackled
with pills if they persist. There are probably some behaviours and
some children that a teacher ignores to some extent because they
find them too evil to face. However, it is also very common for a
teacher to adopt strategies for relating positively towards a child
with the aim of helping the child to progress.

We claim that it is necessary to enforce discipline to enable
children to develop their own for life-long use. I have no quarrel
with this. It is the way in which it is done that is right or
wrong. I think it is right to work towards children forming their
own ability to discipline themselves. But at worst we simply behave
as if they are unformed adults and should be kept subordinate until
further notice.

I would argue that often we inhibit the good potential in
children and go about bringing them up as if they were helpless or
uncooperative, which they may become if treated in certain ways. I
believe a lot more can come from children than we often allow in our
treatment of them in schools - as George Dennison (1972) illustrates
in the following:

The children have come to know each other and to understand with
great finesse where they stand in their various relationships....
If M takes something of E's, E will push until M is on the floor,
at which point E will bawl her out and kick her in the rear four
or five times, moderating the force of her kick very nicely, not
enough to hurt but a jolt sufficient to drive home the rapid
warnings and curses, usually shouted in Spanish. This simple
anger, followed, as it always is, by forgiveness, is so much more
civilizing in the end than a teacher's homilies enforced by
discipline from above.

These children spontaneously exercise a disciplinary process
between themselves that expresses deep respect for personal needs
and for standards of behaviour.

I think that children's relationships with each other should be
encouraged and used in class. I think children should be trusted
more but I am not suggesting a free-for-all. We have, I think, to
beware of a mistake that Jules Henry (1966) vividly describes:

School creates what I have called the essential nightmare. The
nightmare must be dreamed in order to provide the fears necessary
to drive people away from something (in our case, failure) and
towards something (success). In this way children, instead of
loving knowledge, have become embroiled in the nightmare.

In this situation a modern trend to make school the habitat of impulse release and fun is an expected development.... It is a therapy for the cultural obsession; the educators' expression of their own disenchantment with the cultural nightmare ... and they have made the trend synonymous with democracy itself. The vital democracy can be the product of a disciplined and intelligent population only; that disorder and laxity are poison to democracy, they naturally see because they are as obsessed with destroying the nightmare as an older generation was with creating it.

Most teachers are, of course, very caring and sensitive and work hard to see that each child's needs are catered for as far as is possible in their class. Apart from the emotional problems whereby in this process of adaptation there is often an enormous practical problem - namely the human needs that a full acknowledgment of each individual's reality unearths are perhaps impossible to cater for in a large class. Maybe not though, because the children are then contributing, giving, sharing much more, not just receiving, taking.

We must not forget either that it is we, and previous generations of us, who have produced the situation where we cram large numbers of children into rooms and then throw up our hands and say, 'What can you do in such a situation?' I mean it must suit us to be able to blame external circumstances for social/emotional problems....
and it must suit some of us to be able to justify not dealing adequately with the latter.

Meanwhile it is perhaps more than ever necessary to make classroom experience more and more relevant to the process of becoming a person in the world; more than ever because so many of today's children lack support elsewhere in their lives.

Each person, pupil or teacher has a somewhat different version of what goes on between pupils there and it seems to me that each version is valid. It is what we must work with and from, so that where there are children who are being seen as maladjusted we need to hear their version of the situation they are in. Perhaps some of the adjustment needed should come from the situation or other participants rather than the maladjusted child being removed. Perhaps more acknowledgment of individual differences is the key to stopping some long and painful processes of maladjustment, and sometimes to enriching the experience of everyone present.

REFERENCES

Ariès, Philippe (1973), 'Centuries of Childhood', Penguin, Harmondsworth.
Bakan, David (1973), 'On Method', Jossey Bass Publications, San Francisco.
Dennison, George (1972), 'First Street School', Penguin, Harmondsworth.
Hadow Report (1931), HMSO, London.
Henry, Jules (1966), 'Culture Against Man', Tavistock, London.
Holt, John (1974), 'The Underachieving School', Pelican, Harmondsworth.

Lacey, Colin (1970), 'Hightown Grammar', Manchester University
Press, Manchester.
Plowden Report (1967), HMSO, London.

Chapter 2

STUDENT LEARNING AS SOCIAL PRACTICE
Alan Radley

The context of this chapter is set by my own experience as a teacher
of psychology, a subject which makes claim to have some explanations
for what is generally called 'learning'. A survey of the literature, however, shows that much of the work carried out by psychologists in this field concerns how people acquire and retain 'information'. Furthermore, many of my concerns as a teacher, apparently
faced with the task of educating students, relate to problems that
lie beyond the boundaries of information storage and retrieval.
Perhaps this is best made clear by reference to an example of a
particular learning situation.

Students arrive for a seminar having prepared the topic (or not,
as the case may be) and from the ensuing discussion it is clear that
nobody is terribly interested in the problem at hand. Then I, as
the teacher, will often attempt to raise issues or ask questions in
order to stimulate interest. This kind of seminar is a session in
which it seems to me that the group of students are separated both
from me and from the material under study. In the course of the
discussion (or non-discussion, if it is a particularly bad session),
what emerges is the way in which each student is estranged from the
material with which he is working. The topic, its questions, everything about it seems to stand away from him. The ideas are not his,
nor do they invite him to take them up, but instead they stand as
evidence of the task to which he must address himself. The task is
the drudge of 'learning the material', of satisfying the teachers
that he has sufficient grasp of the relevant facts to be awarded a
degree. In this situation the material is experienced by the
student as a fixed product of a discipline that exists quite apart
from his own enquiries. It asks its own questions and gives its own
answers. It often seems to offer no insight on the questions and
problems in which he might be interested. There appears to be a
gulf between them which is not to be bridged; at least not in this
seminar nor in this chapter. The resulting tenor of the session or
of the writing produced is one of a stiff, lifeless presentation,
stemming from an apathy which turns and turns again in its own
vacuum.

How are these feelings expressed, and how do they become tangible
to me, the teacher? Well, I do not have to grasp them by some long

line of inference. Instead, I experience them directly in the
course of the conversation, in which the students' comments are
nearly always directed to me as a focus. In fact, it is a particular form of such sessions that each student tends to operate, with
respect to the material at hand, as an isolated unit who addresses
me as an individual. (However, with respect to the more basic
assumptions about the learning experience, they operate as a group,
obeying certain tacit expectations about the student role in that
situation.)

The form of address in such a situation is that the student will
tend either to report something which he has read in a book, or ask
me a question about it. The basis of his comment or question is
always the specific point in the literature, the external referent
to which he can direct my attention. To make a point, or report a
passage from a book as an isolated statement, is to make manifest
the form of relating in which the ideas of another person have their
existence for the student as ready-made packages of knowledge.
These points may be made in response to a specific question from the
teacher, in which case they are offered as claimants to the 'right
answer'; or they may be said as a way of testing out what it is
that is required by the teacher as appropriate material to be
'learned'. And finally, they may be addressed to the teacher in
order to test whether the speaker's grasp of the concept is the
'correct' one.

The reporting of an isolated passage leaves me, as the teacher,
with the task of having to comment upon it myself, of having to
judge it right or wrong, or of having to criticize the student's
construction of what he has read. That is to say, I find in the
very hearing of his statement that he has placed the ideas as
opaque, isolated entities between us. These ideas, divorced from
their original context, having no apparent linkage to any personal
commitment that the student may have to the matter, are in their
very verbalization a manifestation of the estrangement which exists
between us. And I, in my part, find these ideas in their discon-
nected, disembodied form to be abstractions with which I can do very
little, except perhaps to comment upon them, declare them right or
wrong, or appraise his interpretation of them. Now I can, and I
invariably do, go back to the student to invite him to say more
about what he means - why he said it - what he wants of us in the
group in saying that. But that is when I have tried to break out
of the relationship in which we find ourselves, when I have refused
the roles in which we seem, unwittingly, to be involved.

What is it that strikes one about this example? Possibly the
degree of estrangement of student and teacher from the ideas with
which they work, and the degree of separation between them as a
result of this. Furthermore, there is a separation 'within' the
student, between the material under study and his own interests or
significant questions. Why should this be so, and is the cause to
be sought in the 'student', in the 'teacher' or in the poorly constructed 'curriculum' with which they appear to be struggling?

We could argue that, in spite of the apparent separation between
student, teacher and the material under study, there is an essential
unity between them in the example described above. More specifically, the teacher's selection of questions to be asked, the student's

attempt to frame his answers in order that they be 'correct' and the
'factual' nature of the material are together constituted in a particular mode of learning. On the one hand the working relationship
of student and teacher is expressed in the form of discourse in
which they engage; the ideas that come into existence for them are
an actualization of this relationship in which they stand together.
Similarly, their definition of study as a re-view of established
ideas predisposes them to work with these concepts in ways outlined
in the example. We conclude that the form of the student's
learning, the style of the teacher's presentation and the nature of
the material with which they work do not have compartmentalized
existences, but are instituted in a system of educational practice
that contains them as related elements.

Therefore, if we wish to understand a particular mode of learning
in the context of higher education (or anywhere else, for that
matter) we shall need to appreciate the system of relationships to
which it owes its expression. This calls into question any approach
to a study of education which is premised upon the apparent separation of student, teacher and material as fixed entities. We
cannot assume that ideas have an existence or a status ('fact',
'truth' or 'fiction') independent of how they are produced and
employed by students and teachers together; nor should we seek
for some abstract student-teacher relationship which exists apart
from the educational practice in which they are joined.

We are led to make two further points about learning in this
context. It has a practical basis in that those involved are
engaged with others in particular ways of relating to the material
at hand. This 'relating' is no intellectual matter merely, for by
it we refer to such things as students and teachers being interested, being objective or being imaginative. These terms refer to the
exercise of our capacities as persons engaged in particular relationships to ideas: they do not refer to abstract mental states
nor to those ideas taken as isolated entities. Second, we have
argued that learning is an expression of a social system of educational practice, which is grounded in the ways in which student
and teacher together work with their material. Taken together,
these social and practical aspects refer us to the personal nature
of the learning process. However, by personal we do not mean essentially 'subjective' nor 'individual', although both of these
aspects are often noted as missing from educational situations which
require students only to 'get the facts'. For our position argues
that what can be said and what can be done with ideas is a function
of the practical relationships in which people are involved. Now we
might resort to encouraging students to provide their 'subjective
experiences' (as opposed to the syllabus material), or to placing
accent upon individuals (as opposed to groups of people). However,
to do this would be to continue to participate in the assumption
that students are estranged from the curriculum, and all that would
be achieved is a change of emphasis within that viewpoint.

In order to understand further the unity of the system that we
have proposed, it is necessary to describe an example of learning
and teaching in which estrangement appears to play no part. However, before doing this we need to appreciate something of the
objectives of the learning situation with which we began, particu-

larly as these are defined by the contexts in which the actual
learning situations stand. This is not only to provide a fuller
account of the system of relations to which we have drawn attention
(which is clearly larger than a single teacher instructing a single
student), but also to retain a critical attitude towards what we
mean by the social and practical basis of study. We should point
out that the mode of learning that we are concerned to criticize
here is only one aspect of the educational process, and should not
be taken as a description of the whole. A lecture course, a seminar
discussion or a tutorial might operate at one time in this mode, and
then pass into a different mode of educational practice. However,
to appreciate why this particular form of learning should so often
endure we need to examine the objectives that underpin it, and also
to inquire into why those involved might be resistant to it being
changed.

THE WIDER CONTEXT OF EDUCATIONAL OBJECTIVES

To understand the learning situation outlined above, we need to view
it within the immediate objectives of the student and the teacher.
Such objectives are, in the long term, framed in terms of the
student's performance in examinations, which are the basis of the
award conferred by the institution. In the short term, essays and
tutorial papers may be part of an assessment procedure, providing a
coursework component as part of the overall judgment made. What are
the effects of asking students to frame their learning as prepa-
ration for external assessment? The main effect, well known to all
teachers and students, is to make students focus down upon the
material which they believe to be the likely source of examination
questions and thus attempt to remember it. This 'focusing down'
means that ideas or material extraneous to the syllabus will be
disregarded and that the syllabus material provides the terms of
reference for their learning.
   Before we go further, it is important that we do not imagine that
all students 'focus down' in the same way, nor that the setting of
the examination in itself causes the students to change their
pattern of study. What happens is that students adjust their study
in terms of their understanding of what the assessor (often the
teacher) requires them to know. In their concern to learn what is
being offered to them, in their attempts to please, or even in their
competitive spirit, students are to be seen within the same relationships that were described previously. Here, instead of an
awareness of estrangement from the material, the student may be
quite adept at picking up the ideas which he believes he is required
to learn. He may perform well in examinations and show a keenness
that the teacher finds appealing. However, to the extent that this
student directs his energies only towards grasping ideas which he
believes the teacher requires him to retain, in so far as he allows
his personal questions and problems to be dormant, and in so far as
he strives to learn in order to gain grades higher than those of his
fellow students, then he also is estranged from the learning
process.
   What is happening in this situation is that student and teacher

are living out a relationship in which the teacher exercises a
discriminatory function over what material the student will encounter.   In its institutionalized form we recognize the expression
of this relationship in the primacy of the syllabus.   The mode of
relating within the system is characterized by the teacher exer-
cising his authority (his expertise in the discipline), to select
ideas which he then presents to students.   He may ask questions, set
problems, or present information in the form of alternative explanations within the discipline.   Although not presented dogmatically,
these ideas are taken by students as being in themselves the essence
of their studies, defining for them the requirements and the limits
of their educational experience.   The teacher has before him, or
within his reach, the field of knowledge that he defines as the
scope of the students' studies.   From this he selects what he wishes
to put forward, and he will do so in whatever way seems appropriate
to what he is trying to explain.   The teacher is actively working
with his subject-matter in making such discriminations, although he
may, in his presentation, put forward these ideas (as theories,
findings, questions) in a form in which they are most readily
tangible to the student.   That is to say, the decisions and choices
that face the teacher as he works through his material (say, in
preparing a lecture) will not necessarily be apparent in the final
presentation which he makes to the students.   In effect, the
lecture, the articulation of the ideas upon which he has been
working, is his product and it is this product which he places
within the reach of his pupils.

Presented in this way, the material stands in relation to the
student as a finished product stands in relation to a consumer.   It
arises within a thought process or discourse which is not his own -
in which he has not participated.   The ideas may come to him in a
form in which they appear ready-made, lacking the strands or tell-
tale marks which indicate the progression of thought or action which
gave rise to this apparent end-point or pause in knowledge.   What is
most important is that, within a learning system in which assessment
predominates, the student's orientation to these ideas is characterized by his feeling at one time that:

(a)   these ideas are important and necessary because they have been
      selected by the teacher for presentation;   and
(b)   that the form or the purposes of the discipline result in
      their being separate from his own questions about the people
      or events he seeks to understand.

Students vary greatly in how they respond to this state of
affairs, some overcoming the separation between themselves and the
material, while others achieve an uneasy compromise with their
studies or reject them altogether.

For many, ideas presented in this way do just remain 'foreign' to
themselves.   They work with it as they must, they try to remember it
as best they can, and in turn re-present it back to the teacher at
various times.   The learning function can be described as a process
in which the ideas are opaque in the student's experience, so that
they exist for him as entities with which he has to deal.   Grasping
these ideas means, in effect, making the same selections that were

originally demonstrated by the teacher. But we are not to imagine
that the process of selection for the student is the same as that
for the teacher. The teacher exercises the power of discrimination
in his choice of what he will present: the student, in so far as
his learning is aimed only at making the same selections, deprives
himself of the power of being a discriminating individual. In an
extreme case the student is an operator of a system of abstractions
provided by the teacher, in which he simply maintains the ideas (the
'knowledge') to which he has been introduced. He provides the
living force, as it were, which maintains that system of ideas as
ways of interpreting the world. What I mean by this is that, no
matter whether the student is interested in the subject-matter or
not, the ideas with which he works are kept separate from the
questions which he, as a particular individual, might ask. Interest
in the subject-matter is still possible (and not uncommon) in a
person whose thinking is alienated from his personal life. Such a
student may be skilled in operating with ideas with which he is
acquainted, but he does not actively relate to them. There is no
inter-penetration of ideas with the spontaneous questions, arising
from his life experience, which is at once a personal commitment to
his thinking and also the key to his freedom within the discipline.
    At this point we might ask why, when students and teachers are
engaged in this form of educational practice, they do not seek to
change the circumstances in which they find themselves. Indeed,
inasmuch as there are students (and staff) who do not feel that this
form of learning satisfies what they believe to be a thorough educational experience, then dissent at various points may set in. For
students, it may take the form of a reaction against the educational
system in which they work. They might reject the material (the
given questions), the need for assessment, the views of the staff;
or else this rejection may take the form of an inner dispiriting
reaction. Then the student may feel only disappointment with what
he had hoped would be an educational challenge, and, keeping these
feelings to himself, quietly soldier on with a learning experience
that he now knows to be less than what he wanted it to be. Staff
may also question the function of what they do, and in doing this
realize more fully the apparent contradiction that exists for them
as teachers - teaching for assessment, or teaching for understanding. It is at these points - when some raise criticisms of
current practices - that defensive manoeuvres by remaining staff
and students often illustrate well the nature of the system within
which they operate. Let us detail these below.
    In the face of criticism, there is a tendency for some teachers
to assert the primacy of assessment within the institution. This
function, arising out of the relationship of the university to other
institutions in society, is retained unquestioningly in their
arguments as a basis for determining the internal relationships of
the university, e.g. those between staff and students. Underlying
this is the social prescription that we employ methods which distinguish 'better' from 'worse' performers in academic activities.
In support of this, and as an adjunct to the proper and efficient
implementation of these methods, teachers often appeal to the need
for 'fairness' in their treatment of students. The notion of
'fairness' is often used by academics to justify the various methods

of assessment employed, and indeed as a reason for structuring
teaching in particular ways. Too often, however, it is a necessary
justification because it papers over the cracks of teaching based
upon assessment, i.e. where the criteria of the educational bureau-
cracy are taken as basic premises for learning. So, any teaching
method that has embodied within its own 'objective techniques' the
discriminatory powers which are properly those of student and
teacher together can be justified as being, through its 'objectivity', both more reliable and therefore 'fair'. The argument is made
- attempts at liberal concern notwithstanding - from the basic
assumption that all students need to have the equal chance of
learning the same material under the same conditions, and to be
assessed in the same way as far as possible. That is, there is the
assumption that all should have an equal opportunity to be passed
through the educational system, at each stage operating by its
criteria and eventually being graded in similar fashion. However,
such concern with 'fairness' is surely misplaced, as in this case
it actually depends upon the teachers' failure to examine the educational practices which are the grounds of their judgment.

Many students also react negatively to suggestions that their
studies should not be aimed at direct assessment. Here again, the
need to be assessed is seen by students as part of the necessary
grading of themselves as they are schooled for later employment.
While often resenting assessment at any moment, they accept it in
principle (and, as we have argued, in practice), and will not be
robbed of opportunities to 'do better' and attain higher grades.
They must and will compete with each other, even if gaining a degree
(in the long term) means sacrificing learning experiences in the
here and now.

Assessment and all that goes with it is often defended on the
grounds that it ensures that students come into contact with
relevant aspects of the discipline. Here knowledge is seen as
standing in a ready-made form, as an edifice that the student must
come to know. Implied by this is the argument that assessment
ensures that students know the history of the subject, their discipline, before they begin to try to speculate upon these matters for
themselves. I would argue that it has quite the reverse effect.
Where students are asked to learn selected material they often lack
the very basis of a historical feel for the problems and questions
that underlie the discipline which they are studying. To understand
the evolution of thought within a particular field one needs to have
some grasp of the way in which previous thinkers have formulated
their questions and confronted the problems which stemmed from them.
There is, in my experience, no better way to sensitize a student to
this process than to require him, in conjunction with his own
reading of the literature, to engage in this struggle for himself.
Only by acknowledging the process of inquiry as real and present in
our learning here and now, can we expect students to attain this
perspective upon a discipline in its historical development. When
staff use assessment to present their subject-matter as a 'buffet of
ideas', they do the greatest disservice to disciplined thought, to
their students and to themselves, for they deny the community of
ideas from which knowledge emerges, and to which it returns. And
if a student who has not known this process does come, through an

awareness of his alienation from the subject-matter, to reject the pre-selected set of notions with which he has been presented, then he may also reject with them the discipline itself. This latter possibility is a serious one, the importance of which must not be disguised because it has implications for how students may come to see not only their particular discipline but intellectual endeavour as a whole.

The danger that arises when a student rejects the set of ideas with which he has been presented 'in alien form' is that he believes he has rejected the discipline as such, including its underlying practice. Never knowing an alternative process of learning, he equates the offered patchwork of abstractions (to which he cannot relate) with the very activity of intellectual enquiry itself. Or rather, he rejects with the pre-selected answers provided by others not only the educational practice which he believes to underlie intellectual activity, but the likelihood of ever experiencing study as a worthwhile activity. As an individual decision it is unfortu-nate and to be counted as a failure of the educational process. As a communicated idea - as a standpoint from which he then discusses and appraises education - it is the seed of the deepest anti-intellectualism, of the very distrust and dislike of learning stemming from disenchantment and disillusion. And this seed is bred in the practice which is, I believe, pseudo-learning; edu-cation as the retention of information for the purpose of assess-ment. The disillusion of the student is a very real one and may grow slowly through a vague sense that learning ought to be an endeavour, not a chore; or it emerges suddenly with the student's experience of learning in a different mode.

WORKING WITH DOUBT

As we have pointed out already, the mode of learning described above is not synonymous with the particular educational situations in which it is found. A mode of learning is that aspect - related to the student - of a social process defining the co-ordinated praxis of teacher and student working with the material under study. Therefore, any seminar, lecture or tutorial situation may realize successively more than one 'mode of learning'. Our aim so far has been limited to describing one particular mode as a form of social practice and to indicating, albeit briefly, how it is instituted in the context of higher education.

We must now turn to an alternative form of learning in which the relations between teacher, student and material constitute an edu-cational system distinct from the one which we have described. In this process, the material does not exist for either party as a 'given' - as a syllabus to be worked through and grasped as a product already fashioned by others. Instead, the ideas with which both student and teacher are working have a more transparent quality, in existing for them as pointers towards things that they are trying to express or trying to grasp. I mean by this that the ideas do not stand in relation to the student and teacher as objects upon which they operate, or about which they frame the discussion. The material is not simply the subject of a selection procedure

carried out by both parties, inasmuch as they might reflect upon
these ideas as ready-made 'concreta' to be systematically thought
upon as an end in themselves. Instead of this both student and
teacher are engaged in a two-way process of expressing what it is
that they are trying to formulate and grasping those things which
the other person is indicating. An idea in this sense is no object
to be looked upon, but is a perspective from which the person
anticipates ideas in formulation. It takes on a quality of being a
sign, a felt indicator of things that are not yet fully expressed,
and brings into relation the person's own questions with elements in
the discipline or in the world to which that question points. And
yet this is only half-true because the idea itself - in that form -
is that moment created as an expression of the relationship between
the person (his questions) and those things which he is trying to
explain or to understand. The teacher engages with the student in
the task of exploring a perspective or set of ideas within the
discipline in relation to the student's own basis of understanding.
Rather than being engaged in assembling or transmitting items of
information, their discussion points always from a shared basis of
understanding towards the problem which, together, they articulate.
Again, this use of ideas is seen as the expression of a relationship
between teacher and student, at once emerging from it and making
such a unity of relating possible. Only the willingness (and the
courage) to reveal one's own doubt to the other and to attempt to
grasp the other's doubt sets this relationship in motion. (By doubt
I mean the acknowledgment of one's relationship to those things one
is trying to explain as being partial and open to change - I do not
mean a flinching sense of confusion.) And that relationship's
existence is realized in the mutual exchange of ideas, as described
above. What emerges from such a conversation is often an interchange between student and teacher in which their relating through
the material is established in a form that was not there beforehand.
The teacher now 'sees' and grasps the student's problem, or has expressed his own understanding of an issue in a new way. The student
has a new grasp of the material and now feels that it does indeed
express a real relationship between himself and what he wants to
explain.

Such a learning relationship is often characterized by its
immediate sense of unity, and by the apparent lack of distinct
separateness of each constituent element. Ideas are not sensed as
objects that are 'mine' or 'yours', to be selected and judged as
thought appropriate. Nor is it of superficial interest that both
teacher and student lend themselves to a spontaneous exchange in
which they participate but, as separate individuals, do not operate
upon it. This is a different mode of relating to the one which was
described earlier, being one in which fundamental questions are
often raised, imagination exercised and, equally important, relationships between student and teacher have a particular meaning
for both. Because it is involving and draws teacher, material and
student together, its effects extend far beyond that particular
teaching session. The raison d'être for learning may now include
that relationship, which forms a basis to which the student can
return again in his experience. By comparison, in 'information
learning', which is justified in terms external to the student

(i.e. the syllabus) the mere shift to other activities leaves the teaching situation isolated in his wider experience.

For what the involved student has gained cannot be summarized only in terms of ideas treated as discrete objects. After a problem has been outlined, or subsequent to a discussion in which possible solutions have been articulated, the student can indeed point to particular ideas to justify his claim that something 'has been learned'. However, this information that he now holds in a finished form is the product of the mode of relating in which he engaged, and through which his educational experience was re-formed. The prior, and I would argue the primary gain which such educational experience offers is the student's appropriation of that mode of relating as a practice which he can subsequently initiate himself. There are two facets of this which we can readily describe, and an equally important third facet which at present seems to me to be dissipated. The first two are these. The student who grasps this mode of learning as a practice (i.e. as a personal involvement) is then able to encourage this mode of learning in discussion with teachers and fellow students. He becomes a positive creator of inquiry in his educational relationships rather than being a passive digestor of information. (We do not imply that prior to this students are not inquiring; they are indeed so as individuals, but are powerless to pursue this in an educational practice that denies to them as students the validity of their doubt.)

The second facet that follows concerns the student's relationship to the discipline. The appropriation of the practical relation to ideas as pointers, and the realization of one's power to work with material in this way destroys the illusion of study as the incorporation of information drawn from an edifice of knowledge. There is a real difference (and for teachers, a real pleasure) in seeing a student's own questions interpenetrate with the ideas of the authors in his field. One aspect of this is the student's growing awareness of having his own particular position within the field of study. Indeed, it is the articulation of this perspective alongside those of others which allows him to participate fully in the discourse of his discipline.

The dissipation of the third aspect lies in the present failure for these gains to be instituted within the broader context of higher educational practice. The structures within which teachers and students continue to work are expressions of learning as the acquisition of knowledge and the ability to perform well in examinations. The institution and its administrative superstructure are geared to the syllabus and to the examination as tangible aspects of their practice, about which all questions of education can be framed. And this context remains in existence for those students who relate to ideas as 'pointers' rather than as 'concrete information'. By comparison, the second mode of learning we described may well be similar to the educational philosophy of many university teachers, but it is often not synonymous with the educational practice in which they participate. The point is not that syllabuses and exams are in themselves a hindrance to learning: our approach to student-material-teacher relations denies the usefulness of this form of proposition. It is rather that our treatment of learning and teaching, as if they were wholly individual activities,

leaves us unable to explain why the educational gains made by
students and teachers together may be of great personal relevance
but remain, in terms of the institution, of little practical significance. This is so even though academics will readily agree upon
broad aims which dispute that higher education is merely the acquisition of information. However, their educational practice -
grounded in the dissemination of knowledge and the assessment of
performance - is an institutionalized activity extending beyond them
as individuals who hold particular sets of values.

It is important to realize that educational practice transcends
the individual teacher, the individual student and the individual
idea. As we tried to show earlier on, the form of this relating
between our three primary elements itself transforms them as they
participate; so that separate groups of teachers and students are
changed through their relating to each other. Staff meetings and
student discussions not only arise out of educational practices but
serve also to organize the particular groupings in the relationships
in which they stand. The teacher teaches from a perspective defined
by the group to which he belongs, in relation to students as an
organized grouping defining their own perspective. So it should not
be thought that our three primary elements represent individuals
only - although in the here and now in which we participate this
might be our experience - but that they define in concrete instances
the sets of relationships practised by teachers and by students in
relation to the discipline under study. No teacher exists as an
isolated individual, nor so any single student, and even less any
particular idea with which they work. What we would seek to change,
therefore, is not the relating of isolated individuals talking about
particular ideas, but the mode of relating that exists through the
joint actions of teachers and students together. This aim cannot be
achieved by teachers and students acting only as isolated individuals trying to improve their study. Nor is it encouraged by us
seeking a more personal form of learning in which 'hard facts' are
supplanted by some form of 'subjective experience'. What we have
tried to argue is that learning in its personal form is to be understood as a mode of educational practice, which is essentially social
and concerned with the transformation of ideas. The opposing of
'fact' to 'subjective experience' is a contrast that arises within
that mode of learning in which academic knowledge is treated as
ready made, and which thereby defines all other knowledge as 'mere
subjectivity'. This is a spurious opposition which serves (in the
repeated insistence on 'objectivity') to bolster the practice that
underlies it, and to hinder attempts at change.

In its extreme form, education as essentially the acquisition of
information denies to the student the experience of joining with his
teachers and fellow students in realizing his inquiries within the
terms of their discipline. This denial has its counterpart in the
refusal, within this mode of learning, to tolerate doubt as a valid
basis for inquiry. We should perhaps re-emphasize the words 'within
this mode of learning' in the previous sentence, for they direct us
to the source of our discontent. It is in terms of the practical
and social relations of our institutions that we grasp the problem,
for outside of these terms words like 'doubt' have a most elusive
quality. Taken as an index of individual dogmatism, or as a sign

of a shared 'educational philosophy', the refusal of doubt can both
be denied within current practice ('I always try to make students
critical') or asserted as an immediate and possible remedy ('We
should encourage students to ask their own questions'). However,
neither of these attempts to manipulate the issue in abstraction
from educational practice yields a fruitful solution. While individual teachers and students can articulate the contradiction of
their educational experience, they cannot change, at a stroke, relationships that contain them in their working existence. For the
question is misconceived if we confuse the locus of the problem's
realization (in awareness) with the social matrix of its workings
in the institution.

   That is why it is unfortunate, to say the least, to see research
into teaching and learning, which should reveal our educational
problems, often contributing to their obfuscation by participating
in the assumptions which they should question. To study student-
learning styles as if they were unrelated to teaching; to implement
teaching methods as if they were both content and context-free; or
to appraise knowledge as if it could be contained in a syllabus,
produce results of a kind which perpetuate the practical problems
by giving them a further status in educational theory. If anything,
new contradictions are then introduced, because we then find that we
cannot apply our freshly-gained knowledge in practice. We read a
manual on teaching, but doing it was different; we revised our
syllabus and improved our lectures, but still the students would not
discuss; we changed the coursework weighting, but they still want
to know what is relevant to the examination. So it is that teachers
in higher education who experience these contradictions between
theory and practice seem to be caught on an educational millwheel
that turns annually in the current of the students who stream
through their institutions. For questions about learning, about
teaching and about the status of ideas need to be asked in terms
that recognize the social context that together they create, and in
which they co-exist. And surely of equal importance, these
questions need to be asked in ways which admit of some practical
answers to the educational problems with which we need to wrestle,
as well as to study. For if what is 'learned', what is 'taught' and
what is 'known' are aspects of coherent systems of relations then
our educational endeavours should reflect this proposition. Put
simply, we need to construct contexts in which ideas inform our educational practice, and thereby ourselves as co-participants.

Chapter 3

HANDING DOWN THE MAGIC
Margaret Spencer

> It is from my earliest reading that I date the unbroken
> consciousness of my own existence. (Rousseau)

Whoever reads this sentence easily will have difficulty in imagining
the truth of what follows. This chapter is about reading and
learning to read, and no one who reads fluently can fully enter into
the condition of someone who cannot. Agreed, the writer can make or
mar what he writes, and some writers are easier to read than others.
But after he has shaped his thoughts on the page, the writer needs
a reader if he is not simply to talk to himself. You, reading this,
are quite used to all the ways we make meaning by using signs,
designs, print, special script or anything else that pleases us.
You know how to interpret a road sign or a bus ticket. If you want
to read the advertisements in Piccadilly you have only to look at
them. You may also quote them all. Your security in reading, and
mine, comes from knowing that if we want to read, we can.

So natural is this habit of turning all forms of writing into
something meaningful when we attend to them, its origins in us, more
often than not, are an unrecollected mystery that we barely stop to
consider. Then something unexpected, like graffiti in Arabic script
on the wall of the Underground, or the old man in front of us in the
post-office queue who cannot sign his name to get his pension, makes
us realize that we take reading and writing for granted as an extension of speaking and listening.

We are always shocked by an illiterate, embarrassed even. Our
care for our children includes anxiety about their reading; we want
them to be fully and freely literate. What would their lives be
like if they were not? Every parent who leaves a child at the
school-gate hopes that, sooner rather than later, he will master
these skills that schools exist to teach, and having learned to read
and write, will write and read to learn. Although McLuhan suggests
we have outgrown our need to engage with print, there are still very
few signs that we have given up worrying about teaching children to
read. Deep down in many a British parent is a faint belief that
John Stuart Mill, who could read when he was three, began life with
certain distinct advantages. We would like to know a foolproof
method for teaching children, and the quest for this has used up

more cultural, educational and psychological time, and still does,
than any other issue concerning children's learning.

Why are we so sure that everyone should learn to read? Our con-
viction about universal literacy is still framed in nineteenth-
century utilitarian spectacles. Perhaps we think, as Mill's father
did, that when everyone could read and write and had access to all
knowledge, the golden age of the greatest happiness of the greatest
number will arrive. We know now that there was no time in the past
when everyone could read, not even when everyone knew the 'basic
skills', so the movement that seeks to go back to this imagined era
is chasing a will-o'-the-wisp. Centuries before this one, people
learned to read by looking at familiar texts, often things they knew
by heart. They learned to write by copying, not composing. We have
a picture in our heads of thousands of people reading Dickens and we
compare this with people watching television. The 'fluent' reading
of people in Dickens's day came from reading the Bible, which was
commonly heard rather than read, and although more people in the
nineteenth century could read than had been taught in school, it
was by no means the entire population.

It is difficult to imagine that the kind of reading people do
nowadays is something very new. We have an abundance of printed
material that tumbles out of sophisticated machines and expects that
there will be readers to make it meaningful in a way that has no
counterpart in any previous generation, here or elsewhere. That
everyone should be able to read up to a given 'standard' is equally
novel. The reader as an autonomous interpreter of text is a modern
figure. If he undertakes to teach himself by using a book, especially in the matter of inferential reasoning, he is as skilled
as a medieval philosopher. What seems so obvious to us now that
books are all around, that everyone can be taught, that schools,
libraries, that agencies of all kinds promote literacy, is very new
in the history of literacy, and we are sometimes so busy looking at
learning to read that we fail to see its links with what is to be
read. When children have difficulties we look at them to see what
is wrong but rarely examine the consequences of living in a literate
society. The general belief is that everyone has the same view of
what is involved in reading and a common agreement about why it is
important.

But when we learn to read we actually see the world differently
because what we read changes our view of it. Our experience is both
confirmed and extended, and the limits of where we are are not the
limits of what can happen to us. To see ourselves as readers is to
enter a universal brotherhood but it is still in some ways a curious
thing to do. As the process of learning begins in the first months
of school (the agency designated for the initiation of our children
when a great many things are changing for them) they may not be
particularly surprised by this new linguistic encounter. It usually
happens as children are learning the inner speech of thought, that
curious way of talking in the head, and reading may well seem to be
an extension of this process. If it happens later, it may happen
differently.

Learning to read in our day is strangely paradoxical. Everyone
is expected to learn. But to learn successfully is to be able to
read, not known texts, but new texts, material that carries messages

about the way our lives are organized. Newspapers, manuals of
instruction, records, sales promotion, and post-office print are
all about how our society coheres, how it operates and changes in
our technological age. Public print - the income-tax demand,
passports, pig licenses - informs social behaviour and interprets
society to itself. Information has to be 'retrieved' by reading.
To be effective readers we have to know how to understand what is
written, to think about it and act on the basis of what we understand. People talk of literacy as 'functional', meaning that we
read and write for those functions that concern us so that society
may function. Employers demand this kind of performance and call it
efficiency in a work-force of clerical assistants who are to 'read
off' computer printouts or the results of other mechanized
processes. The contemporary model of a successful reader is of
someone who can scan, review, extract, process and précis information contained in printed text; he is a consumer, the mirror
image of successful twentieth-century economic man.

As our society becomes more complex, technical and abstract, so
does the reading matter, and the successful readers are those who
have stayed longest at school to handle confidently as much of it
as they can. Curiously, our most literate students become specialist readers in a narrow rather than a wide sense. They understand
best only a very small proportion of what is there to be read.
Lawyers rarely read medical journals. But the distinction that sets
a competent reader apart from someone who is illiterate is that he
does not worry about what he cannot read. The illiterate is in a
different case; he may imagine that to be able to read will solve
his problems but he also fears he may have to be able to read everything.

Amongst the many problems of learning to read nowadays is that a
great deal of public print is notoriously difficult or just plain
boring or long-winded. This is not an accident or failure in the
writer. Our complex social systems make a deal of what is written
into something legally or contractually binding. Whoever writes
about food on a container offered for sale, describes a house in a
conveyancing document, gives instructions about a gas fire or sells
a ticket, enters the realm where the words are weighed down with the
authority of Acts of Parliament. The main concern of the writers is
that they should not be caught out saying what is not the case so
they take care to be legally in the right rather than easily understood. To be 'functionally' literate now means that you can deal
with this public writing and all that goes with it, and be neither
duped nor dismayed.

What confuses us most is the idea of a reading 'standard', especially when we hear people say that standards are falling. In
fact, there has never been only one standard of competence in
reading. The 'civic-national' literacy we have been discussing is
constantly changing, but it has never been the same as being 'well-
read'. This is the traditional description of a literate elite.
What we have not decided is: does the raising of our standards of
literacy mean a rise in the general civic-national level of competence to meet the vast array of printed matter by which society
interprets itself to itself, or does it mean an extension to more
people of reading standards that are the traditional inheritance of

a few? (1) Whichever decision we make will affect the teaching of
reading in school. This is a new problem. We are not even sure if
people see this as a choice they can make for themselves.

Part of the paradox is that, alongside the rapid growth in the
amount and kind of printed matter closely associated with people's
lives, there is a significant lack of interest in reading it on the
part of large numbers of the population. Members of Parliament,
employers, educators and others discuss the standards of literacy we
are said to need to function in a complex society, but there is no
evidence that people want to be able to read so as to read public
print. When we have to read complicated documents we get help from
those who know how to read them. The hire-purchase agreement may
be threatening for an illiterate, but those who cannot read have
their own strategies for keeping away from trouble of this kind.
The strongest reason for reading, as opposed to learning to read,
is that it is a special kind of activity with its own reward; it
is generally pleasurable, and does what nothing else can in quite
the same way. To call someone a reader is to suggest that he reads
because he wants to, even when he is not obliged to.

In trying to make sure that everyone can read we have now to look
more clearly at what we are doing. The main reason offered to
children, implicitly in the early stages, explicitly later, is that
to function well in society we have to be clerically competent. A
non-reader is a social failure, someone who is blind in a special
way. We talk about learning to read as necessary for getting a job;
and that is, in the end, true. The barrier comes down there. As a
result, our view of functional literacy narrows still more. We
worry about spelling and punctuation before the learners know themselves as potential writers. Reading is a worry before it can ever
become a pleasure for many children because it is so bound up in
their future in a way they can barely understand except as a vague
menace if they fail. Some children, worried by the early stages,
develop rituals of evasion that stay with them for the rest of their
time in school.

Because we think a child learns to read in the infant school we
are confused when he does not, and the subsequent processes are to
'remedy' what has apparently gone wrong. But, curiously, whatever
else we look at we seem to think that the material is the least
important part of the operation. The general belief is that a child
learns to read by some method unrelated to the kind of reading he
might want to do, and then he can read what he likes. It is a
strange view of the process. We never wonder about what it is to be
'well-read' nowadays, and the notion of a body of common literature
is impossible now when publishers have to produce new stock, or old
titles looking like new titles, or go out of business. Reading has
assumed a curious role in a consumer society, with public libraries
as primary patrons.

Even those who earn their living by reading can cover only an
insignificant number of the thousands of new books published every
year. They read to support their bookish roles and have a wide
choice of books to neglect. As we said at the beginning, literacy
nowadays means knowing what you need not read. But the inexperienced adult or child knows nothing of this choice. For them the
option is to learn to read or not to learn to read, and if they

cannot see what is in the operation for them they simply opt out.
Truly to learn to read is to come to know how to make reading
meaningful in the sense of significant. This realization comes only
when we take the task in hand for ourselves rather than at the
behest of others. In the end, we learn to read because we know,
however vaguely at first, that reading will somehow make a great
deal of difference.

What of the teacher who welcomes the child we left at the gate; how
does her view of reading inform her teaching? Whatever her
training, she knows she has about two years in which to see that the
child satisfies at least some of the parents' aspirations. She sees
the home as 'background'. Within a month she will begin to predict
to herself who is likely to be a good reader. Usually, the child
who prefers the book corner to boisterous playground games catches
the teacher's eye; he is like her, so she confirms him in the role
of a reader.
    The teacher knows that, in a class of thirty children, she will
never have to teach them all to read. Some will already be able to
and their example causes others to imitate them and thus win adult
approval. Some need a period of practice, while others, already
'anticipated', will rarely sit down long enough to engage with a
book. Her college tutors told her that children learn at different
rates but the variety of responses of children to print still comes
as a shock. Infant-school teaching is an exhausting business from
which escape is necessary, especially into sleep. But our young
teacher may see, even in her dreams, her classroom with its ordinary
children, all different, some whose mother tongue is not English,
encircled by the reading experts. There they stand, powerful and
numerous as the troops of Midian, conducting theoretical and
empirical debates about methodology that teachers are expected to
turn into lessons. The children vanish and turn into figures on a
chart.
    Let me testify that these nightly visitings are more than figures
of speech. Whoever has taught a child or an adult to read knows
that the array of offered expertise, the demand for rigorous sequential instruction, is as bewildering as the apparent intracta-
bility of failure. Teachers believe in what works, and every
teacher of reading knows what works for her. No amount of contrary
research evidence will make her give up a teaching strategy that
seems to have some rewards in the pupil's success. The trouble is
that successful practice, to be acknowledged, has to become a credal
statement. There follow local skirmishes between adherents of
various 'methods' and these can develop into national battles
between 'phonics' and 'look and say', with the children in the
middle, their heads bowed over a new writing system, or testing and
screening exercises for research studies that lead to published
reading standards, and the whole cycle of operations begins again.
Teachers can be easily humiliated by national surveys or great
debates. Their natural pragmatic eclecticism in classroom practice,
what they call 'a mixture of teaching methods', has somehow to be
given the cachet of respectability by being embodied in a ritual if
it is to stand beside other reading liturgies which are backed by
orders of service and special books. Teaching reading is now part

of the consumer society. It is an industry with investments of
millions in all kinds of devices, expertise, materials and machines,
the modern consequences of literacy. But in the end, the operation
of teaching someone to read is a collaborative understanding with a
fixed term and known outcomes. The teacher, as in everything else,
teaches herself to the child; the first thing he learns is the
prospects the teacher has of his success. If she is at all uncertain of herself, the child picks up this uneasiness and transfers
it to himself.

Many teachers believe that they are the victims of circumstances
over which they have no control and that the children's success or
failure is unrelated to school. John, aged 7, reads Treasure
Island. His choice of book conditions the teacher's response. She
knows he comes from a 'good' home with many books. He responds to
her view of him as 'a good reader'. Joe, who never engages with
print, even under threat, has 'a poor background'. You can't get
through to Jack because he is away too often. Asad speaks no
English. Teacher and child, especially the child who seems to be
making little progress, are right at the interface of theory and
practice, and teachers have most faith in what gives them least
trouble to do or to administer. The records of the possibilities
of failure are manifold. Almost anything will do as an alibi for
a child's failure to learn, anything, that is, except that he
doesn't want to, that the book bores him, or that the language of
instruction is incomprehensible. Studies of failure range from
linguistic inadequacy to imperfections in binocular vision. It is
so much easier to find a child who does not know what a word is than
to show him. The pathology of reading failure is an exact science.
Yet we are almost unaware of what makes a child learn without help.
It is, in the end, easier to give a test than to teach, so that the
result can be the reason why the child fails. Thus the teacher's
concern that teaching should be a source of pleasure and freedom
shrinks to a preoccupation with the reversal of letters or the
decimal position on a test result. The situation in which the
teacher and the child find themselves, where they engage in the
business of reading together, dwindles to a set of limp-covered
reading books, written in no one's language called 'a reading
scheme'.

For all the high theoretical battles of the reading experts, the
outcome is a non-reading experience, the kind of book that no sensitive person would regard as worth a second glance. Yet almost every
child in school has, at some point in his progress, encountered this
formal passage into literacy.

In the 1960s, everyone concerned with reading was taken up with
devising a detailed model of reading skills arranged in a hierarchical structure. 'Look and say' and 'phonic' methods were derived
from a decision about what constituted the smallest unit to be read
- the word or the letter. In fact, there was nothing new about any
of it; we had been using the same teaching methods for centuries
but now there was a psychology of behaviour to reinforce practice
and reading machines to give a technological gloss to the enterprise. The experts talked about the reinforcement of 'reading
skills' and encouraged teachers to believe that children learning
to read are like rats entering a maze with no obvious prior con-

ception of the pathways. Worst of all, the domination of experts
made parents, who were hitherto very happy to read to their children
and to help them to learn, feel that they were somehow confusing the
operation because they did not know the official ropes, the techniques for teaching reading. A great deal of specially-produced
material made reading seem very scientific, and what children had
been doing as well as ever in the past suddenly became a cause of
great concern. 'Remedial' departments sprang up, kits and teacher-
proof materials proliferated, and quasi-scientific scores called
'reading age' began to occupy the place left by the almost dis-
credited I.Q. The teacher's view of her task became clouded by the
belief that in reading, the parts counted for more than the whole,
so that many were convinced that the test score, not the child's
obvious mastery, told her when he could read. While the world
outside school was extending the meaning of 'to read' to include
'to read off' instruments, to read a diagram, a map, even a town,
a film or a situation, and children playing in nursery schools at
cops and robbers said into imaginary walkie-talkie sets, 'Do you
read me, over', schools still made them perform on tests of single
word recognition. Official assessment always lags behind a reader's
engagement with what reading intends and what he intends reading to
mean.

Twice in every century we have a paroxysm of anxiety about
literacy. By the beginning of the 1970s, in response to indetermi-
nate but firmly-held beliefs that standards were falling (they
weren't, but the scare was successful in making the worry general),
a committee was set up under Sir Alan Bullock 'to make suggestions
as to how present practice might be improved'. The committee had
many recommendations, notably that reading had to be the concern of
all teachers, not just the experts. By the time the report
appeared, the notion that reading had absolutely to be learned as a
series of strategies, including 'word attack skills', was giving way
to a view that included the insights drawn from newer studies of how
children learn language and, above all, how they come to know themselves as learners. After all, school is a public place; reading
looks like a social obligation. To fail to learn to read is to fail
at school in a way that is specially noticeable. The idea that
reading was a piece of learning that children could do because they
had already learned to speak came as a relief to teachers who had
always believed this to be so. The problem was, the experts had
already eroded the confidence of both the teachers and the pupils,
with the very best of intentions.

Those who are convinced that children need encouragement more
than skills practice to learn to read believe that 'a child receives
remarkably little credit for his mastery of language. Because he is
given no formal instruction by adults, the magnitude of his
achievement is grossly underrated'. (2) If we look at the young
reader's 'miscues', we see him trying to make meaning from the text
if he is told to do this rather than to 'decode'. Making reading
meaningful now became the concern of those who extended psycholin-
guistic insights to learning to read. By this view, children no
longer have to perform actions with words in ways that bear no relation to what a successful reader does. 'Behave like a real
reader' is the invitation; guess, sort out the meaning from the

text. The young reader is to go about reading as readers do, and
the teacher has to stand behind the child's head to see what the
task looks like from there. Most research and nearly all teacher
training takes its stance behind the teacher's head and the invitation to the child is couched in the terms of the instructor. The
child or his home may be at fault, but the assumption is that the
teaching procedure is beyond reproach. The context of the operation, where and how the teacher and the child come together with a
book, has been largely ignored. The idea that what is read may make
some, if not all the difference, is scarcely entertained. The
collaborative nature of the enterprise does not form part of the
analysis of its success or failure.

What does learning to read look like if we stand behind the child's
head? The view is different for the successful and the unsuc-
cessful. In her study, 'Young Fluent Readers', Margaret Clark shows
how the total context of these children - they came to school able
to read beyond the risk of failure - is significant. (3) They
enjoyed reading in the company of supportive adults, not all of them
middle-class parents. They made sense of the words and seemed to
understand the voice in the page. They spoke a Scottish dialect of
English which in no way interfered with their learning. They
enjoyed the stories they read and tried talking about them. They
expected print to make sense and knew they were successful. As the
result of her investigations Margaret Clark wondered if learning to
read is exactly the developmental process many people think it is.
She was inclined to doubt the 'essential sequential steps' that the
experts insisted were a necessary part of learning to read. Instead, she showed how parents and children collaborated in choosing
TV programmes, for instance, and in enjoying reading together. The
heavy-handed apparatus of school was significantly absent.
    When young children talk about how they learn to read their
explanations seem unconvincing to adults when they say 'one day I
saw what I had to do and I said it'; 'my mother told me the words
and I read it'; 'I suddenly saw what it said and I said it out
loud'. Whatever the early part of the process, and we still haven't
put all the pieces together to understand exactly what happens,
there comes a moment when the learner feels confident that he can
manage on his own. He is still not clear how the reading process
works any more than he knows about speech as he learns to talk, and
his ignorance of words like 'sentence' is notorious. The decision
to go about the business of reading like a reader is so much part of
the action of learning that he cannot even remember it later.
    He is still puzzled by reading, but it is the puzzle of a game,
of a jig-saw, of sorting something out. He can try to read
something 'as if it made sense'. The puzzlement may include uncertainty about the right way up for the book, who actually says
the words, where the eyes go at the end of the line or how to 'read'
the pictures, but because the words and the pictures stay where they
are, the learner can go back to them. It is like the puzzlement of
play, learning the rules of the game, and has the freedom of play,
freedom to engage with the material as we like. The natural rhythm
of verse, the skipping rhymes and street lore, the topsy-turvies of
word puzzles have all accustomed the child to sorting out word

games. The inner speech of thought, just developing, helps him to
put together this intriguing new game of reading. It is so easy to
deceive ourselves into thinking that children learn to read because
of what we tell them to do, that we miss the chance of looking at
all the other things that help them towards understanding how to
make written language meaningful. A picture is the greatest support
in distinguishing outlines that look like what we see in the outside
world even if it isn't exactly the same. When we know what it's
'supposed to be', then we see it that way.

Gradually as he knows a book for what it is, the reader's view of
the task becomes more clearly defined, and mastery approaches. 'I
used to wonder,' said a child, 'who put the sound of the words in.
Then I realized that I did it.' By the time he is 9 or so and
wondering if he will ever learn to spell, the young reader begins
to look at the constituent parts of the words he is writing. Asked
then how he learned to read, he will say and believe he learned the
alphabet first, although at 6 he said his brother told him what it
said and he 'knew how it worked'.

Coming to know how the words mean on the page is only half the
operation of learning to read. The other half is the child's sense
of story. Right from the days of his pre-sleep monologues the child
makes up stories about himself and his world. He begins to notice
that stories in a book have certain recurrent conventions such as
beginnings and endings, the formulae of 'once upon a time' and a
continuous past tense. The stories are about strange people, born
like and unlike the adults in the everyday world, kings, queens,
princesses, witches, clever little tailors and talking animals who
help to sort out the world in the child's head, to organize the
experience of walking alongside that giant adult, to indicate how
the world is ordered, especially in terms of chance and fortune.
Adults are very ambivalent about the process called 'making it up'.
To them the 'fictive' has implications of deceit and lying, and
fairy tales have not always enjoyed popularity with those who see
the picture they give of the world as of dubious relevance.
Rousseau, an avid reader of romances, wanted no fables for Emile
because they presented such a picture of life as led to inevitable
disappointment afterwards. But as their memories are short,
children use stories to organize their thinking so that in reading
they confirm a habit of narrative that is already well established.
Stories help us all to have more than one life and to live our lives
forward in anticipation of the next occurrence of what we have
already learned. A child's early reading (or being read to) is a
place to play, a means of 'assimilating reality to the ego without
the need for accommodation', (4) a source of pleasure and safe new
encounters.

Gradually the printed page becomes another focus of language
interaction, comparable to, but also different from, the interpersonal functions of language in the social world. Sartre's remi-
niscences (always regarded as important, while others are classed as
'mere anecdotage') are helpful in this, as in other ways. When he
realized, as his mother read to him, 'it was the book that was
talking', he noticed how 'sentences emerged ... rich in unknown
words. They were in love with themselves and their meanderings and
had no time for me; sometimes they disappeared before I understood

them: at others I had understood in advance, and they went rolling
on nobly towards their end without sparing me a comma'. Sartre goes
on to describe how he took reading in hand for himself ('I was as
zealous as a catechumen, I even gave myself private lessons'). From
behind a teacher's head this is the future philosopher manifesting
superior intelligence. But Sartre, with a writer's power to give
this experience a reality which, its intensity notwithstanding, it
could never have had at the time, shows us a puzzled child who,
seeking a role for himself in a house where his identity and status
were dubious, saw in books and reading a source of adult approval.
He learned to read by enacting reading rituals, and also by making
reading do what reading does. He latched on where he could, pre-
dicting his way through an unlikely tale. Strange language was part
of the game. The book was the dwelling-place of 'the woodcutter,
the woodcutter's wife, and their daughters, all those little people,
our fellow creatures, [who] had acquired majesty, their rags were
magnificently described, the words left their mark on objects,
transforming actions into ritual events and ceremonies'. (5) We
usually expect language on a page to be like written speech and
think that children can thus understand that reading is words, like
print as speech is words. But if the text is formally different
their attention focuses on the difference and reading becomes a
different verbal rhythm, for one thing. Some children learn by
recognizing what they say. Others by noticing that written language
is in fact different from spoken language. The advantages seem to
be with the latter.

There seems no doubt that children who learn to read early do it
differently from those who come to it later. Stories are always
part of the early process, and knowing what a book is. (6) When a
group of 7-year-old children were discussing with their teacher the
difficulties experienced by another child in the class, one said to
the teacher: 'You see miss, she doesn't know it's stories'. The
crucial point is to 'get into' the story. The author's invitation
is important. The convention tells the child what to expect after
'once upon a time'. Realism, so greatly prized by adults, is not
necessarily essential to the child's understanding of what is afoot.

We can be more sure of this if we look from behind the head of a
child who has difficulty in the early stages or, even more so, in
adolescence. Usually he receives a conditional invitation to engage
with the task, and then only when he comes to school. There is no
need to castigate the home for failing to point out the advantages
of reading; too much emphasis on reading before school can be as
bad as too little, but clearly the terms of the offering are significant. If the usefulness of reading is asserted before the
pleasure is experienced, then the expectation of the learner is
simply different. If the adult demands certain specific responses
to print and excludes the tolerance of mistakes, then the child sees
he is on a perilous path. Guessing, inventing the story, 'having a
go' may be frowned upon so that the child's natural instinct for
discovery is repressed. When he fails to make the process respond
to the instruction he is given, or he lacks the confidence to pro-
ceed, he averts his eyes more and more from the page and looks at
his teacher's face. By this time the process is not puzzling, in
our exploratory sense, it is bamboozling, leaving a trail of un-

certainty in its wake, another adult-imposed duty, where to be right
is to do what one is told. Then the special cards, the vowel
charts, the 'remediation' material, the books with short sentences,
all conspire to convey the message of failure. The learner may be
highly motivated in that he desperately wants to be like the others;
he may do everything he thinks his teacher is telling him to do,
like 'sounding it out', reading every word until it is correct, and
still not 'make it work' because the essential relevance of what he
is doing to what reading is has not been made clear. He may recognize ice-cream signs, cigarette packets and TV slogans. He could,
given half a chance, turn a hi-fi advertisement into a story and the
motor-bike catalogue into another, but as his enterprise is so
dominated by fragments of reading, he never sees the relevance of
what he knows, what he can do, to what he is asked to do. The
teacher's view of the task and the child's view of the task are at
their most disjoint when the things the teacher takes for granted
are those the child needs to know are relevant, namely, his own
stories, in his head, in his family, in his day-to-day encounters.
A determined adolescent, whose progress was being recorded as part
of an investigation into what is involved in teaching someone with
a history of prolonged failure, said desperately, 'I've been coming
for two-and-a-half years and still you haven't taught me to read'.
He could not believe that his strength lay in his mastery of
storying and his total absorption in what he was reading. As this
was pleasant, reading had to be something else. Because he saw
himself as a different kind of person from those he thought of as
readers, he had difficulty in believing that what he did was what
they did. Alienated from the view that he can ever tackle reading
with success, the inexperienced reader builds up a different picture
of the total operation. He sees it as something to do with school.
In any subsequent rejection of school (and without reading ability
he soon becomes a 'case'), reading is rejected too. Books become a
threat. If the pupil is expected to use a book to 'attack' words,
if the words come in sentences he meets nowhere else, wherein lies
the attraction? When a reader 'gets into' a book he withdraws from
the social world into a quasi-social relationship, what D.W.Harding
calls 'the bond with the author'. (7) If the text does not offer
this as a possibility but instead asks questions like 'Where is the
red balloon?' to which the answer is either right or wrong, then the
risk is increased. Highly motivated and sensitive children always
seem to be aware, to a greater or less extent, of this withdrawal
into the story in the book. Asked where they like best to read,
most children say 'in bed', where the physical separation from
social life helps the retreat into the alternative world. Most
unwilling-to-read adolescents know the obscure threat of this separation and prefer the company of their peers or the watching of TV.
What for Proust's narrator was the security of the 'cabinet' at the
top of the house, where he was allowed to lock the door so that he
could weep or read, is for some children a threatening idea. The
problem is to know oneself in the world and in the book, and to be
at home in both.

The menace of 'functional' illiteracy that hangs over the unsuc-
cessful teenager is rarely countered by an invitation to enter the
reading world he may have glimpsed. He must read to get a job, and

the more his teachers realize his plight, so the tensions increase.
The bamboozlement becomes aggression as he enters further education
where he has the right to make more stringent demands on his in-
structors. He now insists that his teacher should do what all his
other teachers had failed to do, and by those same methods. So the
material is changed to 'relate' to his situation, and for reasons
that are never explained. This means he reads short stories which
present, in the name of realism, the lowest level of human relations, gangs, social problems such as unemployment, stealing,
family disruption, all at a time when idealism could be at its
height. No wonder the teenage non-reader sees himself as different.
The reading business is like an impenetrable pocket sewn with invisible string that he is constantly ordered to open. As long as we
show him reading as a form of information retrieved for purposes he
does not see as his own, the less attractive it becomes. His view
of the teacher is of someone with a bag of gold, the secret
knowledge about reading, to be dispensed in exchange for a contract
of good behaviour in class, on the correct 'sounding out' of irrelevant forms of language.

If a pupil has rarely associated the sound of a story with what
it might look like, if he has no idea of what happens between 'once
upon a time' and 'happily ever after', then the first pages of a
novel, with the need to suspend judgment on both the action and the
characters, is bound to be perplexing. How much worse is a text
about an unfamiliar subject? Experienced readers know how books
work; they have forgotten when they learned how episodes are related to each other.

By using videotapes to watch children in lessons we are learning
what it never occurred to us to teach. A 12-year-old reading 'The
Magic Finger' was discussing events in the story with his teacher,
just as readers normally do. 'What were these neighbours like?'
asked the teacher, and was puzzled by the pupil's apparent inability
to understand her question because there was no suggestion that she
was trying to catch him out. She repeated the question, again with
no reply. 'Would you shoot wild duck?' asked the teacher. There
was a pause, then, 'Oh, I see,' said the pupil. His expression
changed from incomprehension to relaxed awareness. His shoulder
tension slackened. He didn't answer the question but he read on
with increased speed and fluency. He had realized that the
judgments the reader makes about people and their actions in the
real world have their counterparts in a story, and are thereby extended. But until we learn to look for these lacunae in the
learner's view of the task, we have not discovered how to help him
to come to know.

The path of the inexperienced adolescent reader is strewn with
hazards that teachers often fail to notice. The act of reading is
an act of concealment; we cannot actually see it happening, except
as someone looking at a book. Teachers usually like to talk to a
class because they believe they can tell when someone stops
listening. When a class is reading a book the teacher has no
certainty that the looking is transformed into understanding. When
we watch any game of skill we look for tips of style or expertise on
which to model our own performance. But the connoisseurship of
reading is invisible; it involves an invitation into silence.

Perhaps every school should have a reading-room where people go to
read in companionable quiet, where the social life is club-like,
quiet with the satisfaction of readers being together although withdrawn into reading.

Another unresolved problem is, who owns the book, especially the
one given to a child in school? A paperback selected and bought
fits snugly into a pocket and has on it the stamp of possession.
A school book is generally unyielding and a library book is stiff
with municipal binding. Both are linked to the institutions with
invisible chains as surely as in a monastery. When the pupil asks
'Can I take the book home?' the answer indicates the relationship of
the teacher and the learner and the adult's view of the child as a
reader. The mechanism of impersonal borrowing and lending cannot be
friendly or casual, for books cost money. The conditions of
'owning' what the school supplies are not conducive to being a
reader, at least not on the same terms as the person who has a
collection of his own. Many young people stay away from even the
most relaxed British public library because they feel their visits
cast them in a role they do not fully understand. Some libraries
are fearsome places which turn books into alien objects. Some
teachers cannot give out books to a class without admonitions about
not defacing or losing them. Thus children can only believe that it
is safer not to incur a book as a debt, therefore they never learn
that it is possible to borrow a book, read it, return it, and still
keep it, in a strange way, as part of oneself. To invite children
to become readers must at some point include unconditional sharing
of books with them on terms of equality and generosity.

In a fine story called Poor Koko, John Fowles tells how a middle-
aged author, surprised at night by a young burglar, discusses with
him the art and craft of being a writer. His mission accomplished,
the burglar ties up the author, and then, in what seems an act of
gratuitous vandalism, burns the author's manuscript, the work of
years, before his very eyes. For a long time after the author
wonders why. Part of his speculation goes thus:

> I must very soon have appeared to the boy as one who deprived him
> of a secret - and one he wanted to possess. The rather angry
> declaration of at least some respect for books; that distinctly
> wistful desire to write a book himself. That striking word-deed
> paradox in the situation, the civil chat while he went round the
> room robbing; that surely not quite unconscious incoherence in
> his views; that refusal to hear, seemingly to understand, my
> mildly raised objections; that jumping from one thing to another
> ... all these made the burning of my book only too justly
> symbolic in his eyes. What was really burning was my gener-
> ation's refusal to hand down a kind of magic. (8)

In the presence of someone who thinks he has not learned to read we
are bound to ask ourselves why we failed to 'hand down the magic',
for that is what it must seem to the illiterate.

The daunting self-assurance of the well-read is a constant threat to
others. It so often looks like arrogance, and we can understand why
the inexperienced reader appears to reject the 'high culture' and

its initiates. Many teachers believe, however, that the training
they received in the elitist tradition is the very thing they must
make available to the discerning few, whoever they are. They want
apprentices of 'proven intellectual stamina' in whom they can 'train
the capacity to evaluate and adjust an individual scheme of values
in relation to personal literary experience'. (9) Other teachers
are equally exclusive in that they reject all that stems from what
they believe to be an elitist construct of literature and the
publishers who support it. They see reading for what they call
life-enhancement as self-indulgent escapism, and they would pin
children down to the hard graft of learning-by-reading. Each of
these views is absolutist. If only the discerning are to be admitted to the mysteries, reading will become the new mandarinism.
If reading is only taught as a part of study skills no child will do
more than he has to. We have already said that no one can read
everything, and as things stand, publishing on a grand scale is
interested in manuscripts that fulfil marketing criteria more than
literary or functional ones. What we need is a new cosmology of
literacy, new maps, new bearings, new means of charting the relation
of reading and writing to the lives of people who will soon have
more time for both. The possibility that more publishing on a
smaller, local scale, can offer to more people a wider prospect of
literacy than ever before must not slip past. The idea that parents
may write books for their children should soon become a commonplace.
Either we genuinely share the best consequences of living in a
literate society or we lose even those advantages we desperately
want to keep. The failing reader is cut off from not only the
economic functions of literacy, but also from alternative ways of
knowing himself in his generation.
    Clearly, we still operate all kinds of subtle exclusions –
social, linguistic, cultural. We have spoken of remedial lessons,
libraries, book ownership, and now the language varieties of a
multi-cultural society challenge us further. Listen to a teacher
talking to children about television and what they read on their
own. Is she condescending, despising, only half-accepting what the
children offer for consideration? Many children believe that
reading is what goes on in the reading lesson, and nowhere else.
This is the greatest bamboozlement of all. Do children in a primary
school, sleepily wrapped in their coats waiting for the afternoon
bell, connect the story the teacher is reading which half lulls,
half enchants them, with the word drill they did in the morning?
What relation has each activity with the homes to which they return
and the language spoken there, the stories told there? Everywhere
there are signs that children, notably in inner-city schools, but
not only there, are given limited and conditional entry to literacy.
Not because teachers want to be exclusive. On the contrary, they
bend over backwards to help, but they do not know how to admit,
first, the total context of the child's learning, and second, the
intentions he brings to the task. To understand the context will
always exercise the imagination but it can begin by letting the
child declare himself and listening to what he says. To validate
his intention is not to ask him formally what his purposes are in
learning, but to harness the energy that comes from a natural inclination to discover how the world is organized in representations

conveyed in writing. The child's language, the processes by which
it develops and promotes his learning, and his sense of story, work
together to make reading a success. If there is any magic, the
teller and the listener, the reader and the author, generate it
between them. This is not to say that reading is like listening;
the context of utterance and text are different. But the reader
and the writer engender between them the fabric that they weave
together; the reader's meanings and the author's meanings make a
pattern that both acknowledge to be meaningful. We have to admit
that, however important reading may be for extracting information
from written records, successful readers understand how 'fiction
does what nothing else can do, how together within a single space
a variety of language, levels of focus, points of view, which would
be contradictory in other kinds of discourse are organized towards a
particular end'. (10) In fact, if we want to see society interpreting itself to itself, we have to read novels rather than the papers
in the records' office. Effective reading is not successful
information retrieval. It is to be free to enter whatever domain
of reading seems relevant to one's intentions.

Sometimes reading serves our immediate ends; sometimes we are
looking for something more holistic. Successful readers know the
feeling of creating the work with the author; they experience
reading as something they produce, rather than something they
consume. Very young readers have this sensation. Discussions with
children about 'living in a book' release evidence of a kind of absorption that seems to come easily to early starters, part of whose
delight is this sensation of 'indwelling' - the word is Polanyi's
but the feeling is common. To be in the book and later to have the
book in us is something we know as a particular experience. We know
the hero or heroine as a familiar friend. We agree with Bacon that
reading makes us 'full' men. Part of our delight is that we should
like to have written the book as it stands. We quote and refer to
it in phrases that are in us as much as in the originator. It is
not, as Barthes points out, that we should like to write like the
author whose work pleases us. Instead 'we want what the author
wanted of the reader when he was writing'. (11) Children understand
this; they write long letters to authors of their favourite books -
writing such as they do nowhere else. In the true tradition of ap-
prenticeship, the material they handle enters into them.

We must begin to be honest with ourselves and admit that, in our
day, the real power of literacy lies not with the reader but with
the writer. In the area of 'functional' literacy, the reader is a
consumer. Most expert readers have another side. They can make
their point in public debate by taking a pen in hand to write a
letter of protest, to criticize a point of view, to join forces, to
express admiration, to discuss or to praise. The extension of
seeing oneself in print now goes on in many local publishing enterprises so that more and more people experience the satisfaction of
'telling it how it is' with them. James Britton suggests that such
satisfactions as learning to form a relationship with a reader,
offering our values, feelings and beliefs about the world for cor-
roboration, challenge or modification, presenting ourselves in a
light we should like to be seen in, or for the sheer delight of

bringing into existence a pleasing verbal object, are the satisfactions that come from learning to write. All young people should
experience these things as part of becoming literate, for then we
could liberate reading to be not a penalty incurred as the result of
growing up in a literate society, but as one half of a double-sided
process, reading-and-writing, by which we realize our own meanings
and those of others.

I suggest now that one way to help this along is to introduce the
young to writing stories very early, and to see that they meet
writers who understand reading-and-writing from their point of view.
There is a special expertise that some authors bring to writing for
the young which is not always recognized by those who look for the
'literary' quality of books for children or by those who insist on
'realism' or 'relevance' in the portrayal of character and action.
It consists partly of an understanding that the language that speaks
to, say, 8-year-olds, has a certain poetic resonance, the words that
children savour rather than say, but would write if they could, and
partly of an awareness that powerful passions inform children's
understanding. 'And it was still hot' at the end of 'Where the Wild
Things Are' is more than a statement about Max's supper; it is a
judgment about the way the world is ordered. Children who read
early escape utterly the desiccating anxiety that permeates learning
to read in many schools; they also circumvent the idea that reading
to learn is a task related to operating on a text like a combine
harvester, producing the crop of information in neat bales for
storage. They discover 'the unfolding of the text as a living
event', (12) an experience which nothing can remove once it has
happened, and it happens best in contact with a writer who is concerned to make it happen. Authors for children who provide this
kind of reading experience, Alan Garner and Philippa Pearce, for
example, know how to take their stand behind a child's head. The
best children's authors create a place where a child can genuinely
be. The worst writers practise a form of adult exclusiveness,
usually exercised on grounds of 'suitability' of language or
content, or 'readability' or 'density of text'. Over and over again
young readers confound their teachers by what they are able to read,
but still we persuade ourselves that we know best what is good for
them.

When we, as adults, help a child to learn to read, we begin with
all the advantages, and the learner knows it. He needs our as-
surance that we shall not give him the lesser half of the domain of
literacy, the obligation to read what he has no desire to read
because, effectively, it excludes the part of him that responds to
what he is reading. He wants to be sure that he can bring to
reading his own genuine intentions and his language, and that we
shall offer him a learning context that does not alienate him from
the task. If we make his entry into literacy conditional on his
taking on our view of what it is for, we must not be dismayed if he
rejects both our terms and our texts. We who have no difficulties
may not imagine that there is another view of the task of learning
to read than the one we know. But we should do well to move our
feet and eyes and try to see what the learning looks like from where
the learner stands, his book in his hand. We might then help him
more.

REFERENCES

1 Resnick, Daniel P. and Lauren B. (August 1977), The Nature of
   Literacy: a Historical Experience, in 'Harvard Educational
   Review', vol.47, No.3.
2 Smith, Frank (1978), 'Reading', Cambridge University Press,
   Cambridge.
3 Clark, M.M. (1976), 'Young Fluent Readers', Heinemann, London.
4 Piaget, J. (1951), 'Play, Dreams and Imitation', Routledge &
   Kegan Paul, London.
5 Sartre, J.-P. (1964), 'Les Mots', Gallimara, Paris.
6 Wells, G. (1978), Children Learning to Read, Research Report:
   the University of Bristol.
7 Harding, D.W. (1971), The Bond with the Author, in 'The Cool
   Web', ed. Meek et al., Bodley Head, London, 1977.
8 Fowles, J. (1974), 'The Ebony Tower', Jonathan Cape, London.
9 Inglis, F. (1969), 'The Englishness of English Teaching',
   Longman, London.
10 Culler, J. (1978), 'Structuralist Poetics', Routledge & Kegan
   Paul, London.
11 Barthes, R. (1976), Sur la lecture, in 'Le Français
   aujourd'hui', No.32.
12 Iser, W. (1974), 'The Implied Reader', Johns Hopkins Press,
   Baltimore.

PART TWO

In this section of the book, all three chapters concern the relationship between who you are and what you know. For Kay Frost the
question is the effect of gender identity on self-perception - how
women experience themselves. Jagdish Gundara, in tracing the story
of his own childhood and youth, examines the way in which his social
treatment, as a Kenyan Asian, influenced what he came to know about
himself and the world. In the final chapter Miller Mair discusses
how people come to know themselves and others in a genuinely personal sense. The common theme in this section is that what we know,
and how we come to know, are inextricably linked with - indeed, are
part of - the kinds of people that we are.

From each of these accounts, the picture of learning that emerges
is of a difficult and often painful process. Certain kinds of
knowledge cannot be achieved at all without doing violence to fundamental aspects of personal identity. Where women's self-knowledge
is concerned, Frost suggests that certain perceptions, however
'true', are simply too dangerous to be acknowledged because they
would threaten the whole basis of living as a woman in our society.
Since this would disturb not merely the individual concerned, but
the social order, there is, as she puts it, 'collusion between the
external social context and internal anxieties and repressions'.
As a result, 'some aspects of the self are actively kept out of
awareness, and some connections are actively avoided'.

Mair also shows that there are reasons why intimate knowledge of
oneself and others is often impossible to achieve. As he puts it,
'coming to know personally seems to be a serious game of hide and
seek ... in which ... seeking often does not result in finding'.
This may be because there is no sense of common ground between
people or because, in trying to know oneself, one does not always
have available even the terms in which to cast some dimensions of
one's experience. But the reason may be of quite another kind.
Deeply personal knowledge can be profoundly disturbing. To achieve
it one has to be in touch with one's feelings; and that itself
means being vulnerable. Entering the world of the personal is also
far less comfortable, and safe, than our usual social transactions;
our 'trading in niceties, evasions or particular practicalities'.
Without the familiarity and the sense of control, of our habitual

dealings with ourselves and others, we risk all the terrors of the
unknown and, perhaps, the sense that we may 'unsettle the foundations of our former selves'. In the face of this we sometimes
retreat from genuinely personal knowing into the safety of a more
trivial engagement with experience.

In his chapter, Gundara offers a first-hand account of one
person's learning history that was full of confusion and pain. As
he shows, the social categorization by which his identity was defined - with the educational fate that followed it - was very
complicated and fraught with contradiction. Early on, the ascription of Indianness involved a violation of his own experience
of himself, which in his pre-school years had been one of solidarity
with Kikuyu children and their milieu; as he puts it, 'we grew up
learning to think that we were part of the forest and of each
other'. Being defined as Indian, however, meant that he could not
go to school with the children amongst whom he lived. Debarred from
the neighbourhood school where all his friends went, because it was
'African', and from the school a mile away from his home because it
was 'European', he was obliged to travel by bicycle and two buses to
an 'Indian' school ten miles away. Ironically, it was only through
the agreement that his favourite 'uncle', a Kikuyu, should remain in
the school compound to give him moral support that he was persuaded
to stay at school. As Gundara describes, his schooling brought
loneliness and self-doubt, a sense of personal fragmentation and a
lack of continuity in his experience. However, as he also shows,
his complex personal heritage gave him a special sensitivity to some
aspects of himself and his world. Being categorized in terms of a
minority group has necessarily entailed first-hand experience of
social stratification. As he says, he became aware early on of
'European domination and oppression on the one hand, and the mediocrity and pettiness of the Indian community on the other'. Yet,
through a painful working through of this experience, Gundara has
been able to forge a personal philosophy which is not cast in terms
of ethnicity, of outgroups or of social hierarchies.

In their consideration of personally significant learning, all
three writers in this section look at conventional ways of understanding and facilitating knowledge. Both Frost and Mair seriously
question the usual assumption that people can know themselves in a
complete, coherent and uncomplicated way. As Frost argues, this
assumption does not seem to square with how things often feel: 'we
have the experience of making decisions, planning our activities, in
an intelligible way, perhaps on the basis of thoughts and feelings
which do not feel chosen and whose origins we do not know'. Our
experience of ourselves is seldom 'all-of-a-piece, unidimensional,
unconflicted'; much more typically, we find ourselves to be
various, contradictory and, to some extent, fundamentally unknowa-
ble. Yet the investigation of women's self-perceptions 'grossly
underestimates the variety and complexity of the processes by which
people set out to represent themselves to themselves ... and ignores
the range of purposes that such representations serve'. As Frost
shows, the findings which result from this simple-minded standpoint
are seldom enlightening. Even the apparently straightforward task
of rating oneself on a seven-point scale of aggressiveness entails
such complexity that the meaning of any rating is profoundly am-

biguous. 'Thus, the statement "I am not very aggressive", when
unravelled, may mean some or all of the following: "I do not want
to behave aggressively; I do not want to feel aggressive; I do not
plan to act on any aggressive feelings I may have; I do not mean to
put myself in situations which might surprise me into aggressive
feelings or acts; I am not going to learn how to translate those
odd twinges I get into actions that I might construe as aggressive".'

Mair is similarly critical of the conventional psychology of
knowledge, for partly the same reasons as those of Frost. Like her,
he questions the assumption that people generally have a clear and
adequate knowledge of themselves and those with whom they interact.
'Much of our living is acted and felt in complexly coherent ways
without any explicit awareness on our part. Within and between
ourselves we remain rich realms of mystery.' Mair also rejects the
conventional reduction of knowledge about people to knowing about
them, on the one hand, and knowing how to influence them, on the
other - a view which, he suggests, is sometimes maintained even in
the psychotherapeutic context. Neither of these kinds of knowledge
can be equated with truly personal knowledge, which means knowing
oneself, or another, as 'an origin of experience, a centre of
living, a place of power in a particular private world'.

Frost and Mair also develop a similar theme in relation to
alternative modes of enhancing our understanding of personal
knowledge. Both writers show how potentially fruitful the use of
images, metaphors and fantasy can be. It may be, Frost suggests,
that in very intimate and crucial ways, women come to know themselves through the portrayals of films, plays and novels, through
the world of secret fantasy and through their identifications with
other people. To allow these modes into our research might, Frost
concedes, be 'an invitation to return to primeval muddle'; but it
might also permit us to 'arrive at a more complete description of
our lived experience'. Mair, too, argues for an enlargement of the
modes we use to enter the realm of personal knowledge. In his
account of the personal journey of discovery made by Margaret, he
documents the way in which images enabled Margaret to grasp aspects
of her experience which had previously been beyond her reach.

A final theme, shared by all three writers, is the creative
quality of personally meaningful knowledge. For Gundara, this fact
became evident by default during his educational experience. As he
describes, the formal instilling of compartmentalized facts and
skills at school, and the absence of any linking of the material
with the personal perspectives of pupils, resulted, for him, in a
failure of school learning to take off. One aspect of the theme
that Gundara terms 'the cultivation of the imperfect' is a Schweik-
like quality of continuous informal learning. It was the entirely
unofficial browsing in bookshops that gave him a feeling for books,
the self-initiated running that led to a sense of 'rhythm with the
earth', and his personal and uninstructed interest in physical
landscape that formed the basis for his appreciation of the visual
arts. As far as school was concerned, the fact that 'Indian'
teachers were obliged to teach an English-based curriculum evidently
drained the material of the creative personal meaning it might have
had; only when, in teaching Urdu, 'they recited the verses from

Urdu poetry with such verve' did 'the far away and long forgotten
land of India become real'.

Frost also shows how personal knowledge is essentially personally
created. As she says, 'self-discovery and self-creation are inextricably entangled.' This becomes particularly vivid in her
account of how she herself 'like millions of other girls before and
since ... experimented with seeing myself as Beth or Jo', from
Alcott's 'Little Women'. In this essentially experimental venture,
'I did not know in advance that I could not become a Beth, though no
doubt anyone who knew me could have told me. In order to find this
out, I had to live in my imagination as Beth for some time. It was
only by doing so that I began to define more clearly the image I had
of her, and, in contrast, the images that I had of myself.'

The fact that personal knowledge must be created is also one of
Mair's major themes. Partly this means that we are continuously
involved in personal action, whether or not we recognize this.
Creation also entails the development of ways· of formulating what
we know, 'ways of giving form to what we feel, such that we may
recognize and come to own what otherwise may seem to control us'.
Finally, to acknowledge the creativeness inherent in personal
knowledge has implications for the way in which psychology itself
should be conducted. This might involve psychologists in drawing
on their own personal experience, their own possibilities of being
creative as persons, thereby taking a different stance towards their
subject-matter. As Mair puts it, 'We will need to develop an understanding of psychological enquiry which will allow and encourage us
to "live in and amongst" rather than "stand over and against", and
become closely and intimately involved rather than remaining
separate and superior observers.'

ON THE VARIETY OF THE FORMS OF SELF-KNOWLEDGE SOME SECOND THOUGHTS ABOUT RESEARCH ON WOMEN'S PERCEPTIONS OF THEMSELVES

Kay Frost

INTRODUCTION

I was recently engaged in reviewing some research on women's perceptions of themselves. I began with considerable interest, and
found much to interest me along the way. Yet somehow I emerged with
a sense of disappointment and frustration which was pervasive, but
whose origins were at first obscure. I have in mind in particular
the numerous studies which appear under headings such as 'women's
self-concepts', 'concepts of femininity', 'sex-role stereotypes',
'sex differences in self-esteem', and the like. Much of the work
relies on rating-scales, requiring people to describe by this means
their views of 'typical' men and women, 'ideal' men and women, or of
themselves (see Fransella and Frost, 1977, for review). My problem
was not that I did not like the findings: in so far as they could
be made to mean anything at all, they had a canny way of confirming
my prejudices. I had expected to learn that women (and men) consider that in general women's personalities are somewhat, not
greatly, different from men's. Of course, the results confirmed my
expectation. I thought that some of these supposed sex-differences
in personality would occur on 'traits' such as 'dominance', 'aggression', 'competence', 'autonomy' (perceived as higher in men),
and in qualities that have been loosely summarized as 'warmth and
expressiveness' (seen as higher in women). And indeed they did.
I anticipated that these differences would be prescriptive as well
as descriptive: that is, that both sexes think that women should
ideally be more expressive and less competent, dominant, etc.
Again, this is what is found. It was hardly more surprising to
discover that, when men and women are asked to rate themselves, they
do so in a manner that resembles (though less extremely) what has
been called the 'stereotype' for their sex.

Now this summary is of course brief and unjust. Research must
sometimes consist in checking up on what seem like well-known facts.
They could, after all, turn out to be untrue. Moreover, the data is
beginning to tell us something about the variations in attitudes
that may occur, and about the way in which these relate to variations in social position, in experience and life-expectations, and
between subcultures. It also points up some interesting discrepan-

cies between the attitudes of women and of men within any given
social group.

None the less, with all this taken into account, I was still left
with a worrying feeling of actually knowing less than I did before.

This realization led me to consider more carefully what it was
that I had hoped to find out from reading this kind of research
literature.

My starting point was, and is, the belief that the way in which
we see ourselves is important. We construct images of ourselves
which influence not only what we do, but also how we interpret the
consequences of what we do. Thus, such images may profoundly affect
what we can learn both about ourselves and about the world around
us. On the one hand, they may direct us towards new discoveries.
On the other, they may rule out whole areas of activity and
knowledge.

One's knowledge of one's sex is a fundamental part of one's image
of oneself. It is also widely believed to imply a great deal about
one's personal qualities, one's intellectual abilities, one's
personal feelings, one's interests, goals, and so on. It would be
immensely surprising if women and men did not incorporate some of
this into their perceptions of themselves as individuals. It also
seems possible that, in the course of 'growing up female', many
women acquire assumptions about themselves as individuals which they
do not see as having anything to do with being female as such, but
which do in fact arise from their experience as women. In general,
then, I am suggesting that a better understanding of women's perceptions of themselves as women is essential for an understanding
of their actions and their choices.

Some of the questions with which I set out were relatively clearly articulated and specific (and of course not first formulated by
me). In particular, there are the huge sex-differences in depression and neuroses. Do concepts of femininity play some part in
this? Could it be that women's images of themselves in some way
unfit them for coping with their experiences? Another area of
interest is the failure of many women to realize their potential
academically and at work. May this perhaps stem not only from
external restrictions but also from barriers that are internal and
acquired? Again, is it possible that some apparent sex-differences
in ability arise from differences in assumptions about the self?

These questions have all the appearance of being empirical ones.
They are of course formulated within the frame of reference of an
existing body of research. It seems as if the fact that we have no
clear answers so far must be primarily because not enough work has
yet been done.

Behind them, however, I had other questions. Do most women
accept the roles in life that they have, and if so, why? How do
people come to choose, by and large, the place in the world that is
laid out for them? Even when that place is, as it seems to me, in
many ways oppressive, limiting, conflictful or even downright disabling? It seems to me that it is often not too difficult to see
why we behave in socially expected ways. What is considerably more
difficult, and more interesting, is to understand how we come to
want to. How do we come to experience ourselves in ways that are
congruent, at least in part, with the requirements of the world in

which we live? How does it happen that so many of the wants,
feelings, thoughts, intentions, dreams, which feel so peculiarly
and personally one's own, are in fact shared in broad outline with
so many others? And that there are others that seem to be so
strangely at variance with theirs? How has it come about, as it
has, for instance, with some of us who see ourselves as feminists
(but also for most people at some time) that we do not quite want
and do not quite opt for the readily available paths, and yet find
it sometimes so difficult to make others?

Now, these questions were obviously too many, and of quite the
wrong kind, to put to the sort of research material that I was
looking at. I suspect that anyone doing or reading research has
some of this sort of fuzzy stuff lying around somewhere at the back
of the mind, be it near the surface or well hidden. As scientists
we are encouraged to exclude it in the interests of 'objectivity'.
It would be possible, I suppose, to conclude merely that I had far
too much investment in the subject and that perhaps, after all, I
should have been reviewing research on pigeons or something else
sufficiently removed from myself. Alternatively, perhaps I should
have spent the time reading great novels, or in psychotherapy.

However, I should like to consider a different possibility, which
is this: perhaps some of these questions were not, after all, so
very inappropriate. Perhaps the disquiet that they aroused does
point to some problems for current research on women's views of
themselves. What they suggest, it seems to me, is that neither
concepts of femininity, nor a person's view of herself as a woman,
can satisfactorily be treated as a set of attitudes. One's experience of femininity is often difficult to convey in any clear and
coherent way, and sometimes difficult even to verbalize. It is deep
rooted and extremely difficult to change. It simply does not feel
at all like beliefs about remote matters of fact which we can
examine objectively for their accuracy and discard if they are
faulty.

In essence, my discomfort is not primarily with the data and
methodology per se (though there are many problems there). Rather,
my unease concerns the framework of assumptions, often implicit,
from which the research springs, and within which it is understood
and used to explain women's choices. It seems to me that this
framework grossly underestimates the variety and complexity of the
processes by which people set out to represent themselves to themselves. It also ignores the range of purposes that such representations may serve.

My reservations can be grouped, roughly, into two main categories
of rather different kinds. They may appear to be contradictory,
though I do not believe them to be so.

On the one hand, I want to suggest that we should take more
seriously the data on what women have to say about themselves. We
should consider more carefully the possibility that what they say
may be true in important ways and not for trivial reasons. We
should also look for the ways in which it may have a sensible and
intelligent relation to the lives they are trying to lead.

On the other hand, I shall go on to suggest some ways in which
such accounts may be incomplete and misleading. Verbal self-ratings
give disproportionate attention to one particular way of knowing and

representing oneself. A great many things that people 'know' about
themselves are not of a kind that can be told in this way or in this
context. One may have different ways of seeing oneself at different
levels, and there may be contradictions and conflicts between them.
There may also be aspects of the feminine self-concept that remain
outside awareness, but which none the less influence the form and
content of the conscious images.

I had better say at once that I do not have a solution to the
problems that I am raising. I hope only to make the whole business
a little more perplexing than it sometimes appears in the research
literature.

SOME REASONS FOR ADOPTING THE VIEW THAT WOMEN'S SELF-CONCEPTS MAY BE
BOTH AN ACCURATE ACCOUNT OF EXPERIENCE AND A REASONABLE APPROACH TO
THE WORLD IN WHICH THEY LIVE

I shall begin with my complaint that investigators do not take
seriously enough the descriptions of themselves that women give on
the rating-scales and questionnaires that the research provides. It
is not, I think, an accident that so much work in this area is so
often discussed under the heading of 'sex-role stereotyping' and
that the developmental accounts of how these 'stereotypes' are
arrived at are often referred to as 'sex-typing'. (The term
'stereotypes' is frequently used even when referring, not to
accounts that people give of the other sex, nor to their descriptions of their own sex in general, but to their ratings of
themselves.) The implications of this sort of terminology are that
such self-presentations must be, in some simple sense, untrue. The
respondents must be lying in conformity to some social prescription
or other; or, they must be misled as to their own true nature by
some process of brainwashing. An alternative assumption which often
seems to be lurking behind the use of such language is that other
people are passive tabula rasa; their beliefs about themselves are
true, but only because conforming personality traits can be stamped
onto them in the tender years by the culture.

Essentially, the assumption behind all these views is that self-
concepts are arrived at passively, as a simple product of external
social pressures. They are not seen as part of an active attempt to
understand and cope with the world. Viewed in this way, 'self-
concepts' seem to float in mid-air like some curious mirage; it
becomes difficult to see what possible relationship they can have
to the person behind them or to the life around them.

Suppose, however, we take seriously the possibility that these
women's self-descriptions (and perhaps even their descriptions of
women-in-general and men-in-general) contain some sort of truth.
The problem, of course, is what sort of truth?

To examine this, we should have to look at how it is that we get
evidence about our own characteristics and how we arrive at schemes
for interpreting that evidence.

Consider, for instance, the request to rate oneself for 'aggressiveness' on a seven-point scale. When women students on
average rate themselves lower in aggression than do men students,
they may be recording a simple and accurate observation of their

own behaviour. They may also be taking into account the frequency
and intensity of what they consider to be 'aggressive' feelings; in
which case they are making an implicit comparison with what they can
guess of others' feelings on the basis of what they can observe or
are told. In both cases their observations may be honest and
accurate in one sense, yet at the same time profoundly influenced by
the social world. For that world provides very different opportunities to women as opposed to men for behaving in an aggressive
fashion; and it also constrains their exposure to situations which
might elicit aggressive feelings. Not only that, it teaches us what
behaviour, feelings, fantasies, to count as evidence for 'aggressiveness' in the first place. And it provides differential
opportunities for learning how to behave in ways which others, and
we ourselves, may construe as aggressive.

It could also be argued that verbal self-descriptions are not
simply retrospective summaries of observations. They may at times
be statements about values and future intentions. Thus the
statement 'I am not very aggressive', when unravelled, may mean some
or all of the following: 'I do not want to behave aggressively; I
do not want to feel aggressive; I do not plan to act on any aggressive feelings I may have; I do not mean to put myself in situations which might require aggression from me, or which might
surprise me into aggressive feelings or acts; I am not going to
learn how to translate those odd twinges I get into actions that I
might construe as aggressive.'

In other words, a self-description may be in part an implicit
plan of action. As such it can often be successful in guaranteeing
its own truth at one level. Determining its truth may not be a
simple issue of honesty or deceit, self-awareness versus denial.

Moreover, if we assume that women's self-descriptions do have
this sort of function, we can look to see whether they are formulated with an eye to what is practical and acceptable and congruent
with the world in which they anticipate living. Perhaps the self-
concepts of the above-mentioned college students are, precisely, all
of these things. They anticipate being wives and mothers, and they
describe themselves as more warm and expressive of tender feelings
than men do. They anticipate putting motherhood and the needs of
husband and family before academic work and careers, and they describe themselves as less aggressive, assertive and competent than
do men. Given their own expectations, and the expectations that
others will have of them, it would be irrational indeed to set out
to make uncomfortable discoveries to the contrary, or to develop in
other directions. Several researchers have found that women who
make 'unfeminine' life-choices (studying sciences, for instance, or
maintaining a serious career) tend to describe themselves in less-
traditionally 'feminine' ways (see, for example, Fogarty et al.,
1971, pp.205-6; Richardson, 1975; Steinmann, 1963; Vogel et al.,
1970).

The tendency is to take this as evidence that women who already
have deviant personalities make deviant choices. May it not also
be, though, that those who can foresee a future in which 'unfeminine' qualities might be acceptable or even required, are more
prepared to admit them? They may also be more prepared to put
themselves in situations in which they may discover more of these

qualities and learn how to develop them. That is, future plans
influence present self-knowledge, as well as vice versa. Such
'knowledge' may involve dishonesty, self-deception, conformity to
social conventions, wish-fulfilment, but it may be based on hard
evidence. It could even be both.

SOME GENERAL PROBLEMS WITH THIS APPROACH

I have been pursuing the notion that we should look for the sense in
women's descriptions of themselves, and of femininity in general,
rather than dismissing their descriptions as 'stereotypes'. I have
argued that such descriptions may be treated as accurate reports of
some aspects of the evidence available. I have also argued that
there is no necessary contradiction in treating them also as purpos-
ive, as guidelines or plans for acting in a particular social world.
Viewed in this way, they may offer some basis for understanding
behaviour. (I am influenced, of course, by the point of view expressed in Kelly's much-quoted comment that, if you want to know why
someone does something, ask him, for he just might tell you.)
    In the remainder of this chapter I want to discuss a number of
different ways in which these kinds of accounts may be incomplete
and misleading. (Perhaps I should say that many of the difficulties
that I shall mention are not confined to rating-scale research.)
    Shotter (1975), in the course of elaborating an approach to
understanding human action in terms of reasons and intentions,
raises some important problems. He begins from the position that
'people's actions are not to be explained casually, as sequences of
objective events linked by causal principles, but intentionally.
That is, in general people's actions are to be explained as attempts
to help in the realisation of projects, goals, enterprises or ideals
which they have invented amongst themselves'. He goes on to point
out that the notion of explaining people's actions by their reasons
is an everyday, common sense one, but also that it is a complex one.
For one thing, when we ask the reason for a person's action, we may
want to know: (1) what it is he is or might be trying to do; and/or
(2) why such efforts are valued, that is, the place such a goal
occupies in relation to all the other goals he might have tried to
realize in the situation but did not. Much of the time we do not
lay out to ourselves what we are trying to do before we do it. We
just act 'naturally' or 'spontaneously'. However, spontaneous
actions may be transformed into deliberate actions. Shotter
suggests that one way in which this happens is in social interaction
(he gives the examples of teacher and pupil and mother and baby) and
he argues that what is communicated is partly reasons for action.
Thus, for instance, a baby learns from mother a meaning or a social
use for a movement he can make any time.
    Thus, according to Shotter, if one wants to find out a person's
reasons for acting as she or he does, one may have to go beyond the
immediate situation:

    On the basis of very fundamental attitudes to the world, people
    do all sorts of things quite spontaneously, without deliberating
    upon them at all; their actions have, nonetheless, a character-

istic structure, informed as they are by such beliefs. To understand people's different overall styles, we must elucidate these
beliefs. How can this be done? (pp.101-2).

He points out that one way of discovering some of these beliefs is
by self-interrogation - since we are members of the same culture and
share at least some fundamental reasons for action. This involves
not simply introspecting our own feelings but discovering our own
reasons for action. These reasons may not be obvious to us until we
sit down and think about it. We may indeed have to construct
hypotheses about our own reasons for actions.
      However, Shotter goes on to say, such analyses of the immediate
situation can only be carried so far:

> To understand the deeper reasons why I act as I do, I must study
> the history of my culture to discover the genesis of this reason
> (and, in the study of mother-child exchanges, we can investigate
> its transmission); I cannot discover the reasons for its coming
> into existence in any form of self-interrogation (p.103).

Now, my reason for introducing Shotter's comments here is that they
seem to throw some light on the complexity of what is involved if we
are to try to understand women's accounts of themselves as bearing
some meaningful (to them) relation to their actions and to their
world. It suggests, first of all, that even when people in a very
real sense 'know' what they are about, there are levels of this
knowledge that may not be immediately available, and that may also
be difficult for them, and us, to discover. It also clarifies why
some such reasons may not be discovered from the persons themselves
at all. For our goals and our accounts of ourselves are at one and
the same time our own and not our own; we learn them, we have to,
they become part of ourselves, in order to be able to live in a
social world at all, and in order to be able to organize our own
lives in a way that is intelligible to us. As long as we live
within a relatively coherent culture, there may never be any need
or purpose in speculating on what life would be like if we did not
have certain taken-for-granted purposes and meaning-systems that we
share with others. In such a setting, the pursuit of culture-
appropriate feminine roles and goals, and of a 'feminine' self-
concept that will fit those goals, is not likely to appear as
something that needs explaining; it presents itself as the natural
order of things. The reasonable response to questions as to why one
does these things and is as one is would be bewilderment. To be
otherwise would be not merely impossible, so it seems, but incomprehensible. At best, we ourselves as individuals would be at sea. At
worst, there would no longer be any basis for a social existence at
all, and thus no coherent frame of reference within which anyone
could pursue any purposes whatever.
      Shotter's approach, it seems to me, helps us to pinpoint two
major (and related) areas of difficulty that arise when we try to
account for women's actions in terms of their perceptions of themselves and their purposes.
      First of all, there is the difficulty of eliciting from them the
'fundamental attitudes', the 'characteristic structures' and beliefs

that inform their actions. Precisely how do we go about doing this?
Shotter suggests that we draw on self-interrogation, with which I
agree; but he also recognizes that this does not entirely get us
out of the problem. Essentially, it seems to me, the problem is
this: what kind of framework of assumptions, what model, are we
using in the process? For this will determine what questions we
ask and the sense we make of the answers. It may be that we, the
investigators, do not know how to put our questions in such a way
that they can be given answers which both accurately portray the
person's experience and are intelligible to us. There are theoretical issues here as well as practical ones. For my present purposes,
the one that I want to draw attention to is the question of whether
we are to assume that people's knowledge of themselves and the world
they live in is 'all-of-a-piece', unidimensional, unconflicted. Can
we really take it for granted, for instance, that any given woman
has only one clear and coherent picture of herself that is un-
changing, or only one way of looking at 'femininity'? I do not
think that we can, and I shall try later to say more about this.

      For the moment, however, I want briefly to sketch the second area
of difficulty that is suggested to me by Shotter's approach. It is
this. He suggests, and again I agree with him, that some questions
about our intentions, reasons, and so forth, can only be answered by
a study of our culture and our history. There is again, however,
the problem of what questions to ask and what framework to use. Are
we to assume that the intentions, reasons, purposes, that we acquire
from our culture form a coherent whole with no internal contradiction? That they are transmitted between people deliberately?
That they are all entertained consciously? Is it not perhaps the
case that the images of femininity-masculinity that are abroad in
the world are various, that they exist at different levels of
awareness, and that they may conflict with one another? If we take
the second view, then this vastly complicates the business of understanding how it is that the child takes them on. It may be that a
good deal of what the child learns about sex-roles is not deliberately transmitted. It may also be that what is taken on and how it
is integrated depends both on the inner needs of the child (which
change in development) and also on the context in which the information is presented and the child's relation to it.

      It may be that a good deal of what children and adults learn
about themselves is not 'known' consciously by anyone. There is a
good deal in our experience that feels neither chosen nor questionable.

      How is all this relevant to research on women's self-concepts?
To answer this question, let me begin by returning to the 'sex-role
stereotype' questionnaires.

SOME PROBLEMS FOR THE PRESENT USE OF RATING-SCALES AS MEASURES OF
WOMEN'S PERCEPTIONS OF FEMININITY

One problem that I have mentioned is that the questions we ask are
too narrow. The person's answers are forced into too simple a
mould. That is, there may be aspects of these women's experience
of which they are well aware, and which they are well able to put

into words, given the opportunity, but our methods prevent them from doing so. This arises particularly with rating-scales, at least those in current use. They make several assumptions about women's knowledge of themselves which I believe to be false.

First, they use language supplied by the researcher and not by the respondents' own concepts. Yet the terms used may have quite different meanings to individuals. I doubt, for instance, whether the term 'aggressive', when applied to the self, has the same connotations for women as for men. However, I do not want to go into this at length partly because it has been argued frequently and at length elsewhere, and partly because it does seem to me that there is a case for using standard terms when one is trying to find out about culturally-shared beliefs. That is, it makes some sense to see whether in fact people do use language in a way that is consistent with each other.

Some of the other assumptions may be more important, however. One is that a person can easily sum up her experience of herself in different situations into a single answer. Fogarty et al. (1971) report some of the comments made about themselves by the wives in dual-career families:

> When I'm at work I'm very authoritarian. I wear a white coat at work and I try to hang up my working personality with it when I leave the office.

> I am two different people at home and at work.... I am much more domineering and aggressive in the office than I am at home in that I will fight a point in the office in a way that I would never fight in a domestic situation, or want to.

These women are asserting that different behaviour is appropriate in different contexts. They adjust accordingly, in a way that is deliberate, conscious, and relatively conflict-free. Yet one wonders just how, without distortion, they could convey this on a seven-point scale. One individual might encapsulate the work-experience, concluding that it is 'not really me', but merely a performance required by the work setting. Another might cheerfully integrate it into her total self-image, as much-needed evidence that she really can stand up for herself when she needs to.

Another mistaken assumption involved in the use of ratings is that the self is generally experienced as unitary and noncontradictory. Most of us see ourselves in different ways at different times. Often we see ourselves in contradictory ways at one and the same time. The extent to which we become aware of the conflict as a conflict may vary.

If I am gentle and mouse-like in all my social exchanges, but have a taste for films and novels overflowing with blood and thunder, am I to describe myself as 'gentle' or 'aggressive'? My conclusion may depend on quite other things than the degree of my gentleness at home or the violence of my feelings in the cinema. It might, for instance, depend on my own personal psychological theories. It might depend on rather obscure anxieties about the implications for me generally of being a 'gentle' or an 'aggressive' person. It might also be influenced by very specific concerns,

conscious or otherwise, about the consequences of being aggressive
towards particular people or in particular situations.

One effect of these kinds of assumptions is the tendency to see
self-images as static rather than evolving. Indeed, given the
'unitary' nature of the account elicited, it is hard to see how it
could be otherwise. In so far as change is incorporated, it is seen
as a one-way impact of the environment. In contrast to this, Dana
Breen, for instance, has shown how pregnant women change their image
of themselves in the course of pregnancy and birth. She is able to
show how the kind of new picture that emerges draws on past experience and particularly the women's relationship with their own
mothers. It seems as if they use old knowledge that was always in
some sense there, to create a new picture (Breen, 1975).

Difficulties also arise from asking people to describe themselves
primarily as a series of separate traits or characteristics, thus
very much simplifying the kinds of structure that we may experience
ourselves as being. The consequence is that we see women's
knowledge of themselves as it is filtered back to us through 'trait'
psychology. It seems to me that we also come to know ourselves
through roles, persona, visual images, metaphors, in the ways in
which we dress, cook, and decorate our homes, and by many other
means, as much as through discrete verbal labels. To illustrate
this, let me mention a few instances of other modes of self-representation.

A BRIEF LOOK AT SOME OTHER MODES OF SELF-REPRESENTATION

One way in which we all discover ourselves, especially in childhood
and adolescence but by no means confined to it, is in adopting the
persona of a real or fictional other person. At the age of about 10
or 11, for example, I, like millions of other girls before and
since, read Louisa May Alcott's 'Little Women'. Like many others,
no doubt, I experimented with seeing myself as Beth or as Jo. (For
some reason not too unfathomable, Amy and Meg never appealed to me.)
Beth was my first choice as alternative personality. She seemed to
embody all the goodness to which one might aspire, she seemed to
have only good feelings inside, and she kept it up all the time; she
was adored consistently by everyone; and she died tragically at an
early age (before she had time to spoil her image?). I nursed the
image of myself as Beth for quite some time. The inner feelings of
goodness and spirituality were elusive, so I focused on the ex-
ternals, little acts of self-sacrifice, in the hope that spirituality would follow. It did not, of course, and by and by I gave up
Beth in favour of Jo. Perhaps it would be more accurate to say that
I recognized Jo as a better fit; she was turbulent, moody, not
always well-intentioned, prone to doing the wrong thing and to
subsequent fits of remorse. There was more to it than that, though,
for, despite her misery over her 'scrapes', she really did seem
after all to have a better time of it.

There are several points about this sort of identification that
I want to draw attention to. One is its experimental quality: I
did not know, in advance, that I could not become a Beth, though no
doubt anyone who knew me could have told me. In order to find this

out, I had to live in my imagination as Beth for some time. It was
only by doing so that I began to define more clearly the image that
I had of her, and, in contrast, the images that I had of myself.
Another point to notice is the global quality of the identification.
I would have found it hard then to define the precise qualities that
Beth and Jo had for me; and this despite the fact that they were
first introduced to me via written descriptions in a book. I did
not look at their attributes one by one and then decide to emulate
them. On the contrary, I found myself being them, in my imagination, and then began to discover their (my) various attributes.
Each in turn represented a whole complex way of being in the world,
together with a complicated set of consequences which I could
explore through them. I was constantly making up continuations of
the story. I was also constantly running into real-life situations
which were not at all like the ones in the book. In both cases the
characters became somehow elaborated as I attempted to imagine what
they would have done. This, I think, had something to do with my
relinquishing Beth for Jo. I kept finding that I just could not
imagine what Beth would have made of my world. When I could, I
could not see my way to imitating her. She was an ideal, but what
she represented for me and the means of achieving that state, were
obscure to me. In the end, I suppose, I did not know how to want
to be like Beth. Whereas, in the character of Jo, I found something
sufficiently familiar to elaborate on and sufficiently sympathetic
(neither too good nor too bad) to live through. She provided me
with the means to construct plans of action for myself. I could
invent her and then imitate her.

Akin to this, perhaps, are some sorts of identifications with
real people whom one knows. In early adolescence, one identifies
first and then tries to observe in specific situations what the
person does and feels. Picking out a specific quality in someone
else to imitate seems to be a rather late development. Helene
Deutsch (1973) describes very interestingly this sort of global
identification in adolescent girls' twosome 'best-friendships'.
She also points out how the image of the person with whom the girl
identifies is in fact her own fantasy or projection, but one which
could not be realized in any other way. In this process, self-
discovery and self-creation are inextricably entangled.

Somewhat different, but perhaps not unrelated, is the experience
in adult life, when one becomes immersed in certain kinds of novels,
plays, films. One becomes, temporarily, the characters, feeling
with them in a global, non-reflective way. In the course of doing
this one discovers, as it were, the parts of oneself that could be
that person. Gradually, usually in retrospect, one comes to see
them from the outside, as characters; and in so doing, one comes
to know oneself in quite a new way without necessarily recognizing
that this is happening.

In contrast to the exploratory immersion of these forms of
identification are the images which somehow sum up a whole complex
of thoughts and feelings into something that appears well-defined at
the outset, but may have to be unravelled very laboriously. One
thinks, for instance, of Komarovsky's student who remarked, 'It
seemed that my family had expected me to become Eve Curie (sic) and
Hedy Lamarr wrapped up in one' (Komarovsky, 1946). I doubt very

much whether one could spell out in a short space the significance
of these two famous people for this girl. To be sure she is contrasting an 'academic', 'studious' personality with a 'glamorous'
one; but is she not also summing up different life-styles, quite
different ways of relating to others, quite different futures, with
very different consequences for herself? Another example is the
woman who said to another interviewer:

> I think of myself as a housewife, but I don't think of myself as
> a cabbage. A lot of people think that they're housewives and
> they're cabbages; I don't like to think I'm only a housewife....
> I usually say "I'm a wife and a mother and I've got a part-time
> job." People look down on housewives these days (Oakley, 1974,
> p.48).

The images used here are public, and the speakers are explicitly
concerned with how they are seen by others. The images chosen
represent a public persona and the implications of adopting this
persona in social life. They serve to define and explore what one
might wish to become in the eyes of others as well as oneself, which
possible selves one might wish others to see as really oneself.

Other forms of self-representation have perhaps a quite different
function. Consider, for instance, sexual fantasies. Hariton and
Singer (1974) report on the most common sexual fantasies admitted by
141 upper-middle-class married women in a New York suburb. Around
half admitted to each of the following: 'Thoughts of an imaginary
romantic lover enter my mind'; 'I relive a previous sexual experience'; 'I enjoy pretending that I am doing something wicked or forbidden'; 'I imagine that I am being overpowered or forced to surrender'; 'I imagine that I am delighting many men'.
Around one quarter reported that: 'I see myself as a striptease
dancer, harem girl, or other performer'; 'I pretend that I am a
whore or a prostitute'; 'I imagine that I am forced to expose my
body to a seducer' (Hariton and Singer, 1974, p.317).
It is, of course, an essential part of these sorts of self-repre-
sentations that they are fantasies, and experienced as such. They
do not, on the whole, form part of even a potential life-script.
One imagines that most of these women would react with horror to the
suggestion that they should in real life put themselves in the position of being overpowered, delighting many men, or becoming harem
girls. (It still seems to be relatively unusual for many women to
admit to having sexual fantasies at all; most of us, I think,
censor rather carefully what is shared with friends, or even
lovers.)
Not only are such fantasies not publicized and acted on (at least
outside the bedroom), but they seem to hover on the borderline
between that part of the person which is embraced as the 'self' and
the parts which are not.
What function do they serve? It is, I think, a popular notion,
but a false one, that fantasies, and in general those parts of
oneself which one hides from oneself and/or from others, are in some
sense more 'real' than those one makes public, and that those wishes
which emerge more or less disguised in fantasy are somehow more
truly one's 'real' wishes.

Even if one does not take this view, however, one can still ask
why the fantasies have the content they do. Why are these particular fantasies sexually exciting for so many of the women? One
noticeable feature is that a very traditional 'feminine' role is
maintained, even though the surrounding circumstances are exotic.
These women represent themselves, in secret, to themselves, as
weaker, as desired rather than desiring, as overwhelmed rather than
powerful, as passively rather than actively sexual. There is no
need for them to comply with social norms, since fantasies are
private. If they are merely trying to remove themselves from the
real situation, why should they do so in this way? Why should they
not picture themselves as actively seductive, or as maternal and
tender in their sexuality, or in some other way?

Why are some representations so persistently entertained and so
persistently and explicitly rejected?

I am not here about to embark on an elaborate theory of women's
(or anybody's) sexual fantasies. I want merely to suggest both the
interest and the problems that they illustrate in the understanding
of women's self-knowledge. Here we have a form of self-representation that is nurtured, but secretly and ambivalently, and appears
to be in marked conflict with other, more publicizable, representations. Moreover, I suspect that most of us would have some difficulty in explaining why we have our own particular sexual fantasies.
At the least, we should have difficulty in doing so on the basis of
introspection, without going outside our own experience to draw on
our favourite psychological or sociological theory. We might say
that the fantasies heighten sexual arousal, but then we should be
stumped. Whereas the woman who did not want to see herself as a
'cabbage' would be likely to be able to give a more elaborate
account of her reasons in terms of what she was about in the world
in general.

It does seem to me that to pursue this one is having to make use
of some sort of concept of a dynamic unconscious. That is, one is
having to assume that part of the person's experience is being
actively kept out of awareness, and is finding expression in a
disguised form.

One can think of many images in novels, plays and films which
rely for their power on this process. In a German film of the
thirties, Fritz Lang's 'Metropolis', the two women embody two prevailing and related fantasies. One woman is first seen surrounded
by children; she is beautiful, gentle, maternal and caring, and
entirely devoid of active sexuality; her presence awakens the
hero's better self, but she takes no direct part in the action. The
other woman is a robot constructed as a facsimile of the real one,
for reasons which I shall not go into. She is aggressively sexual
and pitiless; in speeches that are strongly sexually seductive in
style she arouses the men to an attempted revolt which can only
destroy them. These two contrasting and complex images do not exist
in isolation; they maintain each other. A high level of anxiety is
generated precisely by the fact that the women appear to be identi-
cal (played by the same actress). At an unconscious level it seems
that the 'good' woman can somehow turn into the 'bad' one. Indeed,
there is a long sequence in which the 'good' woman is pursued by the
villainous magician. The storyline justification for this is that

he wants to hold her prisoner so that the 'bad' woman can take her place and by this deception lead the men into destruction! However, the sequence strongly, though very covertly, suggests the possibility of rape, in other words that she will be contaminated by sexuality. The maternal image can only be preserved if she remains sexually pure and passive. The actively sexual woman is destructive herself and arouses destructive passions in others. (This film is made by a man, yet so far as I can observe, it is no less involving and disturbing for women in the audience than for men. This, I think, is important. No theory of women's perceptions of women can ignore the fact that many fantasies are shared by both women and men, at a very deep level.) Such simultaneously existing images may play a part in structuring social institutions. Thus, for instance, Katherine Arnold, in a study of a Peruvian brothel, argues that the existence of the brothel, and the way that it is set up, expresses an image of women which is complementary to the respectable image of the 'good' woman in Peruvian culture. Susan Lipshitz summarizes it thus:

> This study of a brothel as a social institution suggests that its rituals articulate with unconscious and ambivalent ideas about women. They are either the Madonna or the Whore, a split described by Freud in his essays on love and a dual image which develops in the context of the child's relation to its mother. For she is both the provider of satisfaction and yet is discovered to be separate and sexual in relating to the father. Such currents of fantasy, in which one woman is worthy of love and another is sexual and to be degraded, form romantic love's images. They persist into adulthood and seem to be part of the activities of this brothel. The men need the prostitutes and yet fear and degrade them. So do their respectable wives. For the morality of the conventional Peruvian marriage seems complemented by the place of the prostitute. She is feared and hemmed in by health rules and regulations and is literally placed on the outskirts of town. But she is also accepted as having a place. Sex for pleasure and sex for reproduction are clearly split between the home and the brothel (Lipshitz, 1978, p.7).

What is to be learned from all this? In a brief and sketchy fashion I have tried to show that the ways in which women represent to themselves the knowledge that they have of themselves may be various, complex and contradictory. Even some of those which can be communicated in words do not lend themselves to rating-scales. Some are neither likely to be communicated to others, nor readily owned by the self; they appear only in disguised form and with crucial elements missing. It is often easier to see them more clearly in artistic creations which the audience can enjoy with the freedom to choose what is taken as relevant to the self. Any individual woman (or man) may entertain different images of femininity at different levels of awareness. Sometimes these will be experienced as conflictful and contradictory, sometimes not. Some images of femininity will be accepted as applying to oneself in particular, others will be repudiated. For those that are repudiated, external evidence sometimes suggests that the person does, at some level,

recognize them as reflecting thoughts and feelings of her own. One
is driven to the conclusion that the preservation of a relatively
stable 'core' sense of oneself as a woman does not occur out of
inertia, but through an active process. And that this process involves keeping some things outside awareness. What precisely is
accepted or rejected depends on a great many factors internal and
external.

In addition, we have to recognize that in attempting to organize
and integrate different aspects of her experience, a person is
drawing on images that are public, but that are themselves neither
simple nor unidimensional. The concept of 'femininity' elicited by
sex-role questionnaires is one, and only one, of the images available. It is also likely to be the one that is least problematical
for the individuals concerned.

SOME SPECULATIONS ON THE INTERACTION BETWEEN SOCIALLY ACCEPTED
CONCEPTS OF FEMININITY AND THE SELF-CONCEPTS OF INDIVIDUAL WOMEN

It seems to me possible that one reason why it is so peculiarly
difficult to tease out these issues in relation to women's images of
themselves is that there is, as it were, a collusion between the
external social context and internal anxieties and repressions.

Leaving aside, for the moment, the fact that society, through
child-rearing, plays a part in establishing specific repressions,
there are, I think, a number of ways in which social systems of
behaviour and beliefs may permit the resolution of some such
conflicts and hinder the resolutions of others. In other words,
even for adults, the social world can influence the range of experience of oneself that is accepted into the conscious self-image.

Take, for example, the Peruvian society referred to earlier, in
which sex-for-reproduction is kept firmly separate from sex-for-
pleasure, the one being allocated to wives and the other to prosti-
tutes.

Without speculating about origins, I should like tentatively to
suggest that, once such fantasies are there, and institutionalized,
they not only influence what people do, but also in some sense
ensure their own truth. That is, there no longer exists a way in
which, for instance, women can be both 'good wives and mothers' and
actively sexual. Female sexuality becomes not only a source of
personal anxiety for both women and men, but also a real threat to
real institutions. When 'good' women lack the experience and the
means for safe sexual expression, it becomes uncharted territory in
which the emotions and fantasies aroused are new and really uncon-
trollable, and the consequences unforeseeable. In such a setting,
people are more likely to do harm to themselves and others. And
hence they are likely to provide themselves with new evidence that
female sexuality is indeed dangerous and that sex-for-pleasure is
indeed incompatible with feminine motherliness and with lasting
relationships and marriage. (This in addition to the fact that in
such a setting the sanctions imposed on women who transgress against
social mores are savage.)

One could develop a similar point as regards the college students
whose self-concepts were my starting point for this chapter. Let us

suppose that English and American women enter college with deep-
seated and partially repressed anxieties about their own aggressive
potential. They are coming into a world in which self-assertion,
competitiveness, academic success in women, are construed as aggressive, as well as threatening to the social fabric; a world in
which these traits, in a woman, are experienced as personally
threatening and attacking by the men. Is not this a world in which
self-assertion, career interests, achievements, are likely to remain
linked, in the minds of the women, in a diffuse and subterranean
way, with their own destructive aggression and with whatever repressed hostility to men they may have? (In some women they might
even become the means for being hostile, if they are not so
already.) In such a setting, reality testing becomes difficult.
That is, it becomes hard to check out realistically what one's
potential for damage is. (I am assuming that in 'healthy' development one learns, among other things, that, however destructive one
may sometimes, consciously or unconsciously, wish to be towards
those whom one loves, one's power really to hurt them is in fact
limited; one learns how it is done and thus how it is avoided; and
one learns to be sufficiently aware of such impulses not to be taken
by surprise by them and not to act on them when one 'did not really
mean to'.)

In so far as reality testing is possible, these women will be
likely to discover that their assertive and achievement-orientated
behaviour is construed as destructively aggressive even when that is
no part of their own motivation. It may even be very difficult to
discover what exactly their own motivations are. (How easy it is
for any of us to be absolutely sure, when we turn out to have hurt
or threatened someone, apparently by mistake, that that was no part
of our intention? Especially when we know that we may well wish to
hurt at other times?)

A further complicating factor is that the same social forms may
be used by different people in different ways. Many women students
at this stage in life are likely to have a reasonable level of insecurity about their own fundamental femininity; that is, that their
bodies and sexual organs are intact and satisfactorily functional,
that they are capable of bearing healthy babies and becoming good
mothers. If self-assertion, achievement, aggression, etc., are
construed as 'unfeminine', then by the same token avoiding these
things can become a means to indirect reassurance about the other,
more fundamental matters. For other women, perhaps with greater
anxieties, behaving in a 'socially masculine' way can become the
means to avoiding those other conflicts. But the same behaviour
might also be facilitated by a secure confidence that one's 'true'
femininity is not in question.

My general point here is that it can happen that the real world
is so organized that particular repressions continue to be experienced as too dangerous to work their way into consciousness, and
also that they are likely to retain inappropriate conscious and
unconscious associations.

Such repressed material is likely to be in reality more dangerous
when it does find expression because the individual concerned has
had no opportunity to learn either about consequences or about means
of control. (This might be one reason why women fighting are so
notoriously more terrifying than men.)

Could it also be that the same line of argument is relevant to
some aspects of neurotic disturbance, at which women excel men in
the ratio of about two to one? It is commonly assumed by clinicians
that anxiety about repressed aggressive fantasies plays an important
part in the aetiology of some feminine psychiatric disorders. Might
it be that in many cases they do indeed play a part, but that they
remain repressed and therefore problematic, not because the fantasies are unusually prevalent, but for the sorts of reasons that I
have described with regard to the college students?

The relationship between the individual's unawareness of her
feelings and the social world that I have tried to describe, is
elaborated much better by George Eliot, in 'Middlemarch'. Dorothea
frets at the triviality of the activities permitted to her as a
woman in the small town. She nurtures powerful but entirely vague
aspirations to greater fulfilment. She marries Casaubon in the
belief that sacrificing herself to his work will make her life more
meaningful and worth while. Casaubon, not surprisingly, turns out
to be not at all the man she took him for, and in no way capable of
helping her to realize herself. When she meets Will Ladislaw, she
falls in love with him in a way that she has never been in love with
her husband, but remains entirely unaware of that fact long after
her husband is profoundly jealous. Not only is extramarital love
taboo in her community and unthinkable to her, but also she entirely
lacks the experience that would enable her to recognize sexual love
when she finds it in such an unacceptable quarter. It is implicit
in the novel that love and desire can emerge only indirectly, and
are confused with all her other yearnings for expression and self-
fulfilment.

SOME SPECULATIONS ON THE IMPACT OF THE CHILD'S SOCIAL WORLD ON THE
WAY THAT WOMEN SEE THEMSELVES

Research on sex-role development has tended to focus on the acquisition of sex-typed behaviour (see Maccoby and Jacklin, 1975, for
review). Less attention has been paid to the emergence of self-
concepts, and of the sense of the nature of one's own masculinity/
femininity, which guide this behaviour. Very different theoretical
approaches ('shaping', 'modelling', even Kohlberg's 'self-social-
ization') seem to make a number of similar assumptions: that the
evidence available to the child is on the whole presented
deliberately and that it forms a single coherent picture. Essentially, even Kohlberg seems to treat the child in certain
respects as a sort of mini-adult: to be sure, the child is presented as inducing the rules that govern behaviour appropriate to
his/her sex, but her position in the world, and her purposes, are
accepted as rather like our own. It all looks rather like an
adult's attempts to determine the customs of a foreign country. It
is also assumed that the final picture is a simple one. If, however, I am right in thinking that each of us entertains a complex
set of images of herself, her feminine nature, and of femininity in
general, with varying degrees of conscious acceptance, then perhaps
we need a different kind of model of what is happening in childhood.
We need to pay more attention both to what the context is for the

child, and to the ways in which the means available to the child for
making sense of that context may be rather different from our own.
How is it that we come to have the coherent and consistent sense of
self, feelings, wishes, thoughts, appropriate to our gender-role?
How is it that we also remain able to entertain images that threaten
to disturb and conflict with them? None of the above theories help
us to understand either of these things.

An approach to this problem which I find helpful is that outlined
by Nancy Chodorow (1974) in her paper 'Family Structure and Feminine
Personality'. She starts from the assumption that neither explanations based on biological difference nor explanations based on
deliberate socialization can account for 'the extent to which
psychological and value commitments to sex differences are so
emotionally laden and tenaciously maintained, for the way gender
identity and expectations about sex roles and gender consistency are
so deeply central to a person's consistent sense of self' (in
Rosaldo and Lamphere, 1974, p.43).

Her approach is essentially a psychodynamic one. She proposes that
a crucial differentiating experience for male and female development
arises from the fact that women, universally, are largely responsible for early child-care and for (at least) later female socialization. Thus, without teaching, the context is different for the
boy baby and the girl baby. The girl is being cared for by a person
of the same sex, who also has the gender role that she will ultimately have. For the boy, neither of these things is the case.

She suggests that this may have a number of consequences for the
way in which the self is structured in the two sexes.

First, during the period of 'primary dependence', when the child
experiences herself/himself as one with the mother, with no
awareness of differentiation, the positions of boys and girls differ
because of the mother's involvement with the child. The mother is
more likely to identify with the daughter, experiencing the daughter
as herself. She is consequently less likely to push her daughter
into differentiating from her, with the result that issues of separation and individuation are more difficult for girls. Whereas the
mother is more likely to emphasize the son's masculinity in opposition to herself and to push him into playing a male role in relation to her.

Other consequences of the mother's role in child-care come into
play in the period in which gender identity is being established;
that is, when the child is finding out, not just which sex she/he
is, but what it means to be of that sex. For the girl:

> femininity and female role activities are immediately apprehensi-
> ble in the world of her daily life. Her final role identifi-
> cation is with her mother and women, that is, with the person or
> people with whom she also has her earliest relationship of infan-
> tile dependence. The development of her gender identity does not
> involve a rejection of this early identification, however.
> Rather, her later identification with her mother is embodied and
> influenced by their ongoing relationship of both primary identi-
> fication and preoedipal attachment. Because her mother is
> around, and she has had a genuine relationship with her as a
> person, a girl's gender and gender role identification are medi-
> ated by and depend upon real effective relations (p.51).

By contrast, says Chodorow, masculinity becomes and remains problematic for the boy, since the father is less available and it is less
immediately clear what it is to be a man. Moreover, in order to
become masculine, the boy must more clearly differentiate himself
from mother and deny his early attachment and dependence. This
seems to involve repressing and devaluing 'femininity' in himself.
(It may also lead to the devaluing of women in a defensive fashion.)
Finally, if, as is commonly the case, the father is relatively
absent, the boy's identification with him is not based in a satisfactory affective relationship. He is, as it were, having to
identify with a position rather than a person, and the requirements
of that position are known in a rather abstract way.

Chodorow proposes two general consequences of this combination of
factors in the social context. First, 'feminine personality comes
to define itself in relation and connection to other people more
than masculine personality does. (In psychoanalytic terms, women
are less individuated than men; they have more flexible ego boundaries.)' (p.45).

Second, issues of dependency and individuation are handled and
experienced differently by women and men. For boys and men they
become tied up with the sense of masculine identity. Whereas for
girls and women, issues of feminine identity are not problematic in
the same way. (It is important to remember that this is not a
theory of gender identity, nor of sexual object choice, as such.
It does not attempt to explain why boys wish to identify with the
father, nor why either sex, by and large, choose members of the
opposite sex as sexual partners. For that, Chodorow seems to
assume that the Freudian model operates.)

Chodorow is not suggesting that one would expect as a result of
all this that women's roles, personalities and experience of themselves would be always and everywhere the same. The mother-daughter
relationship would always be significant, but what precisely the
daughter internalizes from that relationship would depend on many
things. Some relevant factors might be: the mother's personality;
whether the mother has roles and a sense of self independent of her
motherhood; the extent to which other agencies (such as school)
intervene in the relationship; whether other role models are
available; the precise role and relationship with the father; and
so on. What Chodorow is suggesting is that a number of features of
feminine experience may be attributable, not directly to deliberate
role-training, nor yet to the mechanisms by which gender identity
and sexual preference are established, but to the context in which
they occur.

There is of course insufficient evidence for this or any other
theory. However, Chodorow suggests some that would be consistent
with it. It helps us to understand why women accept their gender
role sooner (they want and expect to become mothers and to have
babies sooner than boys do). It may also be one reason why women
tend to define themselves primarily as mothers, with extrafamilial
concerns coming second: the maternal identification is established
early and firmly, in a very concrete way, and other roles have to
fit in with that. The theory is consistent with the findings that
the same parental behaviours have different consequences for
children of different sexes (e.g. the finding that maternal warmth

increases the 'need for achievement' in boys but has the opposite
effect in girls). The tendency in many cultures for women to remain
embedded in kinship relations with strong affectional ties, to a
greater degree than men, and to give these relations as much importance as the marital one, could also be understood partly on this
basis. Finally, the constellation of putative feminine traits which
have been variously described as 'communion' (as opposed to
'agency') (Bakan, 1966), 'interpersonal' (as opposed to 'individualistic') (Carlson, 1971), 'more flexible ego boundaries' and relatively greater subjectivity (Gutmann, 1965), might be seen as
arising from lesser individuation in women.

Weak ego boundaries and lack of individuation have been often
seen as pathological, but Chodorow points out here that there is a
case to be made for the advantages, to the individual and to society, of ego boundaries that are flexible within limits and for a less
than totally individualistic orientation. Such individuals could
well have a secure sense of self in relation to others, be well
equipped to work with others on a co-operative rather than a competitive basis, to help and accept help in 'mature dependency'.

One can speculate on the circumstances in which these qualities
would have problematic consequences. First, this would occur when
the tendency is present in too extreme a form, that is, when the
person has not really developed a secure sense of the independent
self at all. One would expect this when the mother's involvement
in the mother-daughter relationship is simply too great and there
are no mitigating influences from elsewhere. Second, the consequences might depend on the specific demands of people's lives
(Gutmann, 1965, quoted in Chodorow, p.56). A tendency to experience
oneself and to act in interpersonal terms might be an advantage to a
woman in a close-knit community and a positive disadvantage to a
young mother isolated from family and friends in a fragmented urban
community. (It might also pose problems for the person herself in
many competitive situations, or in academic life!)

Note that in many urban Western societies all the ingredients
seem often to be there to make these issues problematic: mothers
who are themselves lonely and without an identity apart from motherhood, and thus likely to be over-invested in motherhood; communities that are fragmented and families that are isolated, lacking
interpersonal support.

To go back to the question of 'feminine' self-concepts, it does
seem to me that some of the research evidence concerning the way in
which Western women describe themselves and the feminine personality
is consistent with this sort of model. First, there are the
findings quoted at the beginning of this chapter that American
college women describe themselves, the average woman, and the ideal
woman, as lower than men in characteristics that seem to be concerned with such things as independence, assertion, competence, and
higher in 'warmth and expressiveness'. Second, there are a number
of studies (Carlson, 1970) which suggest that women are more inclined to describe themselves in interpersonal terms as opposed to
individualistic ones (for review see Maccoby and Jacklin, 1975; and
Fransella and Frost, 1977). Maccoby and Jacklin tentatively suggest
that the basis of self-esteem is different in the two sexes: women
may tend to put more importance on interpersonal qualities, and to

think that they possess them (see also Fransella and Frost, pp. 97-9).

This does not seem to me to be as contradictory as it might at first appear with what I was trying to say earlier about different modes of knowing oneself, and repression of experience perceived as unfeminine. Chodorow's model suggests a context that would facilitate the internalization of the mother's attributes, whatever these might be, and assist the girl in sharing the mother's repressions. If the girl has a less distinctly separate sense of herself as opposed to her mother, and less external impetus to achievement, she is less likely to seek to establish that she has different qualities from her, and perhaps more likely to fail to recognize or to repress those which are different. Moreover, the environment of the girl, her greater and continuous involvement in domestic life and its 'world of women', is likely to provide her with less evidence to disrupt these assumptions. Also, if the mother is more identified with her daughter, she is likely to sanction, or simply fail to see, qualities in her daughter which she hides from herself, thus limiting the available evidence even further.

All of this would place a crucial importance on the intervention of others in the mother-daughter relationship. There is the question of whether the father becomes available to the daughter psychologically as a model for partial identification, and/or as a source of conflicting evidence of other kinds. One would also expect that the kinds of (female) friends available for the girl to identify with in adolescence, as an alternative to the mother, would be more crucial to the girl than to the boy in establishing a separate identity and the form that it takes. Helene Deutsch suggests that these friendships form the basis from which the girl can oppose her mother, experience some degree of necessary hostility towards her, and thus come to establish her separateness. If the people who are psychologically available to fill this need are drawn from the domestic female world, or from other girls in a similar position, then all that the girl can learn about herself in this setting is essentially 'more of the same', even if she does establish a separate identity. This might also be the reason for the findings of some studies that girls who show some degree of 'father-identification' seem to be better adjusted psychologically and also more likely to go into 'unfeminine' studies and careers. (The evidence on this is conflicting: see Tangri, 1972; Fransella and Frost, 1977, pp.84-9; Lifshitz, 1976; Patrick, 1972; Sperlinger, 1971.)

Again, one would expect from this that alternative role models would have a special importance in influencing girls' academic and career decisions, as the evidence suggests that they do (Almquist and Angrist, 1970). In particular, appropriate role models can give the girls evidence that they can in fact achieve their primary goals (becoming wives and mothers) and also be involved in paid work and life outside the home. It is probably still true that the alternative role models available (for instance schoolteachers) provide exactly the opposite evidence: that on the whole women divide into those who have one and those who have the other.

My general point here is that boys have less need of these means to self-discovery, since they already have a greater separateness, their identifications are discontinuous (first mother, then father), and, often practically as well as psychologically, they have a greater range of experience available.

Even though there is room for argument about some of the evidence, there is a good deal about Chodorow's approach that I think is useful. In particular, she is suggesting that in childhood, finding out about oneself is not just a question of acquiring information, but of internalizing a set of relationships. (This of course she is taking from the psychodynamic perspective.) What is being acquired is a relationship to a many-faceted self, and to a complex world. The theory suggests some ways in which the specific context of the child may influence conscious self-concepts. This context structures the way in which conflicting experiences are integrated, some being accepted as 'self' consciously, and others being rejected and suppressed. It also suggests that, in certain circumstances, the girl may be left with very narrow means for representing, articulating, and developing, discrepant experiences.

CONCLUSION: SOME THOUGHTS ON APPROACHES TO RESEARCH ON WOMEN'S PERCEPTIONS OF THEMSELVES

In everyday interactions with each other, most of us make apparently rather contradictory assumptions at different times. Some of the time we assume that other people know what they are about, and that they can give some sort of account of what they are doing and why they are doing it. Life becomes quite unnecessarily complicated if we never operate in this way. At the same time, we are well aware that we run into trouble if we make this assumption in every circumstance.

Correspondingly, we know of ourselves that we can sometimes make explicit the reasons for our own actions. We do so, on the one hand, by referring to what we know of the world, and on the other, by describing ourselves, our personal qualities and our value systems. If pressed, we may be able to defend that 'knowledge' with objective evidence and rational argument. However, we also know that there is a point beyond which it is difficult either to question or defend. Moreover, we may find ourselves feeling and acting in quite unexpected ways, for reasons which we cannot make explicit.

Perhaps there is a case for 'riding two horses' in a similar fashion, when we look at women's perceptions of themselves. In other words, we may need to entertain the possibility that some aspects of these perceptions are rational appraisals of the evidence available and of the enterprises they have in mind, and consequently that, given time to introspect, they may be able to make these clear to us. At the same time, we may have to consider the possibility that there are some guiding assumptions about the self that the individuals concerned can delineate, but not fully explain; and that, beyond these there are some aspects of the self-image that remain persistently inaccessible to introspection, but which none the less influence conscious experience.

Part of the reason for this may indeed be as suggested by Shotter, that many of our purposes and guiding principles are not constructed by the individuals who hold them; they have been in-

vented among people, and are taken on by individuals in order to
make social life possible.

However, this does not seem to be the whole explanation. For we
seem to be able to entertain divergent and contrary images and
purposes that are often integrated successfully. Only in certain
circumstances do they 'pop up' to disturb, as if they had been there
all the time, but buried. Essentially, I am saying that I do not
know how the conscious images of femininity can be understood
without drawing on a concept of a dynamic unconscious, of aspects
of the self that are actively kept out of awareness, and of connections that are actively avoided.

Much of my argument about the ways in which women may avoid or be
prevented from acquiring certain knowledge of themselves hinges on
this assumption. If the women of a particular culture describe
themselves as, say, not very assertive, not very aggressive, not
very competent and independent, or not very much interested in sex,
we might put some of this down to an environment which fosters the
learning and expression of some characteristics and not others. My
question is, is this sufficient? A commonly stated view (see, for
example, the literature on 'fear of success' in women) is that women
avoid certain behaviours because they anticipate social sanctions.
It seems to me that this implies that at some level they must be
entertaining the possibility that they do have the forbidden wishes
and feelings. If these women are really wholeheartedly seen by
themselves and others as having small potential for aggression,
assertion, dominance, then why the need for avoidance in the women
and negative sanctions from the men?

Consider again, the Peruvian town described by Arnold. If the
assumption is simple that 'good' women are monogamous in so far as
they take any interest in sex at all, then why the elaborate re-
straints on their activities which are always found in societies
which hold these beliefs?

In both cases we are dealing with belief systems that actually do
regulate social life. Consequently, members of the culture in
question will be able to justify their views by pointing to supporting evidence, and perhaps also to the evil results of deviance.
Such justifications will be valid, but will constitute only a
partial and incomplete explanation.

Psychological theories which make any serious attempt to encompass experience, including the experience of the self, have this
quality of hovering between frameworks. (Freud, for instance, in
his clinical writings, speaks a good deal of the time as if people
are driven by motivations which are obscure to them, but he also at
times speaks as if they can make choices which bear some rational
relationship to the world in which they live. Conversely, Kelly,
who starts from the assumption that anticipation, planning, is what
we are about, has a good deal to say about the ways in which we may
simultaneously know, and fail to know, uncomfortable aspects of
ourselves. It is probably no accident that such theories are clinical theories, grounded in clinical practice.)

What I am trying to get at is this: perhaps, at present, it is
an advantage, and not a weakness, to be 'riding two horses'. There
may be something to be gained from each of these apparently incomplete viewpoints, and a great deal to lose from attempting to resolve the issue prematurely, in favour of one or the other.

This may sound like an invitation to return to primeval muddle.
Perhaps it is. All that I am saying is that it seems to allow us to
arrive at a more complete description of our lived experience. We
have the experience of making decisions, planning our activities, in
an intelligible way, perhaps on the basis of thoughts and feelings
which do not feel chosen and whose origins we do not know. I do not
know how to resolve this problem, nor how to articulate the perspectives together. But I do know that opting for either, by
itself, results in theories whose capacity to reflect my experience
at a descriptive level does violence to that experience.

REFERENCES

Almquist, E. and Angrist, S. (1970), Career Salience and Atypicality
of Occupational Choice among College Women, in 'Journal of Marriage
and the Family', 32, pp.242-9.
Bakan, David (1966), cited in Chodorow, N. (1974).
Breen, D. (1975), 'The Birth of a First Child: Towards an Under-
standing of Femininity', Tavistock Publications, London.
Carlson, R. (1970), On the Structure of Self-Esteem: Comments on
Zitter's Formulation, in 'Journal of Consulting and Clinical Psy-
chology', 34, pp.264-8.
Carlson, R. (1971), Sex Differences in Ego Functioning: Exploratory
Studies of Agency and Communion, in 'Journal of Consulting and
Clinical Psychology', 37, pp.267-77.
Chodorow, N. (1974), Family Structure and Feminine Personality, in
(eds) Rosaldo, M.Z. and Lamphere, L., 'Woman, Culture and Society',
Stanford University Press, Stanford, California.
Deutsch, H. (1973), 'The Psychology of Women', vol.I, Bantam Books,
New York.
Fogarty, M., Rapoport, R. and Rapoport, R.N. (1971), 'Sex, Career
and Family', Political and Economic Planning and George Allen &
Unwin, London.
Fransella, F. and Frost, K. (1977), 'On Being a Woman: A Review of
Research on how Women See Themselves', Tavistock Publications,
London.
Gutmann, D. (1965), cited in Chodorow, N. (1974).
Hariton, B. and Singer, J. (1974), Women's Fantasies during Sexual
Intercourse: Normatives and Theoretical Implications, in 'Journal
of Consulting and Clinical Psychology', 42, pp.313-22.
Komarovsky, M. (1946), Cultural Contradictions and Sex Roles, in
'American Journal of Sociology', 52, pp.184-9.
Lifshitz, M. (1976), Girls' Identity Formation as Related to
Perceptual Development of Family Structures, in 'Journal of Marriage
and the Family' (in press).
Lipshitz, S. (ed.) (1978), 'Tearing the Veil', Routledge & Kegan
Paul, London.
Maccoby, E. and Jacklin, C. (1975), 'The Psychology of Sex
Differences', Oxford University Press, London.
Oakley, A. (1974), 'Housewife', Penguin, Harmondsworth.
Patrick, T. (1972), 'Motivational and Familial Determinants of
Professional Career Choice in Women', Ph.D. dissertation, Teachers
College, Columbia University, New York.

Richardson, M. (1975), Self-Concepts and Role-Concepts in the Career Orientation of College Women, in 'Journal of Counseling Psychology', 22, pp.122-6.
Rosaldo, M.Z. and Lamphere, L. (eds) (1974), 'Woman, Culture and Society', Stanford University Press, Stanford, California.
Shotter, J. (1975), 'Images of Man in Psychological Research', Methuen, London.
Sperlinger, D. (1971), 'A Repertory Grid and Questionnaire Study of Individuals Receiving Treatment for Depression from General Practitioners', unpublished Ph.D. thesis, University of Birmingham.
Steinmann, A. (1963), A Study of the Concept of the Feminine Role in Fifty-one Middle-Class American Families, in 'Genetic Psychology Monographs', 67, pp.275-352.
Tangri, S. (1972), Determinants of Occupational Role Innovation among College Women, in 'Journal of Social Issues', 28, pp.177-99.
Vogel, S., Broverman, I., Broverman, D., Clarkson, F. and Rosenkrantz, P. (1970), Maternal Employment and Perception of Sex-Roles among College Students, in 'Developmental Psychology', 3, pp. 384-91.

Chapter 5

FROM A MARGINAL MAN
TO A PLURAL PERSON
Jagdish S. Gundara

THE FOREST AS A HOME

My home was Kenya where I was born of Indian parents and spent my
first eighteen impressionable years in an atmosphere replete with
contradiction. My father, a Sikh, was a forester at Ngong, an area
on the outskirts of Nairobi and neighbouring its elite and exclusively European residential area of Karen. My father's position
as a government officer seemed to me to have a certain glow of respect, but it was not long before it became abundantly clear to me
that, although he was a dedicated forester with a passion for flora
and fauna, he would, under the colonial system, receive no recognition of his dedication or advancement in his career. This made me
believe that ambition was a fruit devoid of sweetness and that I and
my like would in the fullness of time be allotted similar positions
in a closed social and political system based on racialism. The
concept of a proud but independent egalitarian Sikh nurtured through
bedtime stories of the Gurus, told to me by my mother, thrived only
in the dusk of my imagination.
    The recognition of being an Indian child, however, did not
receive any strength outside the home. We were an isolated Indian
family living in the forest, and I did not receive the support of
other members of the Indian community because of this isolation.
    I naturally turned to African children who were my neighbours and
we spent a lot of time playing together. I picked up their
languages - Kikuyu and Swahili. I grew up with mainly Kikuyu
children and I learnt a lot from them about the forest. We grew up
learning to think that we were part of the forest and of each other.
This was a collective milieu consisting of older and younger
children. My brother, sister and I had many common interests with
these children as we felt the sounds of the woods at Ngong. The
smell of the earth and the rain flies after the rainy season had
started are a particularly vivid memory. This rural life had many
thrills and charms for us.
    I attempted to reconcile my friendships with my African and
European peer groups initially because of our like interests and at
a later stage with the initiation of the rather nefarious activity
of smoking. I was the main instigator of running a smoking club

which was housed in the ante-room of what was my study. We had papered the windows of this room so that no one could look in. It was furnished with slatted boxes used for growing plants. We used them as seats and for hiding the various brands of cigarettes which made their way into the den. Two very clear things happened. The first was that it was I who took the risk of providing these premises and of bringing together the African and the European children. Ironically, it was precisely I who was barely tolerated by them. I never quite got over this very odd treatment of me by these two groups of youths. After all, was I not one of them, and did we not do many interesting things collectively? However, in a den created by me it was I who was treated as an intruder. I did not quite fit into their respective worlds. This was a painful experience because I was wrenched from my peer-group friends by their indifference to me.

The second element about this episode was that my father accidentally discovered this smoking den and was so livid with anger that he slapped me extremely hard across the face. He then realized that he had hit me too hard and he put his arm around my shoulders, while we walked around the acrocarpus and chestnut trees - with him explaining to me why smoking was a bad habit. Interestingly enough he did not refer to the religious sanctions (Sikhs should not smoke) during his discourse. The head of the family had thus asserted his authority and protective role, and this integrative aspect of the Indian family system made it extremely difficult for me to break away from what was a cohesive and functional unit.

There were various aspects of living in colonial Kenya which affected one's social learning. Going on holidays was impracticable and therefore non-existent during my youth. Indians were not allowed into hotels and it was an indication of Indians' inadequateness and inaptness not to cater for these needs. During this period there was no broadening of one's own environment and vision through travel or contact with other people. A substitute I found it exciting to be allowed to stay at the homes of various friends overnight or for a weekend. In this way I was able periodically to escape from home and at the same time to value its worth.

While there was a dam near our house, we never went for a holiday to the sea till I was sixteen. I have since learnt to appreciate the value of being near the sea but I missed doing it in the country where I was brought up.

There was another aspect of home which bothered me. In a stratified Kenyan society, our living in a thatched house in the forest seemed to me to reduce our status in society, which I felt was further eroded by our having no electricity in the house, although power-lines only four hundred yards away from our home supplied the neighbouring Karen area. I tended to be embarrassed by our house and refrained from mentioning to my city friends that we had to use paraffin or gas lamps. It was an issue about which I as a child could do little and about which I should not have spent time worrying, although associating with city children made it seem an important issue. The one significant memory which remains in my mind is a dream, in which a lovely thatched house appeared. The thatched house had a long verandah of wire mesh which was used for keeping the chickens out. In my dream, the posts on the verandah were used

for hitching tortoises. It seems, on reflection, that all these
useless preoccupations and concerns about status had reduced me to
a tortoise.

Another peculiar feature of my early life in Kenya was that in my
family we did not celebrate birthdays. This was a historical and
cultural feature which probably only applied to my generation, since
my youngest sister did celebrate her birthdays. Consequently, I do
not remember how old I was when I learnt certain things informally
or formally. Since lots of social learning took place before I
entered school, it is very difficult to pinpoint in chronological or
linear terms how old I was when I learnt various skills. It was
only when I entered school, and I was promoted from one class to
another that I became conscious of my age. Certain aspects of life
and learning continue to seem amorphous till this day. Things seem
to weave in and out of the mind, and thoughts and events merge into
a whole at various levels of the consciousness, which I find difficult to disentangle.

Upbringing at home also played a complex role in my learning
processes. Our family was basically a nuclear unit which was reinforced because of our geographical isolation. However, a web of
family and parents' friends drifted in and out of the home. My
father tended to be strict, loving, authoritarian and prone to
discipline, including an occasional thump. These periods were
softened by various other members of the family, and my mother was
particularly kind, loving and giving. These complex elements of relationship within the family considerably dampened my teenage anger
and rebelliousness towards my father. This dual adult authority and
affection mutually and continually reinforced the superior status of
parents and other adults and relegated peer-group relations to a
secondary position and importance.

HISTORY OF SCHOOLING

Until this point learning was done in conjunction with others on a
spontaneous basis. I was not instructed why certain things in the
forest had to be learnt. Somehow what the parents taught also
seemed to be valid. It was the school-oriented teacher-learning
that was agonizing because the information imparted had no immediate
relevance. Teacher authority did not make this knowledge any more
relevant.

Parental authority was not the only agent of fragmenting my peer-
group relations. As an Indian, I could not attend a school in my
neighbourhood because it was an African school, although all my
friends attended this school. I was also debarred from going to a
European school which was only one mile from my home – I had to go
ten miles into Nairobi to attend an Indian school. I had to travel
to the city and operate singly as an individual outside of the collective milieu I understood. These new relationships were based on
the personalities of individuals and I particularly became very shy,
insecure and depressed, having to cultivate newer relationships.
This sense of insecurity led to depression which manifested itself
on Sunday nights when I had to prepare to go back to school on
Monday morning.

I had to travel to school by bus to the centre of Nairobi and
then further towards a school in an Asian neighbourhood. I can even
now recollect African and European children travelling in the
opposite direction to their respective schools. The urban school I
went to contained Indian children whose interests did not necessarily coincide with those of my own. We were supposed to share common
cultural and linguistic norms. However, this did not necessarily
turn out to be a rationally-planned policy. As a Punjabi-speaking
child I was not taught my own mother tongue but Urdu, which, unlike
Punjabi and English, is written from right to left. This made for
extremely difficult hand and eye co-ordination. This was particularly true because the teachers did not understand this aspect of
teaching language. The result of this haphazard teaching of
language is that I can neither read nor write Urdu as a scholar
and do not write my own mother tongue to this day. Younger generations of children have the (further) problem of not even being able
to speak their mother tongue. This dubious advantage of being sent
to an Indian school, for cultural and linguistic reasons, became
particularly suspect when we were told to speak in English throughout the school day.

Going to school was a painful experience from the very first day.
My father, a driver and Ngure Maina - my favourite 'uncle' - were
driven by lorry to this neo-classical, white-washed re-tiled-roof
structure. To induce me to stay I was given sweets (as was my
teacher), a hundred-shilling note and Ngure Maina, a Kikuyu who
worked with my father till his retirement from the Kenya Government,
was requested to stay in the school compound to provide moral support. This was, in fact, an interesting paradox because I as a
child was cross-culturally attuned and only stayed on in this Indian
school because I felt secure that Ngure Maina, my trusted African
'uncle', would not forsake me. It is possible that had Ngure not
acted as the important link between my rural home and this urban
Indian school, I would not have adapted to this school environment
supposedly created for the benefit of 'Indian' people like me.

The teacher was a rather severe Indian lady who was, however,
kind to me. City children, nevertheless, taunted me as a 'hick',
pinched me, and were noisier - with different games than the ones
I was used to. However, I had to unlearn some of my earlier skills
and learn new ones to become functional in the school milieu. I
continued to be withdrawn and never quite mastered skills like
marbles with which my school contemporaries played. After school,
my classmates walked to their homes in groups. In my case, it was
Ngure and I who had to make our way back home to the forest. We
must have appeared strange to these city children, and my relationship with them ended after school. For them there was a
continuity, in terms of their social and school life, for me it
was a fractured experience.

My discomfort at school was not made any easier by being
constantly late because I lived so far away and had to use a bicycle
and two buses to get there. The bicycle trip was three miles to the
nearest bus, then a five-mile bus ride to the centre of Nairobi and
a final bus trip to the school. Buses were late but the class
teachers did not appreciate the reasons for my unpunctuality. They
often humiliated me in front of the class by hitting me with a long

ruler across the hands. My performance and interest varied from
year to year depending upon how understanding my teachers were.

However, basically I had rejected this sort of racially segregated schooling, at least subconsciously. I deeply resented the
fact that I could not go to school with those children amongst whom
I lived. While it was the urban children, because of their group
solidarity, who felt that I was an oddity, I secretly rebelled
against their narrow city-interests. I was particularly averse to
those children who displayed no rebelliousness and slavishly emulated their parents. Whereas I felt that had the school and the
children been responsive I would have something to contribute to it,
their rejection of me made me feel bitter and fatalistic. I feared
that we would never be able to rise above the narrow framework
within which we operated, and that my generation was doomed to
mediocrity.

Peer-group solidarity, however, did not emerge as my school life
stabilized. I could not identify myself with one single group of
children, but tended to hover between those whose academic performance was good, those who were good athletes or cyclists, and a
group of rebels who rejected school altogether. These three groups
were not part of the mainstream of school life and they were mutually exclusive. In retrospect, I felt that no one group had the mo-
nopoly of the learning experience and only by relating to these
diverse groups would I be able to re-establish some integral
learning conditioning which I had initially brought to school. The
mainstream, it seemed to my rebellious friends, had accepted their
marginal role in society and the narrow norm laid down for them
without question. To preserve this precarious balance at school I
had to keep my parents as far away from school as I could.

Contacts between parents and school at primary school were
extremely limited. There were no parent-teacher get-togethers.
Many children only managed to get educated by sheer dint of effort.
In my own case, the home-school distance in geographical terms made
school remote for my parents, a fact not assisted by my deliberate
manipulation.

Home-school contacts in my case were limited for another reason.
As a forestry official my father dressed very simply in khaki shirt
and trousers. This would not have aided me in showing off to my
friends that my father was an important person. Along with a
thatched house, khaki clothes did not signal one's social importance
in stratified Kenya. As long as I had remained only in the rural
context I was not aware of these issues. However, once I started
attending school in the city I became increasingly aware of subtleties of social status, based on the clothes one wore and the type of
houses and parts of the town in which one lived.

At another level my parents and our home in the forest were a
secret haunt. They were protected from the narrow and mediocre
status that I felt we as Indians operated in. Inasmuch as I respected and admired my father, I wanted to protect him from this
social milieu which I did not particularly accept. This has become
increasingly apparent to me as I realize that I too feel comfortable
in simple cotton clothes, while as a youth I fancied dressing up. I
was also having such a difficult time developing my own particular
approach to combining various diverse and sometimes contradictory

strands, which I felt my father would not understand, that I preferred him to stay away from school altogether.

On the occasions when my father did visit school on a prize-giving day, especially if I had won a prize, I remember pressing him to dress up in a suit and tie.

However, this lack of contact between my family and the school was not due to their lack of interest in my education. In contemporary terms it is asserted sometimes that children fare badly in school because parents lack contact with the school. In our own case, my parents had such implicit faith in the ability of teachers to perform their duty as dispensers of knowledge that they felt they had no right to interfere in this activity. As a matter of fact my parents always ensured that we did our homework and attempted to help when they could.

I managed to pass the public examination at the end of my first seven years in the primary school. I had started school in the intimidating neo-classical structure. However, before I appeared in the primary-school certificate examination, we were moved to two other structures because of increasing rolls in school. The first one was referred to as the 'bandas'. These were classrooms constructed of bamboos, with hessian walls and corrugated metal roofs. These barrack-like structures were homelier, perhaps even charming (if barrack-like structures can be considered charming). They had the advantage of having low windows so that one could look outside into the playing fields and direct one's attention away from the rather strenuous academic activity in the classroom. The linear style of these buildings did not particularly allow for a feeling of integrated learning in the school.

During the middle years of my primary school we only went to school for half a day because the school was used for a second shift in the afternoon. This practice was abandoned, however, when more new schools were built and during my last year in primary school we were transferred to one such modern structure. I did not particularly like this nondescript building, particularly because we now had to attend school for morning and afternoon sessions. I had preferred the one session in the mornings because it allowed me to go back home in the afternoons and play with my friends in the forest without the constraints of the school.

I managed to pass my public primary-school examination and was not sent to a technical school but to an academic secondary school, which in retrospect architecturally appears quite grand. It was a neo-classical structure with classrooms and corridors along a quadrangle. Unlike the primary school, this old structure with its quadrangle created a cohesive learning atmosphere in the school. Parts of the building were covered with red bougainvillea climbers and in the front there was a grassy island with a palm tree and a flag-post. On one side of the main building stood the science laboratories and on the other side a carpentry shed and the playing fields. The main building initially seemed cold and intimidating, particularly since one could hear the reverberations of the teachers' voices in the corridors. The urinals and the canteen situated behind the school were devoid of the presence of teachers and were a welcome relief.

POLITICAL AWARENESS AND IDENTITY CRISES

Kenya was in a tremendous amount of political ferment during the 1950s, and one was inevitably aware of it. In my own case it caused a lot of emotional problems because it raised issues of identity and one's belongingness. This provoked a fair amount of thought that was not directly related to academic and classroom learning.

The first four years in my secondary school were extremely difficult years. However, once I had passed the Cambridge School Certificate Examination and was accepted to complete my Cambridge Higher School Certificate, the school became more acceptable. Once I had completed my sixth form successfully, the officious aspect of my schooling, for some strange reason, seemed to have evaporated and I was left with a rosy-tinted image of what had been extremely difficult years of learning and growing up. I particularly remember, after accepting a prize at the last prize day, fondly walking away from my secondary school with its avenue of purple jacaranda flowers which carpeted the driveway.

The teenage years were difficult because I became increasingly aware of the pressures of living in a racially and a socially stratified society. I continued to live in the rural African world, and more marginally with my European friends. However, these friendships were now not very strong because I had been attending the Indian school in the city, and I had begun to develop a complex set of relationships at my school. My complex responses to my Indianness at home and at school led to conflicts at both these places.

One of the inflictions of this era that impeded my academic pursuits was a disdain of my apparent Indianness. Since I operated in an inequitable society and I could not shed the colour of my skin, I felt that I ought to change my name, at least when I had grown up. I thought that perhaps if I anglicized my nickname it would assist me in assimilating, and some of my problems would disappear. At the same time I felt ashamed of contemplating this, and it was only many years later in North America, when I realized that other people considered doing this, that I began to feel less ashamed of these youthful attempts to break out of a prison imposed upon me from outside. From my point of view at that time, I thought that I might be able to relate better with my European and African friends, from whom I was increasingly being alienated. Perhaps identification with the dominant group was the easiest answer, while in effect I instinctively identified with the Africans. However, since the issues were not easily resolvable in the context of complex Kenya, they caused a fair amount of dilemma which could not be easily resolved.

This involved a lot of thought and a tremendous amount of learning time was spent day-dreaming. It inhibited my relationships with those of my friends who worked hard academically. They did not spend time on this superfluous activity, perhaps because they came from more cohesive Indian neighbourhoods and did not question their identity as much as I did. It is also possible that I indulged in self-pity and questioning because I perceived things from other perspectives. Many of my schoolmates came from homes with fewer advantages and they therefore had a clearer sense of direction and

commitment to perform well. For whatever reason this happened,
there was a group of youth who developed into an academic elite and
did well in their public examinations. It would probably be true to
say that, in proportional terms to public expenditure on European,
African and Indian education, Indian schools did relatively well.
This is perhaps because education was seen as the only avenue that
would lead out of the complex middle position of the Indian minority
in Kenya. I particularly admired these academically bright
students. I, however, could no systematically apply myself to
formal learning as they did and therefore did not spend a lot of
my time with them. I did, however, accept this peer group as a
model to be emulated and even to this day have some warm friends
amongst this group of students.

Another group of friends whom I associated with simultaneously
rejected the dominating elite and the adults from amongst our own
community. Hence parents and teachers were subject to rebellion
partially because of a generation gap but partially because they
accepted the appallingly objective conditions. Many of these
friends were not from my peer group, they were more senior to me.
Their rebellion took the form of enhancing physical stamina, or
asserting premature adulthood by staying out late and drinking. A
small clique of us used to play truant from school to play snooker
and drink beer, although my skills at the snooker table are no
indication of a misspent youth. Others became good cyclists, scouts
or hockey players. However, apart from an occasional act of bravado
like driving a car fast without a licence, I preferred the more congenial pastimes of sitting in coffee houses or watching celluloid
during school time.

This deviation, however, had to co-exist within the constraints
imposed by parental authority. In that social situation one could
not become an out-and-out deviant without serious repercussions. In
my case I was rapped on the knuckles both at home and at school for
these deviations. Parental authority ensured that these pleasurable
pursuits were curtailed and more time was spent on academic work,
and the school reinforced it.

A third group of people who I associated with were either adults
or senior to me and had either qualified in their field of special-
ization or were adults who had returned from England and rejected
the mediocre anglicization of our parents' generation. I found this
group of friends to be fascinating because they had returned from
the metropolis and were critical of it and its norms. A relative of
mine in this category and I used to take long walks in the evening
'to sort out the world' and he introduced me to other interesting
friends. My parents, however, did not object to this aspect of my
life even though it injected new and critical ideas.

My feelings about European domination and oppression on the one
hand and the mediocrity and pettiness of the Indian community on the
other, were lent credibility by a friend and relative of my parents'
generation. I respected him more than my father because I considered him to be my intellectual mentor. Mr N.S.Mangat, Q.C., was
a leading criminal lawyer in East Africa and the president of the
East African National Indian Congress during 1954 and 1956 when I
was in secondary school. During the first year of his presidency
of the above organization he criticized the Europeans for their

arrogance and presumption of superiority. This clarified some of my
earlier dilemmas and the errors of my ways, and I began to realize
why we, as Indians, were placed in such a peculiar position. In
1956, however, on a similar occasion, he took the opportunity to
criticize the Indians for their narrow-mindedness, pettiness and
lack of vision. This too struck a note which was real and I felt
more relaxed about issues that had hitherto perplexed me. However,
there were no channels where I could constructively involve myself
in any political activity. It was merely the assertion of views
felt by me during my own youth, by a respectable adult, which I
found useful.

Needless to say Mr Mangat was not re-elected to the presidency of
this august organization after this second speech. He was a tall,
proud and humorous man and probably made the speeches in this order
purposively, since he took the whole thing in his stride.

This sort of exposure at home had made me politically conscious
and obviously made me look critically at my teachers and the school
system. On the whole we were taught by Indian teachers but literature was taught by an English Oxford graduate. He took great
dislike to me because I did not conform to his stereotype of the
docile Indian youth. He referred to me as a 'lesser Caucasian',
being himself blond and blue-eyed. I did not know what this meant
and in an attempt to protect myself from this sort of insult my
parents papered over the incident. When I did realize what it
meant, it elicited an extremely complex response. I began to read
avidly, partly because of the fear that I might not do well in this
subject. This avid reading was reinforced by the fact that this
teacher persisted in treating me invidiously by openly taunting me
when we neared the examination that I would fail in my final Higher
School examinations. As it turned out, I was the only pupil who
obtained a distinction in literature, but this teacher never con-
gratulated me even at this point. I, however, was exhilarated by
having done well and my headmaster and other teachers became
extremely friendly and affectionate. This included two English
teachers who taught history and geography and who were quite different from the literature teacher.

The above incident provoked another personal response. I had
been brought up in a cross-cultural framework despite the sectarian
and racial divisions which cut right across Kenyan society. I was,
however, turned by this teacher to think in terms with which I
basically disagreed. I became an inverted snob after this teacher
had rebuked me.

This personal attack provoked an opposite reaction to the earlier
one of emulating the dominant culture. It was only when I saw the
Gandhara sculpture in the Boston Museum of Fine Art many years later
and realized that this civilization, which existed from the first to
the fourth century A.D., was a synchronization of Greco-Roman and
Indian cultures in North West India that I established a realistic
sense of personal identity. The realization that I belonged to an
old culture gave me confidence and an ability to function as a
composite person. The inverted snobbery and somewhat false pride
in being a Punjabi did not then need assertion.

I, however, became conscious of the general problem of how dominant cultures wiped out the identities of minority groups. The pre-

dicament of the black Americans came into prominence in the 1960s and I gave some thought to their problems as one group which had been forced to lose their African identity. I felt that the dominant American society had done a dis-service not only to the American Indians and the black Americans, but to themselves by denying themselves a real possibility of becoming genuinely American. They had, it seemed to me, in fact imposed a fragment of a certain period of Europe on the North American society and were destined to remain a Euro-centred paranoic community which had imposed itself but not allowed itself to take root in this new, varied and fertile landscape. Problems of my own personal identity paled into insignificance compared to these mammoth issues.

The above discourse to explain the results of being labelled as inferior as a result of my teacher's remarks, has been to demonstrate the long and tedious process it took to examine issues of personal and cultural identity. The school in Kenya was the obvious place which should have obviated in hierarchical terms a judgment of certain groups as culturally or racially inferior. The ideal task the school had to perform was to show the differences between peoples and not label them as 'better' or 'worse'. This teacher in particular and the school in general, in fact, had succeeded in reinforcing differentiation on a qualitative basis rather than on a basis of equality. As far as I was concerned the school created problems of identity and therefore failed in educating us with open and sensitive values. This particular incident turned me against the English academy, perhaps incorrectly, and I felt I could not count on it to solve the grave issues that linked up in my mind.

DIDACTIC LEARNING AT SCHOOL

We were mainly taught by Indian teachers trained in British India or Kenya. They, however, taught us on the basis of a British-centred curriculum and through books which stressed the British role in civilizing the world. For the life of me, I could not understand why I was not allowed to attend an English school if the purpose of it was to teach an English-based curriculum. When I was sent to an Indian school and was taught by Indian teachers, I might have expected that the content of education would also be Indian. I now feel that by teaching us an Anglo-centred curriculum, using Indian teachers who only understood it in secondhand terms, was unfair on the teachers and the pupils. After all, these teachers had no close experience of England to perform a first-rate teaching job. However, the other side of deficiency in the teachers really manifested itself when the teachers taught us subjects like the Urdu language. They recited the verses from Urdu poetry with such verve that momentarily the far away and long forgotten land of India became real. If any real aspect of India was taught in the school it was Indian languages. It was the preservation of this aspect of Indian society which allowed Indian culture and poetry to thrive in Kenya. My generation did not adhere to the temple so it was mainly the linguistic aspect taught at school which put us in touch with the variety of India.

A few teachers were either radical or nationalistic and attempted

to correct the imbalance of the curriculum and the books, particularly in history lessons. However, the inspectorate of the Education Department rendered such teachers powerless. Those teachers
who accepted the mores and norms of the English dominated department
got promoted to senior posts. The first Indian inspector in this
department was the extremely anglicized headmaster, who also
happened to be an extremely good Shakespeare teacher. A teacher who
was nationalistic, wore khadi (traditional Indian cotton suits) and
taught Gujerati language remained at the lower-scale post, despite
his ability. He was also given 'low-ability' classes, which in professional terms must have made him feel a 'second-rate' teacher.
Whether this is actually how he felt I do not know but he certainly
did not change either his ideas or his teaching ability - while I
remained at this school.

The same was true of an Urdu, a physical-education teacher, who
was very popular with the students. This Sikh teacher had a strong
sense of Punjabi values and was a good scholar of Urdu and Punjabi.
He did not attempt to operate in the mainstream of the English-domi-
nated Education Department. This teacher was not only not promoted,
but was transferred to another less 'prestigious' school. The
treatment received by these two teachers demonstrated to me that the
enhancement of an emerging Indian self-concept was not acceptable.

The above fact, accompanied by the lower per capita amount of
revenue spent on Indian children's education compared to the
European, demonstrated to me as a teenager the imbalance in the
distribution of resources. It also demonstrated that the organization of the Education Department reflected the wider relationships in society. It rewarded those teachers who conformed to its
norms and relegated to lower positions those who had a social or
national consciousness.

Another aspect of being taught by Indian teachers was that the
teachers replicated paternal authority at home, in the context of
the school. On the whole, these teachers as members of a minority
community were exceedingly committed teachers. They were in the
profession because many felt the genuine need to help children from
this community to overcome the hurdles placed by the dominant community. Rebellion by youth against parents was followed by rebellion against teachers, if they were too strict and used corporal
punishment. Some of the teachers, however, made learning a joyous
experience in a relaxed classroom situation.

My own responses to the stern and disciplinarian teachers only
changed later after some reflection. The harsh responses of
teachers towards those of us who were either difficult, lazy or none
too keen to learn were easy to understand. These teachers felt that
we, as youth, did not see the barriers to our advancement in a
prejudiced society. When we refused to accept rules laid down by
them they felt obliged to point out to us in no uncertain terms the
error of our ways. It was our fault that we did not understand the
urgency of our situation and these teachers then resorted to corporal punishment.

Our teachers felt that the school was the last resort that could
positively change our lives, and they saw us passing this chance by.

I am opposed to corporal punishment, particularly by those
teachers who feel no love, affection or more than a mere profession-

al commitment to children. My opposition to corporal punishment in
general is muted in the case of my own teachers. I hold no rancour
or malice to teachers who punished me, especially when it was clear
to me that I was in the wrong or that it was done out of good and
genuine motives.

Relations between us and our teachers were formal at one level
but informal at another level. This was the level at which they
could relate to us because, as members of the minority community,
we were in the same boat.

Teaching in school was in general formal and based on a syllabus
whose ultimate aim was performing well in public examinations. My
initial introduction to English language in the class was through
teaching by rote. Literature was taught on a similar basis with set
textbooks. Problems of hand-eye co-ordination arising from teaching
of English from left to right and Urdu from right to left were not
systematically tackled. Story telling at home, apart from those
stories with religious connotations, were non-existent. This was a
consequence of the parents attempting to teach us on the basis they
were taught in India - with inevitable remarks about how bad 'per-
missive' ideas were. Consequently neither at home nor at school was
there any opportunity for expanding into learning through stories
and general literature. Although my father was unable to assist in
formulating a sensible pattern of reading he was, however, successful in encouraging an interest in books. He made it a point on
Saturdays to take me to a reasonably good bookshop in Nairobi while
he visited his head office. This gave me an opportunity to browse
and choose books which took my fancy. I used to love the smell of
paper and of dust in these bookshops. This self-selection of literature reading has left large gaps in my reading. For instance,
whereas I had read Steinbeck's 'The Log in the Sea of Costez', I
have yet to read 'Alice in Wonderland'. Similarly my familiarity
with African and Indian literature is very superficial. We were
also not provided with much opportunity to devise our own stories.
Neither was there any hardware whereby we could record material to
make learning more immediate and real. Learning was neither child
nor project-centred and there was neither much variety nor flexibility in the way we were taught.

My interests therefore were directed by what and how we were
taught. This, however, was a selective process because not all
subjects were either well taught or attracted my interest.

Our teachers used traditional methods mainly to impart facts and
skills. Different teachers taught us specialized subjects and the
students had to organize and structure materials to make them
comprehensible. One of the drawbacks of being taught by traditional
methods was that teachers applauded only the work of good students,
neglecting other aptitudes. Those who were not achieving much were
either criticized or ignored. Many of us sat at the back of the
class so as not to attract the teacher's attention. The negative
reinforcement led to many children faring badly in public examinations.

There was no systematic teaching of specialized subjects within
an integrated framework. There was no flexibility in the teaching
system with team-teaching or guidance to younger teachers from the
more responsible and experienced teachers. For instance, no con-

nections existed between subjects like geography and history or the
various sciences and specialisms in mathematics. There appeared to
be no synthesis between these various subjects, and I tended to
choose to focus on those subjects which I liked or found easy. So,
for instance, I studied history and geography more scrupulously and
since I found mathematics and sciences more difficult due to the
lack of a logical explanation as to the workings of these subjects,
I studied them less rigorously. Furthermore, subjects like geometry
were not taught as if they had any practical or technical relevance.
My half-hearted attempts to deal with what I considered difficult
mathematical problems only led to a further lack of self-confidence,
issues that were not clearly understood by my teachers. My performance was extremely poor and I actually failed in my examinations. I am not certain if it was a matter of my lack of aptitude
in this subject or the fact that I did not receive the right kind of
support from my mathematics teachers. My parents arranged for
special tuition during my secondary-school career but I was unable
to improve my performance. Perhaps it was too late for special
tuition to rectify previous reverses, and I continue to wonder if
my career and interests would have been different or more satisfying
if my problem in this field had been diagnosed earlier.

   I was also not consciously satisfied with the way history was
taught, which perpetually reinforced the positive values of the
dominant group and the negative features of India and Africa. For
instance, the 'Indian Mutiny' was taught not to demonstrate its
nationalistic aspirations but to exemplify the disloyalty and
untrustworthiness of the Indians. The Africans and the Indians then
viewed each other adversely and did not assert each other's positive
contributions in historical terms. This subject, in fact, could
have been used to share positively the histories of various groups.
This was not the case and one had to make a special and individual
effort to do this. Another opportunity of a shared-learning experience had been lost.

   This system of education rejected any subjective values of
students. Perceptions of certain subject-matters even within the
limitations in which it was taught could possibly have been explored
from different perspectives; however, even this was not done. All
the arts subjects, it seemed to me, could be enriched by different
interpretations. However, my English literature teacher had illustrated that my interpretation was unacceptable by denying my subjective values and place in learning this subject, by rejecting
interpretations which did not conform to his values. Was it possible, for instance, that literature was considered by this teacher to
be near the core of his culture and since he felt threatened in this
strange country, he imposed his interpretation even more rigorously?
Be that as it may, it denied us as students a genuine opportunity to
interact positively and to learn positive features of each other.
We were lucky at least to have teachers who did understand our
background and to some extent were able to hold as valid a certain
amount of our social experience. They were able to do this only
marginally because the whole schooling system was formal and oriented to English public examinations which they did not want us to
fail.

   I had brought to school a fairly wide and associative linguistic

network, which if it had been systematically tackled might have
furthered my cognitive processes. I was able to develop categories
and analyse issues which became useful in the learning of social
sciences, in terms of devising abstract theoretical frameworks. I
had, however, to wrestle with my mother tongue - Punjabi, Urdu - an
Indian language taught in school, Swahilli - my out of school peer-
group language, and English. Since these were neither systematically taught nor learnt, there were limitations to my ability to cate-
gorize abstract thought. At university level I found it difficult
to cope with linguistic analytical philosophy because I found the
concepts too erudite or refined. Hence my linguistic code-systems
were neither vastly 'elaborate' nor were they so 'restricted' as to
render me completely disadvantaged. Perhaps this was consistent
with my upbringing where certain enrivonmental factors either promoted or inhibited learning.

We were, however, categorized in general terms between technical
and academic schools and streamed according to our examination performances. I did not get used to the formal testing and examination
situation and consequently performed in a mediocre manner in them.
In the formal classroom I learnt slowly because I was afraid of
making mistakes and therefore tended to avoid subjects like mathematics which I could not deal with competently.

The distance between home and school made it difficult for me to
take part in sports activities after school. We did not have a
swimming pool at school and none of the public pools were open to
Asians or Africans. Swimming was more of a European sport during
the period I went to school in Kenya. This therefore curtailed my
activities in sport and the cultivation of a team spirit. At school
I did some running for my house called Mars; however, I did not do
well and disappointed my house and the housemaster by not finishing,
which enhanced my loneliness in sports. It seems to me that I was
not much of a competitor, but I have become a better non-competitive
runner, which has improved my stamina as I have grown older. This
is probably because I was brought up in an altitude of over 6,000
feet and have a good lung capacity at sea level. The one run which
I remember vividly was around an artificial lake in Chandigarta, the
capital of Punjab, India, in 1970. I was building up my jogging
after it had lapsed for some years. The first few miles were
extremely good and I felt that I was on top of the earth. The next
few miles were extremely difficult going and I felt, as on a graph,
that I was sinking into the ground. It was the last few miles which
proved exhilarating because there seemed to be a relationship
between the ground and me as I ran. This feeling of rhythm with the
earth is one of the great joys of jogging. However, inasmuch as
running is an exhilarating experience physically and mentally, it is
not only a personal experience but better shared with another
person. Basically I have a solitary heritage so far as physical
activities go.

One of the few activities which I took part in with others was to
play badminton with my brother and sisters. We did try to emulate
good players but we were not very good ourselves and there were
inevitably squabbles over scoring. The whole family tended to join
in these arguments and they had a tremendous amount of entertainment
value.

In some senses it can be argued that going to school in the city gave me experience of the man-made city environment, in addition to the natural environment in which I lived. My African playmates and I operated in the natural environment of a temperate forest. We combined in our psyche the vertical planes of the trees in the forest and the horizontal planes of the grassland and open spaces. In addition I spent some of my time in the rectangular environment of the city. The combination of these two aspects of learning possibly developed perceptual and inference habits which probably varied from those of the other children I knew in and out of school. If the school had encouraged a systematic fusion of the visual per-spectives, then I would have perhaps developed not only an appreci-ation of various arts but of positively contributing to them. As it is, I attempted to accomplish this through a process of self-edu-cation. Living in Kenya I had, for instance, an interest in the non-perspective African art. I continue to have an interest in the works of various angular and rectangular artists like Albers, Mondrian and the Bauhaus school. Is this a result of the imprint the city made on me? I also like two-dimensional art of the Im-pressionists and the post-Impressionists which entails seeing depth in the intentions of the artist's work, of a 'softer' nature. Is this facility of appreciating or operating in both the two- and the three-dimensional world a result of operating in both the natural and rectangular man-made city at an early age? Furthermore, is the ability to appreciate but not to actually draw a result of the im-balance in the school which stressed verbal learning more than the practical and pictorial aspects of education?

It was possible, if the schools had channelled our perceptual experiences in some systematic manner, that students like me would have been able to relate African, Indian and Western art and liter-ature. This process, however, never took place, and it was left to the individual to syncretize these various aspects of life in what-ever manner he could.

These varied concerns and interests did not lead to an excellence in academic terms in school, and when it came to deciding to embark on higher education and acquiring 'A'-levels in England, I felt somewhat reluctant. One of the reasons for this reluctance was that I had seen many older friends who had returned from England without having completed their education or securing a qualification. Since my father was only a civil servant and there were four of us to be educated, I felt reluctant to accept remittances from my father to continue with education abroad. I therefore re-applied to my old school to complete my Cambridge Higher School Certificate. This turned out to be an excellent decision because as a fifth and sixth-form student I was not one of the many down-trodden and forgotten in the lower forms and streams of the school. It was also the first time that boys and girls in our school studied together. This was a thrilling new experience which I welcomed.

Only two of us studied the arts and we had between us three tutors who taught history, geography and economics. Both of us had to work and produce results because all this attention was directed to us. There was no escape to a bench in the back of the class. For the first time we began to enjoy our work in school since we could discuss it with our teachers. Even the history of Anglo-Saxon

Britain seemed to come alive, remote as it was from contemporary Africa.

ADULT LEARNING

Once I had completed my Higher School Certificate examinations I was again faced with the dilemma of whether or not to study in England for my higher education. Because of the high failure-rate of friends I met from England and my family's inability to finance such a risky proposition and the experience of my literature teacher who was English, I decided against studying in England. I began to suspect that the continuity between Kenya and England was not a healthy one.

I therefore took a job with a firm in horticulture, which I really enjoyed. My brother-in-law, a qualified barrister, at a much later date also worked as the manager of this firm and jokingly remarks, 'It has been downhill ever since'. I was dissuaded from attending a major university to study horticulture by my mother. She came from a farming family in India and had married a forester, and felt that the land took so much and gave very little in return. She wanted her children to move away from the soil, and while I disagree with her now, I felt that the peasantry, in fact, did give more to the soil than they got.

I eventually obtained a scholarship to study in America and this American experience was an eye-opener, particularly since it was a total break from Kenya. As a scholarship student I felt secure in the feeling that I was not risking my parents' meagre savings on this venture. The liberal professors reciprocated in my new awakening and I felt free of the domination one felt in Kenya. After three years in the United States I left the country because I thought that I might become Americanized by default. I had also luckily acquired work-experience, in addition to education, and I was exposed to the extremely brutal form of racialism towards the black Americans. This in my case tended to act as an antidote to romanticizing the United States, which many other students from abroad tended to do. There is nothing like working in a country to find out its positive and negative features and to keep one's fingers on its pulse, particularly since studying at higher-education level is a privilege in a very secluded environment.

I went to Canada to complete my postgraduate studies. The French and English conflict in Canada was an extremely interesting example of a dominant class which was not cohesive. Quebec in the late 1960s was an interesting arena both intellectually and in terms of social conflict which was reflected in the university. On the whole, however, the American domination of Canada and its acceptance by the Canadians, with few reservations, was an experience in despondency.

Learning in North America took place both inside and outside the classroom. It is extremely difficult to evaluate which made the greater impression. Obviously the formal learning spilled over into the life outside the university and it was important to keep this connection so that one was not learning in isolated circumstances, which is a grave tendency at university level.

There were certain assumptions about the teaching of the social sciences in the United States which are legitimized in the Canadian context and which I found depressing. The assertion that the social sciences could formulate 'value free' theoretical constraints and that the mainstream of North American social sciences was based on these was unacceptable. These pseudo-scientific norms which incorporated within their framework the rationale of North American society in no way could have been assumed to be 'value free'. The Canadian academy is perhaps now more chary of these models, particularly since many of their American contemporaries have rejected some of the modes of analysis.

My formal education was completed in Scotland, which was in a similar position to England as was Canada to the United States or English Canadians to the French Canadians. However this provided an opportunity to bring together these diverse strands of social science and law, and to examine them in detail in a proper historical framework.

CULTIVATING IMPERFECTION

Learning in my case neither started and nor has it ended within the formal institutional framework. Learning started informally and socially at a very early age and continues outside this framework. Learning in this social milieu is complex and sometimes contradictory. For instance, how and why did I, having been brought up in a racially segregated school and social system, come out of it thinking differently? It can only be because of a learning process that went in and out of the institutional framework and at a personal level and at various levels of consciousness.

I still tend to respect my father, teachers and mentors who I consider helped me in formulating various aspects of my thinking. My father's sensibility towards nature and life tended to influence my visual attitudes. Our house was simply furnished and devoid of the 'kitsch' objects which decorated the homes of various contemporaries. This possibly was a result of a strong contact with nature. My genuine affection and deep relationship with my mother and women in general, are in direct contrast to the time I spent with male teachers and friends because one learnt from them at both formal and informal levels. My brother is similarly more partial to my mother although we remained committed to my father. Somehow we must have recognized that it was our mother who kept our house ticking and that her more lenient attitudes were really a reflection of her deeper strength than that of my father and of my male teachers. She seemed to have an instinctive understanding of her children's problems and needs as they grew up. I subsequently subscribed to Arnold Wesker's remark that 'men are mere rebels, women are the true revolutionaries', because I felt that in our household my mother was the essential person who loved while she instructed, who placated wild emotions and saved against the rainy day. On reflection, however, I feel that there was a balance of paternal and maternal functions in our household which aided my learning and acted as a backdrop to it.

The most vivid and exhilarating learning experience I had was in

1976 when I spent four months in India because of family problems.
This was the height of the summer followed by the monsoons. I lived
on a farm and started work on the fields by weeding, hoeing and
later planting rice. Since I was unused to manual work I had to
start by doing this at the rate of two hours a day, and within four
months I had built up enough stamina to work six hours a day. The
experience was exhilarating because it exploded a few myths about
how the well-read were interesting and the rest of the populace dull
and could not get along together without their guidance. Here in
these fields ordinary Hindu and Muslim men and women worked with
boys and girls. It demonstrated the solidarity amongst us as
workers, and one of its most delicate expressions was the eye-
contact between us. It demonstrated the sham of the perfection
of the elite in India, because I found this the most sensual and
emotional experience which had intellectual ramifications. I lived
simply without drinking liquor or indulging in eating elaborate
food. The sustenance of the fairly simple peasant food was sufficient. It brought home to me the realization that I could live
happily as a labourer without the accoutrements of an urban society.
Certain members of my family felt that I had imperfections of
character as an educated man.

Inasmuch as I continue to learn, I find that creeping cynicism is
best kept at bay by ensuring a physical and mental integration and
to attempting to relate the abstract intellectual and mental activities to emotions and passions. I find that attempts to do this are
a constantly regenerating influence in personal terms. It is, of
course, an extremely difficult proposition since I live in an indi-
vidualized, sectorized and alienated industrial society. It is
interesting that while I can appreciate art, a sister of mine who
did not attend university and was not deeply inducted into the 'Not'
medium of print as McLuhan puts it, is the one who is most creative
in terms of arts and crafts. The rest of us seem to have relegated
these skills and those dealing with creativity and other physical
rhythms of life to a more secondary place.

One thing which I accept is that one is basically a social animal
and despite one's rejection by the dominant society one belongs to
it. This attitude is based on strength which is derived out of
cultivating a humility towards life. It is unfortunate that the
society I live in misconstrues this for a weakness. Inasmuch as one
is not accepted or allowed to play a part in the way society is
presently structured, I find that contacts can be made at the historical and contemporary levels, as belonging to a collectivity.
For instance, one aspect of British history I was not taught in one
or another skeletal form was the history of pre-Christian Britain.
It also seems to be an aspect of history relegated by contemporary
Britons into a period not systematically studied. It is one aspect
of Britain which is physically manifest in the ancient megalithic
sites dotted over the countryside. An understanding of this aspect
of British history which is so different from the other periods
systematically taught in various institutions might evoke a sense of
awe and insignificance and overcome the chauvinism of many contemporary Britons. First, a continuous link between Celtic Britain and
ancient England does not seem to have threatened the British identity, it only seems to have enhanced it. Second, a realistic ap-

praisal of the historical past which explains the presence of Celts in England has its contemporary dimension. People seem to have an even shorter memory about a more recent but more relevant period of history. The role of Britain as a colonial and imperial power explains the presence of another minority in Britain - the black minority. In the same way as Celtic Britain has enhanced the identity of the country in historical and contemporary terms, so does the presence of another collective group from the black Commonwealth.

This grander historical perspective has ramifications for an individual, within the collectivity. While the institutions have attempted to make me an individual coming out of them thinking that I am different from the collectivity in qualitative terms, the factor of society and of time have taught me otherwise. The element of discrimination has assisted in making me realize that I am not 'perfect' and therefore part of the structural elite. I am therefore subsumed within the larger collectivity. An aspect of this strength of being part of mass was illustrated by a friend who survived the concentration camp by being, as he said, 'a small shit, in tall grass away from the main road'. This is an even more important lesson about survival which I have learnt outside the classroom where I was taught aspects of individual survival by achieving excellence. So perhaps sitting at the back of the classroom was not such a bad idea after all.

The limitation of time has taught a far more bitter lesson. Its finiteness in personal terms has instilled greater fear than that of galloping through the forest anticipating danger. Unanticipated deaths of friends and family, and reversals in terms of social advancement have revealed aspects of imperfection in life and society. As part of the great collective of humanity I have found the capacity to deal with both. This derives from the strength which one acquires through humility. Even the most perfect Persian carpet-maker always left a slight flaw and apparently the same is true of Peruvian and Inca art. In anticipation of the imponderables of life, I have even tried to cultivate imperfection. As a youth, when my friends and I used to meet in our best ensemble to attract the attention of the opposite sex, I remember wearing on top of my immaculate ensemble my father's ill-fitting and out of style jacket. This cultivation of the imperfect resulted in not attracting attention. At a more serious personal and social level, it perhaps allows for the recognition of the actual from the potential.

Chapter 6

FEELING AND KNOWING
Miller Mair

Knowing personally is intimately involved with feeling. Feeling is
a fundamental means of knowing in the realm of the personal. If we
degrade our understanding of feeling we have little chance of developing an understanding of what is involved in coming to know
personally. If we are ever to develop a psychology of personal
experiencing then we need to recognize both different kinds of
knowing and how we are continuingly informed by feeling.

In the realm of the personal we move in invisible worlds, mostly
private even from ourselves. In coming to know ourselves or others
personally we will need to find ways to realize the invisible, to
enter private worlds and get close enough to touch what hitherto we
have refused to feel. In coming to know personally we will need to
speak and listen in such a way that we can hear what cannot normally
be spoken and dare to know through being intimately known.

MODES OF KNOWING

Coming to know yourself or someone else is different from coming to
know about them. To know about someone is to know facts or possible
facts. It is to know that they are this much heavy and that much
tall, have two brothers, are thought to be friendly, believed to be
rich and enjoy Beethoven and fried shrimps. A great deal of our
time is taken up in manufacturing and exchanging knowledge of
varying degrees of accuracy about people and things.

Coming to know someone is also different from knowing how to get
them to react in certain ways. Knowing how to get things done, how
to achieve certain ends, how to have things turn out the way you
want them, how to influence others according to your will, absorbs
much of the time and energy of many applied psychologists and many
therapists. An increasing number of therapeutic approaches these
days are in fact based on claims to better 'know how', or more
effective and reliable procedures of control. It is easy, therefore, to confuse this kind of knowing in a psychotherapeutic
context, for instance, with knowing someone personally. They are
intimately intermingled in relationships of influence, and yet
should be distinguished.

In talking of 'coming to know' in this other sense, I'm talking
of a living personal meeting wherein one knower recognizes and engages with another knower and not just with a thing, an organism or
a supposed representative of some human processes or characteristics. This kind of knowing as living personal experiencing of and
with another knower is often lost sight of and largely ignored in
psychology. It even gets obscured at times in psychotherapy. Yet
this kind of knowing is, I think, of central importance to us in
living our lives, and knowing about this kind of knowing is likely
to be crucial in any psychology of personal experiencing or personal
action (Mair, 1979).

KNOWING PERSONALLY

On any occasion where two people actually engage with each other (or
I engage with myself), some degree of personal knowing one of the
other is involved. However, I want to deal primarily of a more
central meeting wherein I, for instance, sense and engage with you
behind and through your various social masks and roles. Speaking
figuratively, it is as if I sense that I am recognized by and in
touch with the 'prince' in the other's encampment (or community of
selves, Mair, 1977a), even though it may be one or other of his
'aides' or 'courtiers' or 'soldiers' still speaking with me. I have
a sense, which may sometimes be mistaken of course, that I am in
touch with some intimate and sensitive centre of the other's experiencing, rather than being coped with in a polite or otherwise pe-
ripheral manner.
   Coming to know oneself or another personally is not to do with a
distant or intellectual identification of aspects of the person. It
is something closer and more involving whereby I sense and feel for
you and to some degree participate in experiencing something of your
circumstances and experiencing. If we are to come to know ourselves
or others more intimately we need to feel for and inhabit aspects of
ourselves rather than merely identify and manipulate from the
outside.
   To be met and recognized in this personal way can be deeply reas-
suring but it can also be alarming and threatening. This is not
merely because the other may be sensed as penetrating your disguises
and defences, but because you also may come to know yourself in ways
you had previously managed to avoid. A crucial issue in this kind
of personal knowing is that those involved will have feelings and
concerns about being known. The development of mutual trust is
intimately involved here and only in relationships of increasing
trust will we learn more about what is involved in the further
reaches of personal knowing. In coming to know you more deeply I
will have to reach into more of myself if I am to speak more intimately and personally to you. Both of us are therefore in danger of
being known and knowing ourselves and each other more deeply and
disturbingly than we might have wished. The context of psychotherapy is one in which personal knowing is of crucial practical
importance and one in which we can learn something of personal
knowing by engaging in and reflecting on what is there undertaken.
   My main concern here will be to spell out a few aspects of this

kind of knowing as lived into personal experiencing. In doing this
I will be calling on my own personal experience both generally and
in relation to my work as a psychotherapist and psychologist. In
doing this I am struggling towards an honest formulation in words of
what has so far only been tacitly sensed and I am reaching towards
your personal experience in the hope that some at least of the
patterns I sense are recognizable to you. Throughout all this will
be a persistent concern with feeling, leading to a few implications
for psychological inquiry.

First, though, a small example of the kind of knowing I am discussing is presented, drawn from the psychotherapeutic situation.
Over and over again clients prove what excellent teachers, experi-
menters and artists they can be.

GIVING FORM TO FEELINGS

Margaret was about 50 years old and had suffered from persistent and
recurrent diarrhoea for twenty years. Repeated medical advice and
treatment had made no difference. The diarrhoea had started when
she was in hospital after she had been seriously injured in a road
accident in which her only son, a baby, had been killed. Her
husband seemed to blame her and refused to allow her to express any
feelings at all about the whole incident either at that time or
thereafter. Under a composed and well-groomed appearance she acknowledged that she did feel things strongly but had had to 'bottle
everything up'.

Only gradually did she come to let herself feel more and acknowledge more directly what she felt. We tried to find ways in
which she could give form to what she might be feeling such that we
could sense it more clearly and understand more fully what kind of
struggles she was engaged in. My concern here, though, is not to
give an account of her life or of the course of therapy or to
justify the therapeutic approach in any way. Rather I simply want
to illustrate some aspects of coming to know in a living and personally involving way.

On about the twelfth session, after six months, when she was expressing more feeling and her diarrhoea had been irregularly diminishing, she said that she felt an absolute void in herself about
the future. She said that for a very long time she had not allowed
herself to suppose that she had a future, and hadn't wanted one
either. Generally, though, as regards the future she had tried not
to let anything change. She wanted to hold things constant and
fixed.

I asked her if she would pay attention to what she was feeling
about her future. Would she notice how she was feeling right there
and then. Could she now suppose she had these feelings towards a
person she was going forward to meet, rather than to an abstract
notion of 'the future'. Going on the feelings she had, what sort
of person might this be?

Having already had a little practice with me in this kind of
improbable, 'as if', thinking, Margaret was beginning to be willing
to let herself go enough to sense whatever she might.

'It's an old person,' she eventually said, very decisively, 'an

old me. She is lonely and white haired. She's like an old and
disagreeable witch from fairy stories like Hansel and Gretel. She's
all on her own. She's pushing everyone away. I'm trying to get to
her, but she's certainly not wanting me. I see her standing there,
oldish, leaning on a stick and literally in amongst the undergrowth.
She's always inaccessible. She certainly doesn't want anyone and is
very disagreeable.'

'Instead of being your present, younger self approaching this old
woman,' I asked Margaret, 'can you try to be the old woman? Can you
put yourself into her to feel and sense what she might be feeling?'

'This I do feel,' said Margaret without hesitation. 'She wishes
she could let the younger one in, but she is threatened by her. If
I welcome her in, she says to herself, she will overpower me. She
will dominate me. This other person will come and rule the roost.
So the old woman doesn't want her to come in. The only way she can
prevent this is to be entirely on her own, then she has supremacy.
The old woman doesn't have enough confidence. She wants affection,
but she's rejecting it all the time. She is lonely. If the other
one comes in the old woman fears she will lose the little bit of
personality she has. At present she can make a few decisions and
have a certain hold on immediate family surroundings, but she can
do this only by keeping everyone at bay.'

Margaret emerges from the old woman back to her ordinary experience and perspective on herself and things. She says with con-
viction and surprise that the old woman seemed very real. 'I could
see the two of them,' she said, 'the old woman and the one trying to
get in. The one trying to get in was much nicer.' I asked Margaret
if she can tell me something about the nicer one.

She, it seems, is not so clear. There is the feeling that she
would like to help the old woman, but Margaret seems, as she speaks,
to lose any impression of this other figure. It's only the old
woman she sees very clearly. She guesses, though, that the younger
one is very much edging her way in. So far she has only come within
the range of the old one's stick, and was felt as a definite threat.

Two weeks later at our next session, Margaret reported that she
has been feeling much better. She has been sleeping with none of
the panics she had recently been experiencing on waking. She
commented that she had found the experience of the 'old woman'
strikingly real, almost too real. Since that time she had tackled
tasks she would not have contemplated before. She looks, and says
she feels, much more relaxed. The old woman had been often in her
mind since last time. She had been trying not to reject people and
has made efforts to calm down and listen to them and also say what
she herself wanted to say. Previously she had felt that other
people at home couldn't be bothered with her affairs, but she went
into last week with a feeling that people were there to help each
other. She has borne the old woman in mind and tried to let people
in.

I ask if she's had any dealings with the 'nicer' one, but she
apparently hasn't appeared much. Margaret adds, though, that she
is obviously gentle and not at all pushing. This other figure would
like to get closer to the old woman. Margaret says she senses this
other figure as slightly loose and flowing. There isn't much sense
of shape other than a very nice softness about her. She is nice and

flowing and certainly has a sense of serenity about her. She is
smiling and very, very quiet, giving a feeling of no movement and
no noise.

I ask if it's possible for Margaret to let herself be that person
for a little. Can she feel herself into that person to get a sense
of what it might be like to be that person more completely?

Margaret finds this difficult and can get no real sense of her.
Indeed Margaret seems to tighten up and says quite sharply that she
just can't see any of this other person in herself and so can't get
into her at all. She says she can only bring to mind the petty,
nasty things she's done in the last ten days which are completely
against this other's nature.

I encourage Margaret to approach this other figure very gently,
softly and without rush.

Margaret's face and body relax a little. She is quiet for a time
before speaking again, eyes closed. She says she has a feeling of
her being gentle and having a lot of humour in her. She seems to be
definitely smiling and tolerant.

I again suggest to Margaret that she go gently and take her time.

She gets a sense of her enjoying other people's happiness and
wanting to laugh. She is good natured and seems very retiring.

When I ask Margaret how she gets the sense of her being 'retiring' she hesitates and says that the word coming to mind is
'love'. But this person doesn't like admitting it and she can't
voice it. She has a great deal of affection but isn't demonstra-
tive. She's not good at showing it and is frightened of it coming
back smack in her face. She is frightened that people are going to
say 'leave me alone!' There is much more love in her than she cares
to admit or show. Her serenity, in fact, is to imply love, but she
keeps it in the background.

This softer person feels quite tolerant of the old woman. She is
very, very patient. She seems just to be there when needed and is
not in the least put out by what the old woman is doing to her. She
just comes out smiling all the time.

As we talk I have a strong sense of warmth and easiness between
Margaret and myself. She comments that she still has a clear sense
of the old woman to contrast with the flowing looseness of this
other gentle figure. The old woman is gnarled, cold and hard with
a hard stick in her hand. Everything about her is hard. She is
white haired and angular. We talk further and then, towards the end
of the session, I ask Margaret if she still has any impression of
the old woman.

Now it seems more difficult to identify her. No longer does she
have the sense of her being forcefully disagreeable, but rather of
her loneliness. She is lonely and can't cry for help. She no
longer seems so aggressive and is certainly no longer so clear. She
no longer stands out so clearly over against the other one.
Margaret pauses and then comments that it's not so much that she has
become softer - but rather that she is paler. Still she is not
nice. She is still closed in. She still doesn't want anyone to
pierce her armour, not anyone at all. But since sensing more fully
the other one, this old woman now seems much less clear.

Over the next few weeks Margaret finds that she has been actually
able to get annoyed at home and show it there and then. In a

trifling situation where she would previously have walked out in a
'tight' way she in fact said what she felt and then burst into
tears. She expected to get a reaction of coldness and annoyance but
actually she was listened to and taken seriously. After crying and
feeling very sorry for herself she says she felt a release from
tension and that things weren't so bad after all.

Her diarrhoea has been generally better, but even at bad times
she hasn't felt so desperate about it. She begins to feel that she
will be able to develop easier relations with people at home, and
let her feeling show more than ever before. In recent days, she
says, she's really felt she is getting somewhere. She says she
doesn't feel so depressed and that there is a future for her at
last.

Over the next month or so Margaret reports that she has developed
quite a sense of the more gentle person, or at least of what she
would do and feel if she were more around and available. I ask if
she is now able to get any impression of her and Margaret soon responds that she has a very strong feeling of her at this moment.
There is a feeling of softness, swirling, flowing, curvaceous
movement, with no hint of hardness or squareness. This time there
is no image of a person but only a feeling of smiling and a slight
radiation of happiness.

Can she let herself stay with these feelings, get closer to them?

She says she has an impression of colour, of purples and golden
yellows, but the strongest sense is that it's completely formless
and unimpressionable. It's just softly there, without anything
jarring, with no form at all. Margaret seems to relax more and
says that she feels utterly and completely at ease. The pains she
had been complaining of in her stomach have completely gone. She
feels very good and relaxed and is sure that this kind of feeling
is in her if only she can let it be there.

'It feels like me,' she states with emphasis. 'It feels like a
part of me that I really don't know, a part I've wished was there
and not believed in. A part I've never really met before.' Suddenly, says Margaret, it felt safe to let it be there. 'I felt it now
had a place. It's a very real feeling, though actually nothing I
could pin down. I've tended not to let feelings take any part in
my life. Everything had to be cut and dried.'

Over the next month Margaret was 'marvellously well' for much of
the time, with some bad patches. She has been more adventurous and
more able to stand her own ground. As we talk I ask if she still
has any impression of the two figures we talked of before. Margaret
says she's given a good deal of thought to them, and just recently
the old one has been more to the forefront. Now the old woman seems
a bent creature, angular and still rather aggressive. Margaret has
the impression that she has become rather concerned with herself.
Usually she is cross with the nice flowing figure, but now she's
cross with herself. She's inwardly cross but not showing it. She's
not cross about making a fool of herself or being stupid, but just
about being there at all. She feels unwanted and maybe also that
she has asserted herself more than she should and that now she
should get back a bit.

Previously the old woman had seemed to lash out with her stick at
any approach, but now she seems to Margaret to be more huddled up.

She's not so upright. She's more bent and is standing back more.
In fact she seems to want to stand back more and give the flowing
one more chance. Now she seems not to be rejecting everything but
herself. She's not trying to push anyone else away. She seems to
want to stand down but finds it hard. She's a fairly firm rock,
says Margaret. She's firmly there, ensconced. It's not in her
nature to stand back. She wants not to assert herself but let
someone else have a look in. But as Margaret points out, there
doesn't seem to be anyone else to do that. No one else seems to
be there.

'Actually,' says Margaret after a moment, 'it's not so much that
the old woman wants to go back but rather that she wants to go into
herself. She wants to reduce herself more. She's very firmly there
and wants to reduce rather than go back.'

As Margaret talks, still dwelling in her feelings and the imagery
reflecting these feelings, she begins again to see the other figure.
There seems no longer to be a person but rather more of a sense of
flowing movement round the old woman. There is a sense of flowing,
very watery and wishy-washy ... a purply colour ... beginning to
flow round her. The rocky one is not avoiding as she did before
and is not pushing or hitting with her stick.

I ask Margaret if she has any sense of how the rocky one feels
about this flowing around her. Margaret says that she feels fairly
stubborn. She is staying firmly there but is not rejecting the
other as before. The other is there and all around her. Margaret
feels that the rocky one would like to let the other in but at the
moment isn't doing so.

Margaret continues to give an account of what she senses. The
other one has changed into a flow-all-round rather than someone
coming from one side or cowering in the background. The flowing one
has changed from almost a person in flowing chiffon to moving
circles ... a wash ... a colour wash ... no lines at all. The
impression Margaret gets is of something that's there and readily
available to do whatever has to be done, but never pushing forward.
There seems nothing firm about it, but in some way there is a kind
of firmness because it seems always there when needed. It is a kind
of background thing, very even tempered, almost wise in fact. It
can absorb irritations and annoyances without getting itself worked
up at all. That's the feeling Margaret gets, that it's a kind of
shock absorber.

If that sense was available when needed in everyday life it would
be very useful, says Margaret, but there's always this rock that
comes up to be buffeted and hit, to be disagreeable.

Margaret has the sense that the flowing one is utterly calming
... just is ... with no irritating edges ... is easy and without
ambition ... flows and moves all the time. 'If I put myself into
it,' says Margaret, 'I get the feeling I'd like to do something
positive. It seems to be trying to say something like, "There's
more than just you to making up a life", and I do lead a very
selfish life.'

I ask Margaret what sense she has of the rock-like figure. She
replies that as she has been talking, the rock has gone more into
the mist. It's definitely there but the other one is flowing over
it like mist and in a way is using it. The flowing one is beginning

to feel the rock is there, perhaps to draw on somehow. There is the
sense that whatever it wanted to do it could draw on the rock for
the necessary confidence perhaps. From being a 'baddy', the rock
seems really to be a solid foundation on which the other is re-
volving. Somehow there is a feeling that the two should really try
to go together to do whatever needs to be done.

For the first time, Margaret says, she is seeing the angular one
as perhaps necessary. Previously, she had always tried to push that
side away as disagreeable and unnecessary. Now she senses that
perhaps it isn't like that. She has the impression that the flowing
one is showing her that the rock is needed for her to flow round.
Margaret says that for the first time she has felt that the hard and
angular one should be allowed a little say. Perhaps, she says, the
angular one gives solid guts for the flowing one to do what it feels
it should. Before now, says Margaret, the angular one has dominated. Now perhaps it can learn not to dominate but to be there.
For the first time Margaret says she has felt the two to be on an
equal footing. 'When I came in I felt very queezy,' says Margaret,
'now I feel very calm. I don't think it's the people round me who
upset me. I think it's myself.'

At this point I'd seen Margaret on nineteen occasions in the
course of a year.

ASPECTS OF KNOWING PERSONALLY

This snippet from Margaret's story may help to illustrate some at
least of the issues in knowing as living personal experiencing which
I want to mention here. In the instance I've been outlining
Margaret was the central inquirer, the person coming to know. She
was here mainly involved in coming to know aspects of herself. However, the points I want to make have just as much relevance, I
think, for one person coming to another or others. A concern for
feeling as a patterned, coherent and crucial means of knowing
threads its way through each of the points that follow.

1 To come to know personally you must be personal

For me, being personal is not a matter of sharing or revealing
guilty secrets, divulging details of your personal history, talking
about sex or nose picking or any other private activity. Any of
these might be involved at times but essentially, being personal
means a serious commitment to meeting with the other person centrally rather than socially or politely or manipulatively. In being
personal you are taking a stand such that something central in your
being is available to listen to and speak with and act towards the
centre of the other person's being. Nothing may be apparent in
this, there is no fanfare of trumpets, but you have taken a posture
towards both yourself and the other person (or other aspects of
yourself) such that both are to be taken in all seriousness.

To be personal is to listen and live from where you are most
sensitively receptive, where you are most vulnerable to pain and
where you feel most sensitively. To be personal is, if you like,

to reach out to touch the spirit of man and not merely to trade in niceties, evasions or particular practicalities. To invite someone else to be personal is to ask them to take their own experiencing seriously. It is to encourage them to trust and be moved by what they feel as a vehicle of articulated knowing. To be personal means not only taking your own and other people's experiencing seriously. It also means taking a stand and enduring.

2   Coming to know personally involves seeking and finding the other

Just being physically present with another person, even talking with them about private matters, does not necessarily imply that you will come to know them personally. Coming to know personally seems to be a serious game of hide-and-seek. Often, I think, seeking does not result in finding. The other may remain hidden from you or you from them. Being found in a central way by another (or oneself) may be so frightening that it cannot be allowed sometimes. Quite often the other may be found for a little and lost again, out of reach. Often you may have no sense of where or how to look for the other, es- pecially if the other's experiencing is very different from your own or if you are unable to sense in your own experiencing the form, location or depth of the other's place of living. Often also, I suspect, people try to show signs of where they are and others are entirely blind, searching in wrong ways in quite inappropriate places.

In seeking for another personally, you are engaged in feeling for the pattern of movement of the other, the living shape of the other person's active engagements with and disengagements from the world which may begin to be sensed between you. You have to sense in yourself the touch of the other person's invisible movements. Margaret illustrated something of this in her imagery of the old woman and the flowing figure and the kind of relationship of ap- proach and rejection between them.

3   Coming to know personally involves developing ways of listening to and speaking with the other

Much that is intimately personal may be beyond the range of what we normally say and how we normally express ourselves. It is often necessary to learn to say and feel and think 'stupid' things in the understanding that there is no other way of reaching matters of im- portance which are outwith the range of our ordinary and 'sensible' articulation. In coming to know another, new conventions and jokes, mannerisms and abbreviations will be created to carry something of the shared world growing between you.

In developing and using something of a personal language, a sensitivity to and trust in metaphor in its many modes seems vital (Mair, 1977b). Margaret showed something of the usefulness of de- veloping this kind of trust as she came to be able to listen to and engage with otherwise unreachable aspects of her experiencing. Margaret, indeed, came for help perhaps because she could only express her unrecognized and unarticulated layers of concern through

the warm, formless, flowing, rejected, out-of-control and far from
'cut-and-dried' bodily statement of diarrhoea. Gradually, the many
and interwoven issues of her personal life, scrambled therein,
became articulated and experienced quite differently as she became
able to listen and enter into intimate conversation with aspects of
herself which previously could only be pushed away and dreaded.
Gradually she became able to attend to her feelings in new forms
which could be entered and explored in new ways.

A personal language is not something given, but something which
those involved have to learn to undertake and share and trust and
use in the growing conversation between them.

4 In coming to know personally it is easy and tempting to betray
and deny the other when things get difficult

To be sought and found by another may lay you open to painful reap-
praisal and make you vulnerable where previously you were protected.
Coming to know personally can involve you in levels of feeling
beyond speech or easy articulation. It may lead you into developing
ways of speaking with another person which are strange and far
removed from the ordinary rules of logic, convention or comfort.
From time to time you may find yourself listening with an outsider's
ear to what is transpiring between you and feel alarm at the
strangeness of what you are involved in and the distance you have
travelled from easy public justification of what you are doing.
This is where it is very easy to abandon, betray and deny the
special trust developing between you. The temptation can become
great to rush back to public safety and recognizable ordinariness.

In the context of psychotherapy, for instance, the shared imagery
which has been the vehicle for mutual understanding and the building
of new habitations of meaning may suddenly be abandoned by either
therapist or client. If done by the therapist he or she may
scramble off to talking in terms of diagnostic categories or conventional value judgments to establish safe distance and publicly-
sanctioned difference from this now frightening companion. If the
client is the one who retreats, it is quite likely to be a stab of
panic that his or her worst fears of madness are perhaps being confirmed. The flight of fear may well be accompanied by an exacer-
bation of symptoms which may often be a silent plea to the therapist
to show greater trust in that which is developing between them than
the client can manage at this point.

It seems very easy to become blind and deaf where previously you
could see and hear. Silent betrayal seems very easy when no one is
around to see, and public justification for such an act may be so
readily available. To come to know yourself or another person
personally can lead you into strange realms. Strange, that is, in
relation to our conventional and often trivial notions of normality
which seem often to become such hindrances to our coming more fully
and feelingly to know ourselves and others. To remain faithful in
an undertaking of personal meeting requires, at times, considerable
courage and strength. It takes nerve to stand alone against the
possible invasion of a feared and critical public world.

5   Coming to know personally involves you intimately in learning to
trust and use the clues and evidence of your feelings

The realm of the personal cannot be pointed to or proved by display.
It cannot be picked to pieces, peered at or pickled in convenient
laboratory jars. Coming to know personally has to be lived. It is
created and finds its existence in being lived between us. We are
dealing here with invisible worlds whose reality is the very ground
of our daily living. So much of what happens within and between us
is sensed rather than said. Sometimes it is sensed because of lack
of feeling. In seeking for where you are, I need to follow and to
learn to trust the messages of my feeling and sensing of all kinds.
Sometimes, as with Margaret, these can be made evident in images
which give informative shape to what is otherwise invisible. But
whatever means are used we need to learn to feel our way along and
to discriminate amongst and trust the patterned clues to what may
later become manifest in more recognizable forms of action.
      Yet there is always uncertainty about what to trust, what to
entrust yourself to and what to doubt and question. In coming.to
know personally, we will seek evidence of what to trust from every
source available to us, but often the probable rightness or wrong-
ness of a step forward will be judged by how it feels, by whether
it feels right. How events feel varies so greatly. There is a
complex and subtle range. Personal reality is perhaps founded on
just such feeling. Margaret hinted something like this in becoming
aware that one of the figures she inhabited felt almost 'too real'
and another seemed like a part of herself she had 'never really met
before'.
      We entrust ourselves to judgments based on what we feel in
personal relationships so much that it is truly surprising that our
acts of feeling and the feeling of our actions are so little trusted
in most of psychology.

6   Coming to know personally involves you in giving yourself over
for a time to the form of the other

To come to know you personally, I will have to enter your world,
breathe your air, feel something of the shape of your living, share
something of your pain and your passion, meet the world through your
eyes, with the armaments of your hopes and longings. To come to
know you personally requires that I become pupil to your teacher,
servant to your master, living clay in the hands of your informing
potter.
      This means giving yourself up, surrendering yourself to some
degree, to the other. It means relinquishing, for a time, your
normal base of operations, your usual stance towards the world, the
familiar ground you presently inhabit. It means being humble enough
to lower your head as you enter the doorway of the other's experience, otherwise you will simply collide, recoil in irritation and
take an outside view only.
      In coming to know you, it is necessary somehow to enter into and
inhabit, to feel from the inside, something of how things may be for
you. It is not enough to look and describe the outside only.

Outside appearances and inside realities can be so very different.
To come to know personally requires that you come to dwell within
the form of the appearance. It requires that you dare to feel
something at least of how it may be to stand where the other stands.

Margaret showed this in many ways. When, for instance, she was
able to stop demanding that other aspects of her own reality be met
and ordered within the terms employed by the 'old woman', it began
to be possible for her to know and own aspects of herself that had
previously been outwith her reach. She relaxed and began to allow
herself to melt into the form of the flowing, fleeting figure and to
feel for herself a strange and yet amazingly familiar reality she
had not really owned before. She came to sense as her own,
something of the patience, gentleness, persistence and loving
acceptance she had previously only hoped for.

This kind of willing surrender, entering a personal world personally, again takes a kind of courage sustained by trust.

7 Coming to know personally can be very threatening because change
is involved

To know about someone, or to know how to achieve certain ends with
them can both involve change. However, the distance and separation
here between knower and known allows for fixity, control and the
modulation of movement for the knower at least. Coming to know
personally as a living, present experience is different. Knowing
and changing are here almost synonymous. If you have to step away
from your usual base and surrender yourself to the form of the other
in coming to know them, then movement is intimately involved. You
open yourself to the possibility of change through changing yourself
to the possibility of openness.

Of course, not all change is alarming, far from it. Even when it
is alarming in some ways it can also be shot through with invigor-
ating hope which is exciting and confirming. But when change has
been long feared and fought against and at last has to be somehow
endured because there seems nowhere else to go, then it can be
filled with terror. The very ground of your being may seem to crack
and split and threaten to melt away. The new possibilities are mere
whiffs of scented air, not yet enough to breathe or to sustain
continuing life. No new ground is anywhere to be trusted. All
seems so entirely familiar and as it was and yet at the same time,
so subtly and decisively changing. The best thing, perhaps, is to
clutch back what was before it is too late. You can frighten yourself into such sensible immobility with dreadful phantoms beyond
your normal knowing. You may sense yourself as vulnerable, tentative, easy to panic, fearful, retreating, and yet in the midst of
all, already changed. Almost unbeknown to yourself, the problem
has become not whether to move on, but how.

Over and over again, Margaret experienced the beginning of change
and then retreated backwards into old, tight, angular, 'cut-and-
dried' ways, before tentatively moving on again. Sometimes she
suffered so powerfully that all seemed hopeless, worse than before.
But each time, with renewing trust in what she had begun to experience, she returned to enter again that aspect of her experiencing
through which such movement was sustained.

The fear of change, and certainly change in the invisible web on which we ground our ways of being, seems to evoke in us terrors great and small, direct and indirect, which our ordinary sensible selves can scarcely credit. Sometimes it can seem so strange and unbelievable that even longed-for changes can be harbingers of such fear. Yet it often seems to be so. To come to know another person- ally may confirm and reassure us, but it may also sometimes unsettle the foundations of our former selves.

8   Coming to know personally takes personal time

Sometimes it is possible to have a sense of where someone is person- ally in a very short time, without aid of historical details or particulars of present circumstances. But coming to know and live in that knowing is different from taking a momentary snapshot of a person's stance towards the world. If I am to come to know in a living, personal way, then I am engaging in a continuing process of change, mingling, meeting, adjusting, retreating, reformulating, moving.
    The struggle to trust what is felt and feel towards the substance of new trust, takes time. Different people take different time. If such movement is gripped repeatedly by doubt and responded to by withdrawal, then in the public realm, time may be passing while in the realm of the personal it has been temporarily suspended. Sometimes, in very short periods of publicly-measured time, huge personal steps can be taken. The persons involved may indeed have progressed far ahead of where they can yet stand with any kind of confidence and again long periods of public time may have to be worked through before they are able to live in the place they long ago moved into.
    A feeling for time and timing seems important in coming to know personally. In personal knowing things cannot be forced, or it becomes a different kind of thing altogether. My impression in therapy is that people so very often know for themselves when they need more time, when things must stop and mature, when wounds or new discoveries have to be nursed in stillness. The therapist often needs to remind himself to sense and trust the other's enacted indications of the time they need. If some kind of central meeting of the other has been achieved at some stage, the requirements of personal time can often be sensed to some degree. If no personal contact has been made, then you may find yourself not only working in the dark, but on a different dimension of time altogether from the other.

9   Coming to know someone personally involves acceptance of each other as equal in worth

In coming to know personally, you are not setting yourself over against others, objectifying them, distancing yourself from them or categorizing them. You are rather taking them seriously, sometimes more seriously than they take themselves, as of equal intrinsic worth to yourself. This acceptance of equal worth does not imply

equal abilities or equal value in the eyes of society or similarity
of characteristics. Accepting another as equal in worth implies an
acceptance of them as an origin of experience, a centre of living, a
place of power in a particular private world.

It's not that dangers of tyranny are lacking in relation to
personal knowing. Indeed, many people probably keep others at a
distance, even if in disguised ways sometimes, because of the kind
of dangers Margaret expressed at times of being taken over, losing
control, being exposed and vulnerable. The development of personal
knowing of another is probably always a zig-zag movement between
trust and fear, openness and closedness, acceptance and rejection,
meeting and massacre.

Margaret experienced something of this move towards acceptance
of equal worth in aspects of herself where previously there had been
an enforced and maintained relationship of attempted control and
slippery subversion. Margaret moved towards trusting in her own
experience what she had formerly feared and degraded. Movement of
this kind towards a genuinely respected and maintained sense of
equality in worth, which can be maintained even as circumstances
change, is probably only slowly and partially achieved for most of
us.

FORMS OF MOTION

George Kelly (1955) suggested that we view man as 'a form of motion'
and it is important to notice that he was outlining a psychology of
personal functioning rather than a trait psychology or a psychology
of behaviour which tend to search for static regularities. In the
realm of the personal, everything is in motion. Even when we stand
still or remain stationary in other ways of engaging with ourselves
or others, we are actively going about the patterned business of
standing and remaining. We inhabit personal worlds of continuous
movement amongst and between ourselves. At all times we are silent-
ly and invisibly engaged in moving and forming and reforming and
approaching and withdrawing and transforming and holding and re-
leasing and making and breaking and composing and decomposing our
ways of being in relationship within our worlds. In each and all
of our multiple and subtly changing relationships we are orches-
trations of in-forming motion. Coming to know personally is also
to be engaged in continuous movement. There is no conclusive end
since we are created and recreated as we move and are moved into
various forms of meeting. But this is not a cold, abstract world
of physics that is being conjured up. In the realm of the personal,
this motion has an 'inside' as well as an 'outside'. That is to
say, we are experiencers of motion as well as being in motion. Some
of this movement is undertaken as personal action and some we presumably participate in unwittingly and are variously buffeted and
modified.

Kelly also held centrally to an understanding of man as an ex-
periencer of events, wherein experiencing involves undertaking
personal action and where responsible action involves entering into
and coming to own our part in what is experienced, rather than
resting content as supposed victims of circumstances. The radical

implications of this view have yet to be fully recognized, I think, but it may be that only as we enter into a deeper knowledge of what is involved in being personal and knowing personally will we come to sense what personal powers we have. This may come from entering and finding ways of living from within our deepest relationships, and from being able to come to know personally and intimately what was previously sensed only externally and separately.

We know much more than we can easily say and are engaged in doing much more than we can readily acknowledge. Only a little of what we know do we know that we know, and only a little of what we are engaged in between ourselves do we recognize in the ordinary light of day. Much of our living is acted and felt in complexly, coherent ways without any explicit awareness on our part. Within and between ourselves we remain rich realms of mystery. So many subtle and refined acts of feeling give shape to our personal lives. So many feelings arising from our implicit actions provide the changing texture of our experiencing.

If we are to come to know ourselves more profoundly, we may need to find ways of coming to know about some of the richness of the knowing we already inhabit. If we are to sense more of the patterns of feeling we are engaged in, we will need to find ways of giving form to what we feel such that we may recognize and come to own or undertake what otherwise may seem to control us. If, within the discipline of psychology, we are to come to know more personally, we will need to develop an understanding of psychological inquiry which will allow and encourage us to 'live in and amongst' rather than 'stand over against', and become closely and intimately involved rather than remaining separate and superior observers. And in all of this it will be important to learn to respect, in discriminating and sensitively critical ways, our most delicately informing acts of feeling.

REFERENCES

Kelly, G.A. (1955), 'The Psychology of Personal Constructs', Norton, New York.
Mair, M. (1977a), The Community of Self, in 'New Perspectives in Personal Construct Theory', Bannister, D. (ed.), Academic Press, London.
Mair, M. (1977b), Metaphors for Living, in 'Nebraska Symposium on Motivation, 1976', Landfield, A.W. (ed.), University of Nebraska Press, Lincoln, Nebraska.
Mair, M. (1979), The Personal Venture, in 'Constructs of Individuality and Sociality', Bannister, D. and Stringer, P. (eds), Academic Press, London.

PART THREE

PART THREE

With the last section in this book we come to the question of how
far the accepted accounts of learning and knowing do justice to what
people actually seem to experience. Each chapter in this section
considers, for each of three areas, the conventional wisdom about
the area in relation to what emerges from a freer, more personal
exploration. In each case the writers find that the official
psychological view falls far short of experienced reality. Nick
Emler and Nick Heather, examining the psychology of intelligence,
argue that many kinds of thinking and understanding are necessarily
excluded by the narrow and biased definition of intelligence on
which this psychology rests. Harold Rosen looks at real-life spontaneous drama; he shows us that it is 'ordinary, pervasive and
universal' and yet it is left totally out of account by a psychology
which restricts drama to formal theatrical events. In the last
chapter, David Smail challenges the predominant view of psychotherapy as a matter of technical skills and shows that, on the
contrary, an account which takes experience seriously must see the
psychotherapeutic relationship as inescapably personal. All three
chapters trace the practical consequences of the inadequacies they
consider. As these writers show, a failure to acknowledge in psychology the richness and diversity of human possibility brings
about, in practice, a curtailment of opportunities for learning.

How is this theme presented in each of the three chapters here?
What Emler and Heather are concerned with is the official psychology
of intelligence as this is embodied in the psychometric tradition
and the work of Piaget. They argue that, like any other system of
understanding, this psychology did not arise in a vacuum, but came
into being within a particular social and historical context.
Inevitably it incorporates values and orientations peculiar to that
context. These, however, have been reified as qualities proper to
thinking itself, this being defined by an individualistic ethos, a
detached and sceptical attitude towards belief, and a valuing of the
technical, objective and impersonal - in short, what is taken to be
'scientific' understanding in a technocratic age. Such features are
certainly not characteristic of the thinking of societies other than
our own, nor do they typify many of the ways that we in this society
think - especially in the whole sphere of social understanding. But

because a particular and limited view of thinking is defined as universal, definite social and political biases have been built in as
ideological aspects of our psychology of intelligence. Since this
view permeates our educational system, some ways of thinking in the
classroom are sanctioned to the exclusion of others, and the
problems of mismatch are located in the supposed 'learning difficulties' of particular groups of children. The underlying values,
as these writers suggest, serve to reproduce the technocratic
society. As they say, 'psychology has been recruited to form part
of that complex of influences whose collective effect is the reproduction of society'.

Rosen's case is that to equate drama with conventionalized
theatrical forms is to miss seeing that spontaneous drama plays a
major part in the human repertoire - a part that enables us to know,
and to present our world with richness, depth and delicacy. As
'flickers of mimicry, borrowed gestures, voices, accents', dramatic
activity permeates not only our social intercourse but our inner,
private experience too. The way in which drama interweaves itself
into our talk is, as Rosen shows, very complex and subtle. Yet the
rules of the game are well understood even by very young children;
in being human we intuitively grasp this way of relating to others.
That such a fundamental aspect of our personal currency should be so
disregarded by psychologists seems extraordinary. The consequences
of this neglect reach the classroom where, again, educational opportunities are all too often lost. Because drama is conceptualized in
terms of skill, children are often put through stilted and barren
exercises which make a mockery of the vivid abilities they constantly show in their everyday lives.

Smail, in considering the conventional wisdom about psychotherapy, lays the same emphasis as Emler and Heather on contemporary
technology-worship. Technological values, models and images pervade
our society. Objectivity, impersonality and efficiency are highly
prized. The 'mechanization of human activity', together with the
translation of psychotherapy into technical skills, is therefore
perhaps not surprising. The payoff of such a view is, of course,
the escape from moral pain which it seems to promise. But, as Smail
shows, personal distress and struggle are not to be dismissed so
easily. Since misery and madness arise 'out of human commerce with
the world and the other human beings in it', it is to our humanity
that we must look in order to achieve some understanding of them.
It is the same humanity which defines the relationship between
patient and therapist - its most fundamental feature being that it
is a relationship between persons.

These three chapters, in considering the nature of learning and
knowing, also present a picture which is similar in many ways to
what has been presented in previous chapters. Again, emphasis is
laid on the social nature of knowledge, on the essentially personal
quality of coming to know, and on the crucial importance of engagement.

In the case made by Emler and Heather, the social nature of
thought is shown to be its most fundamental aspect. The very
character of intellect is itself social; ways of thinking are
culturally determined, what counts as knowledge is governed by
social values and priorities, and even the supposedly absolutist

canons of science represent a construction from the limited perspective of a particular social group. As these writers say, 'The
scientific method, broadly defined, is the embodiment of a set of
norms, standards and values which owe their existence not to the
natural inclination of each one of us to appreciate their intrinsic
validity, but to the survival of a particular institutional
structure which sustains them'. But there is another side to the
writers' emphasis on what is social. As they show, our emphasis on
knowledge which is technical, disembodied and impersonal, has led us
to neglect the whole realm of social knowledge. Understanding our
social world is, these writers suggest, an 'awesome task' which is
somehow managed by virtually everyone. Yet it cannot be explained
away as merely the application, to the social sphere, of what is
currently defined as intelligence. For one thing, it does not seem
to be the individualistic exercise of mind that Piaget portrays; it
is essentially a collaborative undertaking and involves the transaction, negotiation and exchange of meaning. The way we manage
ourselves in the complex interpersonal contexts we inhabit calls
for intelligence of a high order; but this is of a qualitatively
different kind from what psychologists have so far defined as intelligence.

Social aspects are equally stressed by Rosen in his discussion of
spontaneous drama. In part, this is because dramatic activity
typically demands collaboration between people; even in the
theatre, the act depends on the audience's knowledge of how to
'take' the behaviour of the actors. The collaboration that spontaneous drama demands is highly complex and creative, as Rosen
shows. It is not just that the roles of performer and onlooker are
fluid and interchangeable. What is also shared, or jointly created,
is a meta-perspective on the whole activity. Those involved - even
very young children - can switch easily into another level of
reality and back again, without disrupting the performance. Another
kind of meta-perspective is the understanding of the intention lying
behind the act, and whether or not the behaviour is meant to be
taken as drama; we must 'read the quotation marks around the performance'. There is also a further sense in which Rosen portrays
spontaneous drama as fundamentally social. This is the fact that
other people feature even in our most private ruminations. In
rehearsing what is past, in fantasy, in pre-enactment of future
events, we draw on our inner repertoire of characters and 'produce
our little dramas in our heads'.

Smail, equally, sees what is social as fundamental to psychology.
In so far as personal distress arises, in some sense, out of our
dealings with others, the nature of psychotherapeutic problems is
itself social. At issue in psychotherapy are the difficulties which
people face in living in an interpersonal world, with 'all its
painful moral implications and uncertainty'. Engaging with these
kinds of problems requires a context which is itself social, and out
of which can be wrought an essentially social kind of understanding
- one which has been worked out jointly between patient and therapist, which has involved real negotiation of meaning, and which both
find to be valid. Genuine learning in this situation involves communication and understanding of fundamentally social processes; as
Smail puts it, understanding is 'a relational quality which arises
between people, not something you can have, or learn to acquire'.

Though it is somewhat arbitrary to draw a distinction between the social and the personal, this seems an appropriate place to note the emphasis which these writers place on the very personal character of learning and knowing. This emphasis is evident in Emler and Heather's account of intelligence, in which they urge that attention be given to the neglected kinds of thinking that are embedded in personal contexts and personal concerns. As they show, to take this kind of thought seriously is to realize that social intelligence takes in its stride far more complex problems than those typically considered by psychologists, involving temporary encounters with strangers, or simplified and generalized moral dilemmas. 'Other people routinely provide for us the most complex problems that we encounter ... the problems of social living, the problems of operating in an interpersonal environment, communicating, co-operating, manipulating, transacting, and relating to others'.

Rosen is similarly attentive to the highly personal factors that are involved in spontaneous drama. Dramatic activity of this kind is dependent for its production on a personal context which nurtures it; it needs a sense of warmth and trust, it is 'licensed by intimacy, informality and a sense of holiday from the workaday world', it 'withers in an atmosphere of coldness'.

Smail, too, is concerned to emphasize the personal. So far from seeing psychotherapy as a set of generalized procedures having nothing to do with the people who apply them, he argues that the personal qualities of therapists are of supreme importance. What sort of person the therapist is, what engagements his/her life has entailed, how he/she has personally come to terms with issues of pain, courage and responsibility - these are crucial questions for his/her effectiveness in psychotherapy. For the patient, it is the highly personal aspects of the relationship which matter most; since learning requires commitment and faith, a sense of trust is indispensable.

Finally, the importance of personal engagement is a theme touched on by both Rosen and Smail. In stressing the spontaneity of everyday dramatic activity, Rosen suggests that this is a mode in which we characteristically launch ourselves into improvisation, without the safety of practised scripts or well-worn roles. This, of course, is why this mode is so dependent on special kinds of personal contexts. But spontaneous drama is also essentially action; through dramatic activity we change things as well as experience them, we 'develop our consciousness by acting in and upon it'.

The idea of learning through engagement is also fundamental to Smail's view of psychotherapy. Personal understanding cannot be passed on from therapist to patient; it must be achieved through the patient's own agency, which, indeed, will bring it into being since, as Smail puts it, 'learning is something someone does, in which he changes himself'. To do this, it is necessary to commit oneself to a physical engagement with events; the patient must, therefore, 'place himself bodily in a new relationship with the world'.

Chapter 7

INTELLIGENCE: AN IDEOLOGICAL BIAS OF CONVENTIONAL PSYCHOLOGY
Nicholas P. Emler and Nick Heather

Conventionally, psychology has had more to say about how people come
to know things (the process of learning), and their capacity to know
(intelligence), than about what people know. This may prove to have
been a serious mistake. It has been assumed in psychology that we
know very well what it is people know and need to know, and this has
shaped our images of intelligence and the learning process. Unfor-
tunately people do not always behave as psychological theories say
they should. One way in which a closer match between theory and
reality might be managed is to attend to the social and political
influences which shape psychological theories. Conventional psychology has been peculiarly averse to this kind of analysis and
indeed blind to the possibilities of such influences. As often as
not the tendency has been to try to make reality fit the theories.

If we accept that theory is shaped by historical context then we
can begin to consider the repercussions for a psychology which developed in the context of contemporary Western culture. The pre-
eminent values of this culture are technological-scientific and one
consequence has been a high premium placed on knowledge that is
technically exploitable, knowledge that can be used to change,
control, manipulate and order both nature and society. Psychology
has itself shown a strong inclination to develop into the technology
of human behaviour. This is perhaps most evident in differential
psychology where techniques of assessment have evolved in response
to the practical requirements of efficient measurement. It is also
evident in a behaviouristic psychology which was always inclined to
equate scientific knowledge with prediction and control, and which
latterly has gone into the business of technologies for the controlled manipulation of behaviour. It is to be found as well in
social psychology where, for instance, a group-dynamics tradition
developed to meet priorities of the productive process: workers
would be more efficient if they were made to be more content;
managers would be more effective if they were made to be more
rational (see, for example, Moscovici, 1972).

In this chapter we shall examine a slightly different issue, the
manner in which psychological treatments of intelligence sanction
scientific and technological values. The manner of psychology's
support for these values not only misrepresents the nature of

science but, more seriously, distorts the nature of human intelligence, a nature that we believe is fundamentally social.

INTELLECTUAL INDIVIDUALISM

The contemporary psychological view of intelligence has its foundations in the intellectual individualism that emerged out of twenty-five centuries of Western philosophy. According to Russell (1946), individualism of one kind or another was an old theme even in classical Greek philosophy but the Greeks still considered people first as members of communities. The modern era really begins with Descartes's claim that the starting point for all knowledge is the individual's experience of his own existence. This laid the basis for defence of the autonomous thinker against interference by Church or State in matters of intellectual judgment. What was true and good was no longer to be determined by collective wisdom or ecclesiastical authority, but by solitary thought. An emergent scientific method based on rules of evidence and inference saved intellectual judgment from complete relativism but science itself therefore represented a retreat from a purely individualistic stance.

Science has always depended on an irreducible consensus - among scientists if no others - about how truth is to be determined. It is accepted that in principle all scientific disputes can be resolved because, by and large, all scientists accept the same intellectual standards. Scientific debate relies on a form of what John Horton (1964) has called 'collective subjectivity', a framework of shared assumptions within which disagreements can be discussed. Now, it is precisely this social and collective character of science that psychological models of intellectual processes omit.

Psychological models of human thinking, including scientific thinking, are based on an unmoderated form of intellectual individualism according to which it is the individual who thinks, chooses and acts, who invents, solves problems and discovers truth. This being so it is the individual that must be studied. This view penetrates to the deepest levels of psychological method thereby ensuring that it will seldom be challenged by evidence. Knowledge is held to be acquired through the direct confrontation of individual intelligence with experience. The solitary individual can arrive at the truth by applying a set of inherently valid rules. Significantly, these rules bear a remarkable resemblance to those that lie at the heart of scientific method. The truth that is discovered is assumed largely to be about the natural order, the material or physical environment. Finally, as in science, such truth is impersonal and universal.

The kind of cognitive activity that has the necessary qualities to produce 'scientific' knowledge is taken to be the most distinctive and most fundamental of human psychological attributes. In other words, science, detached from its social-historical context and interpreted individualistically, becomes the model for human intelligence and in turn the scientific style of thinking is presented in psychology as an intrinsic propensity of human thought.

There are various 'stories' about how the individual comes by the qualities of thinking that are assumed to be most characteristic of

the scientific style. The most influential and extensively developed is, of course, Jean Piaget's theory of intellectual development, and we shall consider this theory later. Here it is
worthy of note that even those areas of psychology that might have
been expected to resist the individualistic and rationalistic
message of cognitive psychologies have succumbed.

The idea that individuals are naturally inclined to be rational
was attacked by Freud who saw reason as an illusion, rationality a
facade, an act mounted by individuals to disguise their true and
publicly inadmissable intentions which were themselves instinctually
based. Intellect, he felt, could only be emancipated from distortion by society and the instincts through psychoanalysis. There
was a time when social psychologists told a similar story. They
showed how in countless ways intellectual judgment revealed its
vulnerability to the biases of values, personal interest, prejudice,
cultural stereotypes, social influence, group pressure, social de-
sirability and interpersonal affiliations. However, both these
efforts and psychoanalytic theory can be seen as forms of moral
fable which accepted that the standards of individualism and ration-
alism were appropriate aspirations. Their concern was to point out
the gap between the ideals and the reality, not to question the propriety of the ideals.

Many of the more recent developments in social psychology and
personology do not even evidence this degree of scepticism. Instead, theory in these areas increasingly mimics the kind of cognitive psychology that prevails elsewhere. And everywhere one encounters the metaphor of man the natural scientist. In social psychology one could instance attribution theory (e.g. Kelley, 1967).
There are similar examples in personality theory (see later). These
choices of model and metaphor all reflect particular kinds of value
judgment.

THE ROLE AND SIGNIFICANCE OF VALUE JUDGMENTS

It is often assumed that in so far as value judgments are made in
psychology some kind of lapse in scientific rigour, some lamentable
departure from standards of objectivity, has occurred. In truth
such judgments - in the case of the human sciences - are closer to
being inherent conditions of the scientific enterprise. Most psychology is based on a clear conception of optimal forms of psychological functioning, though what is considered optimal varies with
the area of human activity under consideration. In questions of
knowledge and intellectual judgment, as we have argued above, the
qualities to be optimized are truth and objectivity. In matters of
skill and technique the optimal qualities are efficacy and efficiency. Corresponding judgments can be found in the literature on
social and interpersonal relations and we shall have occasion to
mention these later. The point is really not whether or not value
judgments are made but whether the most appropriate ones are made.

Not only are these judgments crucial guidelines for psychological
research, they also reflect directly on the self-image of the profession. A complaint that commonly used to be heard against orthodox psychology was that it lacked reflexiveness; the authors of

psychological theories, it was held, did not construe themselves in terms of their theories. (This is not reflexiveness in the restricted sense that George Kelly used it, in which among the phenomena covered by a theory is the theory itself, but in the more general sense in which a theory is seen to apply to its authors and their activities.)

This may have been true of learning theory and the whole conceptual paraphernalia of behaviouristic psychology, which for a time removed itself quite completely from the domain of intelligible human reference. Elsewhere this complaint is less obviously applicable as psychologists commonly seem to construe their theories in terms of themselves, or at least in terms of their ideal professional personas. Nowhere is this more apparent than in differential psychology. Personality dimensions are almost embarrassingly revealing about their authors' and supporters' self-concepts. They also betray clear value judgments for virtually every dimension ever conceived has a desirable pole and an undesirable pole and no one can be in much doubt about which is which in each case. The IQ dimension is only the best-known example; we shall have occasion to mention others.

The prominence of IQ as a dimension of individual differences tells two stories, one about the monopolization of our thinking by the idea that there is only one way to be intelligent, and one about the importance that this particular way has been allowed to assume in our society.

TESTING INTELLIGENCE AND THE EDUCATIONAL CONTEXT

Most features of current psychological approaches to intelligence can be traced back to the interests of the pioneers in the field of intellectual testing. Galton, who did some of the earliest systematic work on human intellectual powers, initiated an abiding concern with the differences between individuals. In this there was a clear Darwinian flavour with its implication of differential biological fitness.

This preoccupation with ordering people in terms of their mental powers provided what have remained the central concerns of this field, the largely technical issues of objective and reliable measurement. The problem was what to measure. Galton apparently assumed that the relevant differences between people were in their capacity to adapt to the natural environment. As this environment was thought to be experienced directly through the senses, Galton's mental tests were actually tests of sensory discrimination.

Those who came after assumed that intellectual fitness was a matter of scientific and mathematical skills. As Ryle (1949) was later to remark, 'Mathematics and the established natural sciences are the model accomplishments of human intellects. The early theorists naturally speculated upon what constituted the peculiar excellences of the theoretical sciences and disciplines, the growth of which they had witnessed and assisted' (p.27).

Academic achievements in the sciences and mathematics were accounted the evolutionary pinnacle of the species; mental tests were devised to identify the peculiar genius underlying these achievements, sampling the skills they were assumed to involve.

The particular mistake in this was to confuse socially-esteemed and institutionally-created differences with biologically signifi- cant differences. Galton remarked (1892), 'There can hardly be a surer evidence of the enormous difference between the intellectual capacity of men than the prodigious differences in the number of marks obtained by those who gain mathematical honours at Cambridge'. In fact, these differences are only evidence for the examiners' success in devising tests which would order the population to which they were applied. It does not follow that the differences measured by such tests had any independent ecological significance.

The environment in which these differences make a difference is that man-made institution, the school, and they do so precisely because the institution was designed that they should. The gra- dations of human ability which determine fitness to compete in schools and universities have no unique claim to be definitive of the essence of human intelligence. None the less, the development of intelligence testing has been directly tied to the practical needs of these institutions and hardly at all to theoretical priori- ties.

Tests were designed increasingly to meet criteria of efficient and reliable prediction. What people mostly wanted to predict was success in school so it was inevitable that test content should be influenced by what goes on in school. Experience has shown that tests which include factors of verbal comprehension, reasoning, numerical computation and some perceptual and spatial components predict school success reasonably well (Nunnally, 1970).

Most research effort has gone into refining techniques. Where theoretical questions have been raised these have had remarkably little impact on the design of tests. For instance, there has for years been a lively debate about the number of factors that go to make up intelligence and the manner in which they are organized. J.P.Guilford (1959) attempted to provide a logical specification of all the possible different intellectual factors and his efforts represent the most systematic attack on this question to date. But in the end, test selection has been dictated by the purely pragmatic consideration of predictive power; the additional factors identi- fied in theoretically guided research such as Guilford's have not added to the predictive efficiency of existing tests.

The more obviously theoretically-inspired research is not without significance, however, for it reveals more explicitly the psycholo- gist's view of the nature of intelligence. Since this research has invariably taken the educationally-oriented tests as its point of departure, the view it reveals is still heavily inclined towards the educational context. It gives particular prominence to skills re- lating to literacy and numeracy as does the orthodox school curri- culum. Broader questions about the nature and function of intellect have received little attention. We still know very little about the capacities people need to function in their everyday environments, what kinds of intellectually-challenging problems these environments routinely pose for them, or what makes people more or less effective in these environments. Guilford included in his model of intel- lectual factors a category for 'behavioural' content to represent the area of social intelligence, but this category was added on a purely theoretical basis. It did not cover any existing knowledge

about this area of intelligence, nor did it generate any new
research. (More will be said about social intelligence below.)
   Intelligence tests sample verbal and numerical skills or, more
accurately, they are assumed to be measures of these things, though
it is probable that success in school and even test performance
depend on much more than the ability to interpret and draw con-
clusions from written materials, or the ability to manipulate
numbers. Nevertheless, the official version of what tests measure
does represent a choice to emphasize certain qualities rather than
others and this choice has tended to stand in for a theory of the
nature of intelligence. Our suspicion that this is a limited and
partial theory is reinforced by the fact that standardized tests of
intelligence are poorly related to forms of success or competence
other than the educational (Jencks, 1972). As Jencks remarks,
'standardized tests measure skills that are useful in getting
through school, not skills that pay off once school is over' (p.52).
Psychological models of intelligence reflect the manner in which
schools have pre-empted definitions of learning in our society, and
to be learned has come to mean, before anything else, to be literate.

THE SIGNIFICANCE OF LITERACY

An appreciation of the significance of literacy is critical to
understanding the social and cultural role of the school, which in
turn reflects on the way that the concept of intelligence has been
shaped and employed. This role includes dissemination of values,
training for participation in the bureaucratic-industrial system,
and social differentiation.
   The values which schools most obviously support are those of the
scholar, the theoretician and the scientist. Schools promote the
privileged status of certain paths to learning, modes of understanding, and categories of knowledge. Less obviously they promote
individualistic achievement values and the styles of social relationship most congenial to bureaucratic institutions. But let us
consider here the connection between scientific values and literacy.
   If it is characteristic of our culture that we accept the legitimacy and authority of scientific knowledge and the propriety of
scientific attitudes then literacy has had much to do with the
conditions under which these became acceptable. The anthropologist
Robin Horton (1967) has suggested that one major distinction between
African and Western scientific systems of thought is the open attitude found in the latter towards established beliefs. It is characteristic of the Western attitude to accept that prevailing theories
about the nature of the world may be misconceived. The only legiti-
mate grounds for continuing to accept such theories is the verification provided by experimental proofs. Such proofs are not merely
considered possible or even desirable; it is proper that they
should be actively sought. The posture of science is characterized,
in other words, by a sceptical and destructive attitude towards
established theory. In African cosmologies, by contrast, there is a
protective attitude towards theory. No one would consider it necessary to seek empirical verification of accepted beliefs.

Horton believes that the distinctively Western attitude depends on widespread literacy. Changes in beliefs are always occurring, from generation to generation and even from year to year. In a cultural system restricted to oral transmission of beliefs these changes will go unnoticed, giving rise to the illusion that truths remain fixed. When, however, the wisdom of the past is 'frozen' in written form it can be directly compared with contemporary views. This undeniable evidence that beliefs do change undermines the infallibility of conventional truths. Literacy therefore stimulates what Horton calls the open predicament. If truths are open to question, a new problem arises - finding a valid method for choosing between competing beliefs. Science offers the promise of such a method.

An established tradition of written transmission of beliefs also has repercussions for the character of knowledge and the individual's relation to knowledge. Reading and writing are thoroughly anti-social activities. Their solitary nature leads readily to the idea that the exercise of intelligence is also properly a purely individual and private matter. Knowledge is no longer to be found now in social relations, in dialogue, but in disembodied form by the lone individual. Likewise the production of knowledge becomes an exclusively individual affair. Literacy conspires to divorce learning and discovery from an interpersonal context and place knowledge on an impersonal plane, as a universalized, disinterested, socially detached, and preferably abstract entity. Knowledge becomes literally disembodied. We are indeed enjoined in science not to consider the authorship of ideas when judging their validity - a principle enshrined by logical positivists in the distinction between the context of discovery and the context of verification. Thought is to be severed even from the thinker.

Our view of language is likewise distorted. Within psychology it has been more common to treat language as a tool of individual thought than as the instrument of social interaction. The considerable emphasis given to verbal skills in tests of intelligence also has very little to do with the use of language in face-to-face communication.

Literacy is itself a social instrument. No advanced industrial societies are known in which literacy is not widespread. Literacy appears to be directly linked to urbanization, and we may surmise that the functioning of social organization at this level depends on a substantially literate population. The effective co-ordination of activity in cities, industrial enterprises, and bureacracies requires that the populace can read signs, instructions, directions, timetables, operating manuals and advertising copy. Postman (1970) has pointed out that a literate population is vulnerable to the instruments of bureaucratic control; the administration of large numbers of human beings can be managed more effectively if they can read and answer forms.

It is not surprising that literacy should also have a political significance. Language differences may mark significant boundaries between communities but within the boundaries competent language users are seldom in short supply. Literacy skills are far more differentiated. They can therefore more readily serve as an axis of social differentiation. This brings us back again to the role

of psychometrics in the educational system for tests are designed to
discover not what everyone can do with reasonable facility but what
some cannot do. A central function of schools is to create and
certify social inequalities. These are further legitimized by
psychological tests which provide common standards against which
everyone can be measured and which show that there are objectively-
demonstrable disparities between people. The method by which these
inequalities are ascribed in the schools, a kind of extended literacy test, also serves to assess the suitability of children to participate in the bureaucratic-industrial system.

One's educational credentials are largely determined by how long
one remains in the educational system and not particularly, as is
commonly supposed, by talent. Therefore, educational credentials
provide a useful guide to one's willingness and ability to adapt to
a bureaucratic regime, to behave properly, suffer the routine of a
timetable, persevere at often meaningless tasks, and do what one is
told by officials who have only formal authority.

PSYCHOLOGICAL ACCOUNTS OF EDUCATIONAL FAILURE AND SUCCESS

Despite or perhaps because of the success of schools in certifying
social inequalities, psychologists have been inclined to show concern over the origin of the differences that are sanctioned by the
educational system. Given a liberal tradition which favoured giving
all children the same opportunities for educational attainment, it
was distressing that so many children should be palpable failures
from the beginning and even more so that these should come dispro-
portionately from the working class and ethnic minorities.

Explanation of these failures in terms of cultural and linguistic
deprivation was enthusiastically endorsed by psychologists and educators alike. The deprivation argument was based on the assumption
that there are certain qualities of white, middle-class life which
stimulate intellectual growth and that working-class and minority
cultures are impoverished by comparison. It was held that environmental conditions in these latter were conducive to severe linguistic deficit. According to one eminent psychologist, James
McVicker Hunt (1964), writing about the black, ghetto child, this
child is likely to grow up in an environment that fails to provide
the opportunity or stimulus for development of linguistic and mathematical skills or the capacity for analysis of causal relations.

The cultural deprivation hypothesis had the dual attraction of
locating the causes of educational failure in the background of the
individual child and indicating both the possibility and the means
of alleviating its effects. It thus deflected any reconsideration
of the priorities of the educational system, and obscured the fact
that educational failure is an inevitable consequence of these
priorities.

Realization that 'curing' cultural deprivation would involve the
elimination of minority cultures, plus the evident failure of com-
pensatory education programmes began to reveal the ethnocentric
assumption of the cultural-deprivation hypothesis. Moreover, the
selective blindness which allowed an individualistically inclined
psychology to diagnose linguistic deficit became more widely recog-

nized. Linguists like William Labov (1970) have demonstrated that linguistic performances must be considered in terms of the social contexts in which they occur; they cannot automatically be taken as evidence for the competence of the individual speaker.

If one end of the intellectual continuum has been identified with the school failures, the other end has been identified with the professional or academic scientist, and in this category of course is the psychologist. As there are questions about the origins of educational failure, there are also questions about the conditions of entry into the category of the intellectual elite. Why is it, some have asked, that there are talented people who make good scientists while others apparently equally talented lack either the aptitude or the inclination? Interestingly, the epitome of adequate adjustment, as revealed by widely-used personality dimensions, seems to be based on an idealized image of the academic scientist. Put the other way around, the message from differential psychology can be read as the claim that the people most likely to make good scientists are those whose personal characteristics most exemplify what is considered psychologically healthy.

We find from the personality literature that the normal, healthy, mature and adjusted person is tolerant, and certainly not anti-intellectual, anti-rational or anti-scientific (cf., 'authoritarian-ism'). He is open-minded, flexible and objective (cf., 'dogmatism' and 'field dependence'). He values academic excellence for its own sake (cf., 'need for achievement'). He has a complex, differenti-ated view of the world (cf., 'cognitive complexity'). He is psycho-logically minded (cf., the 'Py' scale of the California Psycho-logical Inventory). His self-knowledge comes through self-obser-vation rather than through interaction with others and he tends to be more interested in ideas than in other people (cf., 'intro-version-extraversion'). He is basically a decent, optimistic sort of chap, not devious or cynical (cf., 'Machiavellianism'). He is in other words a scientist and specifically a psychologist. He is also probably male (cf., the study by Broverman et al., 1970, of the re-lation between sex-role stereotypes and clinical judgments of mental health).

It was perhaps inevitable that in defining normality and health psychologists should take themselves as models, but in so doing they perform the useful trick of transforming scientific values into a definition of psychological normality. These values are interpreted as inherent properties of the mature personality and by virtue of this device it becomes more difficult to recognize that they are in reality historically derived.

PIAGET'S DEVELOPMENTAL THEORY OF INTELLIGENCE

There is one body of work which directly reflects a theoretical interest in the nature of intellect and that is the programme of research into the development of intelligence directed by the Swiss psychologist, Jean Piaget. However, Piaget's work also seems to have had the effect of underwriting the belief that people are naturally inclined towards scientific styles of thought.

Piaget (1950) supposed that the development of intelligence is

governed by tendencies towards increasing adaptation and organization and towards equilibrium between these two. He felt that for
thought to achieve this equilibrium it must be freed from its dependence on immediate perceptual experience and suggested that this
is managed in two ways, first by a move from thinking that is intui-
tive and based on figurative representations to thinking based on
logical structures, and second by the development from concrete to
abstract thinking.

There are several, for us, interesting features in this account
of intellectual development. First, the focus of Piaget's analysis
is the individual child. As we shall see, Piaget by no means
ignored the role of social influence on intellectual development but
in this theory it is still fundamentally the solitary child who
adapts to his environment, adaptation here meaning the extension of
control over relations with the environment. This focus is given in
Piaget's assumptions about the basic forces that drive intellectual
development. These are internal, the inherent organizing tendencies
of psychological functioning. Thought is auto-regulative and
therefore auto-constructive. The only limiting conditions are the
irreducible objective properties of the environment to which the
individual adapts, a material environment which obeys natural laws.
Second, then, the categories of knowledge with which this theory is
primarily concerned are those that pre-occupy physicists and natural
philosophers: space, time, causality, substance and number.

Third, as implied above, intellectual development naturally in-
clines in the direction of what Piaget called 'operational
thinking', thinking organized around a set of logico-mathematical
structures. Thought is inherently inclined to become increasingly
objective, decentred from the idiosyncrasies of personal experience;
it is inclined towards impersonal knowing.

Fourth, thought reaches its most mature state when it becomes
completely detached from the contexts of concrete applications, when
it becomes purely abstract and formal. Thought at this highest,
'formally operational' level is described by Piaget as hypothetico-
deductive; formal operations are concerned with setting the real or
the concrete in the context of the possible or the hypothetical.

The series of investigations into formally operational thought
reported by Inhelder and Piaget (1958) show how very closely this
style of thought parallels scientific method, and indeed one must
suppose the parallel is deliberate. These investigations demonstrate the development of a set of operations for (a) discovering a
set of laws which generate non-contradictory predictions; (b) sepa-
rating and eliminating the effects of variables by manipulating each
in turn while holding others constant; (c) setting up and testing
hypotheses that are comprehensive and mutually exclusive; (d)
grasping relations of correlation and proportionality; and (e)
understanding the roles of chance and probability.

Our principal objection to Piaget's theory is that it accords so
little significance to cultural factors in the determination of
styles of thought. The content of intellectual development rests
on what are taken to be the intrinsic organizational tendencies of
thought. Particular environmental conditions may facilitate or
inhibit the operation of these tendencies but impart to them no
specific directional bias. In consequence, Piaget takes operational

thinking - logically ordered, decentred, and in its ultimate developmental form, 'scientific' - to be a universal disposition of
the human organism, whereas we see it as largely a cultural invention, transmitted to new generations through processes of socialization. In other words, concrete and especially formal operations
are forms of socialized thinking particularly characteristic of
contemporary Western culture.

Our view is based on recent cross-cultural studies of cognitive
development, and an interpretation of the origins and nature of
science. The history of Western intellectual accomplishments
suggests that what Piaget calls formal operations are among the
fruits of more than two millennia of collective endeavour, not
twelve to fifteen years of individual intellectual growth. The
scientific method, broadly defined, is the embodiment of a set of
norms and values which owe their existence not to the natural inclination of each one of us separately to appreciate their intrinsic
validity, but to the survival of a particular institutional
structure which sustains them.

Cross-cultural research has revealed a picture of widespread and
considerable cultural differences in patterns of intellectual development. It is clear that formal operations are not universally
achieved even in Western societies, but in non-Western cultures
their achievement is generally much more uncommon. Schooling does
seem to facilitate the development of formal operations, but without
school attendance children almost never come to reason in this way.

More dramatic is the evidence concerning achievement of the
earlier stage of concrete operations. Studies of populations from
non-literate and non-industrial cultures have documented numerous
instances of failures to develop specific elements of concretely
operational thinking. Piaget has held that these various elements -
the abilities to seriate and classify, to perform basic mathematical
and logical operations, to represent spatial relations in Euclidean
form, to recognize the conservation of underlying properties despite
changes in superficial appearances, to understand the operation of
natural causality, and so on - are the manifestations of a single,
unified mental system.

The cross-cultural evidence questions this claim, suggesting
instead that each element is a separate skill, acquired separately.
These separate skills only appear to form a unified structure of
inter-dependent operations because the environmental conditions
experienced by the Western child ensure that they emerge more or
less concurrently. In other words, what Piaget has described are
specialized adaptations of intelligence, cultural in origin and
intimately related to the local economy; they are not the uni-
versals of human intellect.

THE SOCIAL CONTEXT OF INTELLIGENCE

We would propose that it is groups, not individuals, that adapt to
their environments and that this is the basis for the peculiar
genius of the human species. We are a successful species because
we cheat; we tell each other the answers. Solutions to the routine
problems of survival are, once invented, conserved and diffused

through the community, and transmitted to succeeding generations.
Not only the particular fruits of science and technology, but
science itself as a problem-solving strategy is such an invention.

Universal to the species therefore, are culture and social organization, the means for preserving, sharing and exploiting in-
ventions. This in turn means that a universal feature of the
conditions of life of every human is the social and interpersonal
environment, the pattern of inter-relationships that makes up his
or her community. Whatever the local particulars of the technology
and the material conditions in which it is applied, the fact of an
interpersonal environment remains a constant. It is to this that
members of the species have always had to adapt.

A Cambridge ethologist, Nick Humphrey (1976), has recently argued
that the high level intelligence of the primates poses a problem for
conventional interpretations of evolutionary theory. This level of
intelligence appears superfluous to the daily needs of these
species; the physical conditions of life simply do not pose
problems of an order that would confer any adaptive advantage to
individuals possessing such capacities. The social environment,
Humphrey suggests, does pose problems of such an order; it does
regularly demand the exercise of high-level intelligence. To the
extent that this selects in favour of such intelligence, it also has
the effect of increasing the complexity of the social environment.
For humans with the added dimensions of language and a shared
cultural heritage the social environment is considerably more
complex than that of primate social species such as gorillas and
chimpanzees.

What is interesting for us about Humphrey's thesis is the implication that it is other people who routinely pose for us the most
complex problems that we encounter in our daily lives. Perhaps what
is most basic and most universal to human intelligence therefore is
the capacity it gives us to deal with the problems of social living,
the problems of operating in an interpersonal environment - communicating, co-operating, manipulation, transacting, bargaining, and
negotiating.

SOCIAL INTELLIGENCE

Traditionally, psychology has had precious little to say about
social intelligence. Social psychology, still wedded to individualistic models, has only begun to provide analyses of social interaction processes and has barely touched on the question of interpersonal relationships. Social psychology tells us other people
are objects of perception but is still inclined to suggest that they
are perceived much as other objects in our sensory field. It has
said something about how we collect information about others and how
this information is interpreted and integrated to form impressions,
but nothing about why the information is collected or how it is
exploited. Communication processes have been too readily assimilated to perceptual processes, thereby blurring essential dis-
tinctions, as in much of the work on the question of so-called 'non-
verbal communication'. Only recently has there been any evidence
that social psychologists are considering seriously the implications

of the fact that people communicate with one another, and only under
pressure from the adjacent fields of sociology and linguistics.

In developmental psychology the question of social intelligence
has emerged in the context of language development and cognitive development. Interestingly it was Piaget who made the seminal contri-
bution here, and he did so in two ways, first by pointing to the
importance of social interaction in cognitive development. Piaget
repeatedly stressed the crucial role of confrontation with the
points of view of others, of argument and disagreement, in overcoming the limitations of immature thought. He even proposed that
much of logical thinking is the internalization of social rules of
argument, rules of non-contradiction, coherence, and consistency.
Second, he initiated studies of the child's insight into its social
world. The child's insight into the intentions and feelings of
others, its ability to take the perspective of others, its appreciation of the function of social rules and the validity of principles
of fairness, are all intellectual achievements that are basic to
participation in the human environment. But research of this sort
on the development of 'social' cognition is subject to several limitations.

First, this is still basically research with the cognitive developmental tradition. This means that social cognition is treated
as but a specialized application of the more basic logical operations to social phenomena. The logical capacities develop first
and the social cognition develops later, building on these foundations. It has, for instance, been proposed that higher levels of
moral reasoning are applications of formal operations in the domain
of moral problems (Kohlberg, 1976). That Piaget was more interested
in the child's understanding of space, time and physical causality
than its grasp of social relations may simply have been a matter of
emphasis but as a result the former has always been considered the
more basic subject-matter of intelligence. No case has been made,
as perhaps it should, that social cognition is as basic a modality
and may occupy a more central place in the child's intellectual development. Neither is there much possibility that we will discover
any fundamental differences between social and other forms of cognition while we restrict the hunt to those features of social
intelligence that mimic the 'general' type of cognitive development
described by Piaget. Such differences are likely, we would guess,
because if Humphrey is right the human animal is inherently disposed
to excel at social problem-solving and because the social environment is so very different from the physical.

This degree of difference is yet barely appreciated in work on
social cognition which is still based on a highly-simplified model
of the social environment that also mimics the physical world. The
cognitive skills involved in representing the perceptions, feelings
and intentions of other individuals have been explored, but not
those involved in representing processes of transaction, negotiation
and exchange between people, let alone those involving representation of the complexities of interpersonal relationships.

Both Piaget and George Herbert Mead pointed out many years ago
the relevance to social behaviour of people's ability to take the
perspective of other individuals, but their model for this process
was the game, where roles are interchangeable and often highly

stereotyped. In most other forms of collective activity roles are seldom interchangeable and identities are far from stereotyped.

We mentioned earlier that in psychology assumptions are made about optimal forms of functioning. A perusal of the literature suggests that in the context of interpersonal relations the current-ly-favoured optimal quality is empathy, while in matters of social relations the leading candidate is justice. It has become popular to devise training programmes to teach childrem and adults, the social skills which will enable them to empathize with others. Presumably it is supposed that if people have more empathy they will get along better with one another. Similarly there are programmes designed to extend children's appreciation of justice concepts.

That empathy and justice should have been pre-empted by psycholo-gists as the central values of social intelligence betrays several things. First, it reflects what Serge Moscovici (1972) has called the social psychology of the nice person. This psychology suggests that social conflicts arise only because people fail to reason adequately or perceive accurately. The preoccupation with empathy in particular seems to us an unrealistic and unhelpful sentimental-ization of human relations. Second, these values urge an individu-alistic bias on the analysis of social behaviour. Empathy concerns perception, not interaction. Justice has also been interpreted in terms of the individual as we suggest below. Third, these values represent a considerable over-simplification of social life.

This over-simplification is evident in even the most developed area of inquiry into social cognition, that dealing with moral reasoning - and therefore of course with development of the child's understanding of concepts of justice. Morality, according to Piaget, is the logic of action. Ever since Piaget made this remark, students of moral development, most notably Lawrence Kohlberg (1976), have been trying to define the nature of this logic, trying to show that moral reasoning is based on the same logical operations as is representation of the material world. There is here an equi-valent of the intellectual individualism to be found in work on cognitive development, in that moral problems are assumed to occur in the context of individuals who act autonomously and independently rather than contingently and interdependently. Moral problems, it is supposed, concern the individual's relations to rules, and only occasionally and in a very limited way his or her relations to other people. The matters at issue in these problems are either formal aspects of morality like rights and authority or material matters like life and property; they are very seldom taken to be about interpersonal resources and deprivations, such as care, love, attachment, belonging, emotional security and emotional distress, grief, loneliness and rejection. Finally, the moral problems with which this research has characteristically dealt represent a vast over-simplification of real-life dilemmas. None of the complexities of dealing with real people who have real feelings in situations which are never static and to which the inputs are numerous and interrelated are represented. It is not surprising that the con-clusions from this research should prove to have had limited utility and that for political and interpersonal dilemmas, for real-life dilemmas as opposed to hypothetical dilemmas, other models of moral reasoning and decision-making should be needed.

There are at least two reasons why the social environments in which we participate are so much more complex and the problems they pose for us so much more demanding than the social cognition literature suggests. One we have mentioned above; social environments are in a state of continual flux. The second is that our interactions are not just episodic transactions with others who happen to share the same language but little else. They occur in the context of a history of such encounters with these same people, and thus a history of mutual acquaintance. We almost always know, if not know of, the people with whom we interact. This is profoundly at variance with the dominant assumptions of social psychology where, if one takes its research methods to reflect its model of social life, it seems to be accepted that we interact only with strangers; what is problematic in social life is figuring out and relating to strangers. Recent research on social-skill training may show how people can be taught to interact more successfully with individuals they have never encountered before but the more challenging problems of life are those of dealing with people we do know. In reality our acquaintances pose far bigger problems for us than strangers, because we know so much about them and we know they know so much about us. Keeping track of the information regularly exchanged in the interpersonal networks where most of us live - who knows what about whom and about the current condition of the various coalitions, antagonisms, commitments, rivalries, loyalties and conflicts - is by itself an awesome task by the standards of conventional psychological models of human thinking. We commonly despair at our ability to deal with life but perhaps we should marvel at what we do manage.

CONCLUSIONS

We have argued that psychology has been deeply, perhaps too deeply, involved in the game of defending a cultural invention - science and its system of priorities. Of two major psychological approaches to intelligence, the psychometric and the Piagetian, the former more pragmatically oriented has been directly shaped by the needs arising out of existing educational arrangements and has indirectly sustained the scientific values which the formal education system supports. Differential ability to excel in this system has been the guiding preoccupation, and this ability has been taken as synonymous with intelligence.

The Piagetian approach, more theoretically inclined, transforms the culturally relative standards of science into inherent developmental tendencies of the individual child. Science, we believe, is a specialized adaptation of an intelligence which is fundamentally social but psychological theory has achieved a peculiar inversion whereby 'social intelligence' becomes the specialized application of a fundamentally scientifically-inclined intelligence.

The psychology of intelligence is not generally viewed as having been vulnerable to ideological distortion, possibly because the ideology in question exercises such a potent hold over contemporary Western consciousness. It is taken for granted that the standards of science have a universal and absolute validity (except among

those with little education); the claim that the human intellectual
apparatus is inherently inclined to develop in this direction evokes
little surprise. Psychology has been recruited to form part of that
complex of influences whose collective effect is the reproduction of
society.

There is nothing intrinsically reprehensible in this. It is to
be expected that bodies of knowledge with official standing should
reflect powerful cultural images and thus reinforce their power.
However, we rightfully expect of psychology that it do more than
mirror its culture. In the field of intelligence we need to separate what is basic to intellectual functioning from what is historically relative and culturally generated. Apart from anything else,
this would lead to a better appreciation of the sociological significance of intellectual forms and styles. But it must also be
recognized that an analysis of intelligence that is less culturally
relative may precipitate political questions about our own society.

The implications of our discussion for education are not at all
straightforward. A conclusion that might be indicated is that there
should be more sensitivity to the social character of learning in
the educational system. Curricula could give more weight to the
teaching of social and interpersonal skills, in particular the
skills of dialogue, discussion and argument that are critical to
the effective evaluation and sharing of knowledge. Correspondingly
less emphasis could be placed on those individualistic values which
might be expected to frustrate the exercise of social intelligence.
Finally, the schools might do something to develop the child's
appreciation of the relativity of intellectual standards as they
have begun to do with respect to the relativity of moral standards.

Most of those innovations, however, would radically change the
nature of the educational system; they are antithetical to many of
the social functions this system has evolved to serve - for
instance, social differentiation and social selection. Furthermore,
it may be judged important that schools continue to foster intellectual skills that would not otherwise readily develop, rather than
switching their efforts to those that develop anyway. For we have
implied that social intelligence develops because it is part of the
human organism's system of adaptation to features of the environment
that are all-pervasive. We are not yet in a position to give definitive answers to these questions because we have only begun to
appreciate, let alone explore, the social nature of intellect.

REFERENCES

Broverman, I.K., Broverman, D.M., Clarkson, F.E., Rosenkrantz, P.S.
and Vogel, S.R. (1970), Sex-Role Stereotypes and Clinical Judgments
of Mental Health, in 'Journal of Consulting and Clinical Psycholo-
gy', 34, pp.1-7.
Galton, F. (1892), 'Hereditary Genius', 2nd edn, Macmillan, London.
Guilford, J.P. (1959), Three Faces of Intellect, in 'American
Psychologist', 14, pp.469-79.
Horton, J. (1964), The Dehumanization of Anomie and Alienation, in
'British Journal of Sociology', 15, pp.283-300.
Horton, R. (1967), African Traditional Thought and Western Science,
in 'Africa', 27, pp.50-71,155-87.

Humphrey, N.K. (1976), The Social Function of Intellect, in Bateson, P.P.G. and Hinde, R.A. (eds), 'Growing Points in Ethology', Cambridge University Press, Cambridge.

Hunt, J.McV. (1964), The Psychological Basis for Using Pre-School Enrichment as an Antidote for Cultural Deprivation, in 'Merrill-Palmer Quarterly', 10, pp.209-48.

Inhelder, B. and Piaget, J. (1958), 'The Growth of Logical Thinking', Routledge & Kegan Paul, London.

Jencks, C. (1972), 'Inequality', Penguin, Harmondsworth.

Kelley, H.H. (1967), Attribution Theory in Social Psychology, in Levine, D. (ed.), 'Nebraska Symposium on Motivation', University of Nebraska Press, Lincoln, Nebraska.

Kohlberg, L. (1976), Moral Stages and Moralization: The Cognitive Developmental Approach, in Lickona, T. (ed.), 'Moral development and behavior: Theory, research and social issues', Holt, Rinehart & Winston, New York.

Labov, W. (1970), The Logic of Non-Standard English, in 'Georgetown Monographs on Language and Linguistics', 22, pp.1-22,26-31.

Moscovici, S. (1972), Society and Theory in Social Psychology, in Israel, J. and Tajfel, H. (eds), 'The context of social psychology: A Critical Assessment', Academic Press, London.

Nunnally, J.C. (1970), 'Introduction to Psychological Measurement', McGraw-Hill, New York.

Piaget, J. (1950), 'The Psychology of Intelligence', Routledge & Kegan Paul, London.

Postman, N. (1970), The Politics of Reading, in 'Harvard Educational Review', 40, pp.244-52.

Russell, B. (1946), 'History of Western Philosophy', Allen & Unwin, London.

Ryle, G. (1949), 'The Concept of Mind', Hutchinson, London.

Chapter 8

THE DRAMATIC MODE
Harold Rosen

Forgers, imitators, counterfeiters - we don't think much of them.
'Copy-cat!' children still cry in angry contempt. Aping our betters
or anyone else never won admiration. Imitation is for the dull
plodders devoid of originality and the creative spark. Imitation
has had a bad press. Cassirer (1953) writing of the language of
gestures and in particular the gestures of imitation says, 'In imitation the I remains a prisoner of outward impression and its
properties; the more accurately it repeats this impression, ex-
cluding all spontaneity of its own, the more fully the aim of imitation has been realised.'
  For Chomsky (1959) the use of language is creative precisely
because it cannot live off imitation. A speaker must actively apply
his knowledge to create and understand novel sentences. Imitation
it seems is humdrum; freshness, originality, invention are what we
prize.
  But imitation will not let itself be pigeon-holed quite so easily
along with the most routine and unimpressive behaviour. What are
theatres but temples of imitation? Willingly, eagerly we sit and
watch these fellows imitating other fellows and, what is more, we
know they are feigning ('They do but poison in jest'). They are
licensed to imitate the rest of us and we have built elaborate
places in which they may perform their esoteric, specialist antics.
The covenant between actors and audience is known down to its last
clause; no recital is necessary. And yet there is no need for us
to go to theatres to see and hear such things. In any children's
playground the actors will be at work. A few hours after men on the
moon had shown us the weightless plod they needed to move across its
surface thousands of children were plodding across their playgrounds
in similar manner. 'Who's been sitting in my chair?' they will
repeat in three different voices, each of them different from their
normal voices, each an imitation of an anthropomorphized bear. And
it is not as though as adults we put away such childish things.
Without our even noticing it, our speech and actions slip into imitation: we dip into our repertoire of other voices to present
someone of another class, from another place, of a different age-
group, of the other sex. As an integral part of the performance
there will be gestures, postures and actions. What immediately

comes to mind is the comic performance, the caricaturing of acquaintances or public figures; but we also perform to make a
serious point in a serious way, to report disturbing or disastrous
events, for instance.

Why do we do this? Are our own bodies and voices not enough for
us that we must disguise and distort them? I was goaded into
sorting this out for myself some years ago. I had been watching
student teachers of drama. I grew increasingly dismayed as I
watched them putting classes of children through their paces,
carefully worked out dramatic 'exercises' which were in all respects
inferior to what the children would have done spontaneously. I was
reminded of some of the strangled exchanges which passed for oral
discussion amongst pupils who in another setting were lively, fluent
talkers. I started scribbling on a scrap of paper. What took shape
on the paper was the first version of the model which appears in
Figs 1 and 2. What I was trying to do was to understand the essence
of dramatic behaviour or activity because it seemed to me that in
their anxiety 'to develop skills' (1) and fashion a respectable
syllabus for themselves, the students had somewhere, somehow, lost
the core, the heart of the matter. As I tried to sift my experience
and observations what emerged more and more clearly was that dramatic behaviour was ordinary, pervasive and universal. More than
that, it was not an optional extra grafted on to human activity by
the talented or exhibitionist but a common human resource intrinsic

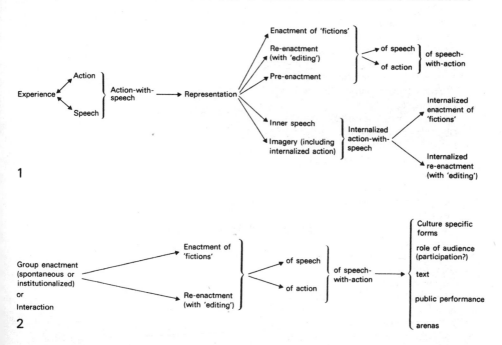

A theoretical model of the location of dramatic activities (very
tentative). Figure 1, from experience to dramatized thought and
externalized drama; Figure 2, from informal spontaneous improvi-
zation to public spectacle.

to language and bodily movement.[*] It can and does exist independent
of theatres, stages, drama classes and dramatic texts.

What we call play has received close attention for a long time
(Bruner, Jolly and Sylva, 1976) but mostly this has been part of the
study of the early development of children. Play will change with
maturation into games-with-rules (Piaget, 1951) or inner-speech
(Vygotsky, 1962) as though it has served its developmental turn and
can be forgotten. Dramatic behaviour may be a form of play but
there are many other non-dramatic forms. It may not, in any case,
be play at all. A serious narration of a terrifying experience may
include dramatic behaviour - replication of the threatening voice of
an unknown assailant, his curious gait or posture. None the less,
some of the studies of play are relevant to my exploration. Then
there are those who have concerned themselves with play-with-
language (e.g. Cazden, 1976; Weir, 1962; Chukovsky, 1968). But
play-with-language is not the same as play-through-language though
the distinction may be difficult to draw simply because it may be
both at the same time or one may slide into the other. At 38 months
Simon shows this very clearly (Boomer and Spender, 1976). The
extracts are taken from a pre-sleep monologue made by his father
Garth Boomer, 'inspired by the late Ruth Weir's study of the monologues of her son':

1 I told yoi
   A piggy nick
   A piggy back
   A piggy back on me
   Right under there (chanting)
   Right under here on my head
   I don't know what to do
   I don't know what to do
   Pat her
   (indistinct sounds)
   Oh, no you can't
   Oh, yes I can
   (repeated three times)
   Oh, yes I can
   Oh, no I'm not
   (repeated three times)
   That's the slip
   It is the slip to go in the water

   That's the water down there
   and you jump
   jumpy, jumpy, jumpy (chant)
   (sound like R,rrr ...)
   A piggy nick
   A piggy nick?
   Oh, that's another good word

Anyone would be hard put to it to allocate with complete confidence
all utterances either to play-with-words or dramatic play-through-
words even with access to the tape. It is much clearer in this
sequence: 'Earlier that day, Simon had fallen off a makeshift swing
... children from the flat downstairs comforted him'.

2   That won't hurt
    Look at that
    P'yoopy, yoopy, yoopy, yoop
    (indistinct whispering)
    Sit down, sit down (dramatized)
    Why you crying
    Oh hosh hosh

    We don't mean to cry do we
    NO
    That's right

3   We have a swing
    O pee doodle
    Fell off the swing
    ... clumsy
    Why you crying, don't cry, hush don't prosh will
    you don't cry

A whole literature has sprung up which deals with body language
(Birdwhistell, 1952; Argyle, 1967; Goffman, 1959; Hall, 1963) and
non-verbal communication, but it does not deal with our capacity to
'quote' from these 'silent languages' much less with our capacity to
use our bodies to imitate machines, things and animals.

    I was drawn into my speculations the more easily because I had
lived a long time with the idea that poetry and fiction have their
roots in everyday speech, that highly-wrought, complex, intensely
conventionalized written texts can be found in both embryonic and
sometimes highly developed form in spontaneous speech. (2) It was
a short step to take to the idea that drama too was intrinsic to
everyday social behaviour; perhaps since it was rooted in imitation
it was even more fundamental than poetry or fiction.

    Though it takes many different forms, can be momentary or sus-
tained, can be dominant or merely contributory, I did not intend
dramatic behaviour to be understood in the metaphoric sense of 'all
the world's a stage', nor in the sense that we are acting out roles,
nor as encapsulated little dramas which crop up in daily lives.
What I was concerned with was almost the opposite: it occurred when
we stepped out of role but paradoxically maintained a role in doing
so. If we insist that all the world's a stage (I don't) then what
I'm talking about is a play within a play. We do not merely speak
and act but also speak the speech of another and intend to be understood as such. Our speech is peppered with invisible but detectable
quotation marks. We also perform the actions of another and intend
them to be perceived as such. This is imitation of quite a different kind from Cassirer's ('devoid of spontaneity') and from
Chomsky's, which he dismissed to refute the Skinnerian behaviourist
model. Chomsky was concerned to demonstrate that language could not
be learned by imitation with reinforcement but that children needed
to derive and internalize the grammatical system. For him imitation
meant the straight copying of the language of others.

    But there is a richer notion of imitation which was, in fact,
explored by Cassirer himself in a passage which follows closely on
the one I cited at the outset: 'If we consider only this factor of

pantomimic imitation of given objects of sense perception, we do not seem to be on the road to *language* as a free and original activity of the human spirit.' He takes us back to the Aristotelian idea that all reproduction presupposes an internal productive process and is therefore more than a repetition of something outwardly given. Cassirer then proceeds to develop this view of 'apparently passive reproduction':

> For this reproduction never consists in retracing, line for line, a specific content of reality; but in selecting a pregnant motif in that content and so producing a characteristic 'outline' of its form. But with this, imitation itself is on its way to becoming *representation*, in which objects are no longer simply received in their finished structure, but built up by the consciousness according to their constitutive traits. To repro- duce an object in this sence means not merely to compose it from its particular sensuous characteristics, but to apprehend it in its structural relations which can only be truly understood if the consciousness constructively produces them.

This is to reinstate imitation as an active creative process, to accord honourable status even to trivial acts of impersonation, the use of special voices readily recognized as departures from normal speech, the altering of normal gesture to render a grotesque version of a type. Nevertheless to reinstate imitation is not entirely to exonerate it. There is still affectation which makes judgments difficult. We can deliver a meaning in a particular way by repre- senting another. There are quotation marks around the performance. There is the other extreme at which the behaviour of another is imi- tated in order that the imitator may pass himself off as such a one. The two processes can come close to each other so much so that no hard-and-fast line can be drawn. But dramatic behaviour as I am presenting it, nearly always distinguishes itself by being embedded in other behaviour. This serves not only to signal it but also to affect its meaning. Put less abstractly we might say that for drama to be effective we must know it for what it is. For affectation to achieve its goal we must fail to detect it. (3)

There was for me another starting point. I had for several years been involved in the debate on linguistic deprivation, which still rages (Rosen, 1972). In essence this became an intellectual confrontation between those who argued that many working-class children failed in school because the language of their social milieu could not carry certain critical meanings, and those who argued that no such limitation had been demonstrated. There is no point in following the debate here. I mention it because in ex- ploring the relevant literature I had been struck by the frequency with which people whose research work had been confined to studies of young children confidently made assertions about the language (and much more) of adult working-class people without anything more than anecdotal or second-hand or even conjectural 'evidence'. A group of us for several years collected tapes of adult working-class speakers and studied them. Of the many observations we made two emerged very strongly. The first was that working-class speakers had a very strong tendency to use narrative when they wished to make

a theoretical point, to clarify an idea or exemplify a general-
ization.   Second, in the course of these narratives, or outside
them, they invariably used dramatic dialogue, i.e. dialogue in which
the speaker became each of the participants and acted out their
voices through direct speech.   They were using the same resources as
novelists (4) and poets frequently used but with the powerful
addition of voice quality and the rich and flexible sound system of
the language.   This is a 75-year-old ex-building labourer recalling
his work experience:

> So one day I says to him - he calls us in a ring - he said, 'I
> want you all to come in a circle.'   In the dinner hour that was
> from one to two o'clock.   So we said, 'All right.'   So we all
> went down the lobby, and er - so he said, 'Now,' he said, 'now
> all you,' he says, 'are here, I want to talk to you.'   So he
> says, 'I want you - er - all down here to do a few more blocks a
> day, as it's not paying,' he said.   'I'm also - want to see the
> years come back when there's four deep on the dole, and a mile-
> and-a-half queue.'   That's what he said.   'Well,' I said,
> 'governor -,' because I put my foot in it.   I got so wild that
> I had to let it come out - I said, 'Well, Governor,' I said,
> 'allow me to tell you, you'll never see them times again.'   He
> said, 'I won't?'   I said, 'No, you won't,' I said.   'The gener-
> ation's coming up now,' I said, 'they want easy money, and
> they're getting easy money.'   So I says, 'And on the other hand,'
> I said, 'the whip's finished: the masters have had their day.'
> (Rosen, 1, 1974b).

I am not, of course, suggesting that working-class speakers are
unique in their use of dramatic dialogue;   on the contrary, it is
central to my argument that it is a universal resource.   I want to
suggest that for social and cultural reasons they use it more readily, more frequently and to fulfil functions which other speakers
satisfy by discursive methods because, in Cassirer's words, their
dramatic dialogues were 'built up by the consciousness according to
their constitutive traits'.   Far from being 'context-bound' or 'tied
to the here-and-now' they were able to deliver a general significant
meaning.
      Finally, I was strongly influenced by Brecht.   Somewhere in his
poems he had said all this.   I went and found it in one poem, 'On
the everyday theatre' (see p. 165) :

> Actors
> You who perform plays in great houses
> Under false suns and before silent faces
> Look sometimes at
> The theatre whose stage is the street,
> The everyday theatre
> Common, unrewarded with honour,
> But of this earth, living,

The whole poem enlarges this theme and displays for us actors in
everyday life, the man at the street corner who has seen an accident
and is re-enacting it, a scarf-seller, who cakewalks up and down
behind his stall dressed in hat, false moustache and scarf:

```
    ... the theatre of the street
    Has uses
    And dignity.
    Not like parrot or ape
    Do those men imitate for imitation's sake,
    Unconcerned with what they show
    Save that they themselves are imitation well,
    They have their purposes in mind.
```

Brecht had seen this link between theatre and dramatic behaviour and also the difference between parroting and aping and having purposes in mind.

Let me now return to those student teachers and my hasty scribblings as I watched them. They had forgotten, or perhaps never knew, that spontaneous dramatic behaviour is affected by the performers having purposes in mind. Drama in schools is well-established and it takes a multitude of forms - mime, 'Movement', improvisation, dance-drama, dramatization of texts, dramatic texts. Do these activities have common roots? What exactly are the participants doing? What are the functions of their activities? Is drama a separate clearly-identifiable activity which needs to be clearly marked off from other kinds of learning? As soon as we distance ourselves from younger children's dramatic activity it does seem a little odd. A little girl in a long cloak taken from the dressing-up basket ('dressing-up', there's an idea to grapple with!) stalks round the room and declares apparently to no one, 'I am a queen and I am outrageous'. It seems less odd when we remember that as adults we dramatize in our heads situations just as remote from our lives.

Inevitably great writers have observed and used the dramatic impulse not only through the use of dialogue but by portraying someone caught in the act of dramatizing, a tertiary. Remember Trabb's boy in 'Great Expectations', who, though he makes only a fleeting appearance on a page or two, and namelessly at that, leaves a memorable mark. Pip has been changed by the effects of his unexpected affluence and his great expectations. He returns to his home town rather full of himself and enjoying the deference and wonder of the townsfolk until Trabb's boy, the tailor's errand-boy, with his large blue bag, approaches:

> I had not got as much further down the street as the post-office, when I again beheld Trabb's boy shooting round by a back way. This time, he was entirely changed. He wore the blue bag in the manner of my great-coat, and was strutting along the pavement towards me on the opposite side of the street, attended by a company of delighted young friends to whom he from time to time exclaimed, with a wave of his hand, 'Don't know yah!' Words cannot state the amount of aggravation and injury wreaked upon me by Trabb's boy, when, passing abreast of me, he pulled up his shirt-collar, twined his side-hair, stuck an arm akimbo, and smirked extravagantly by, wriggling his elbows and body, and drawling to his attendants, 'Don't know yah!'.

What is important in this fragment of drama is that Trabb's boy is

not being Trabb's boy. He is in the presence of Pip and is Pip or
rather Pip as he has interpreted him to be, not re-enacting anything
he has heard or seen. Through enactment he delivers the message to
Pip and us that Pip is becoming a snob who will reject his humble
background. The imitation of a few gestures and a single phrase can
make an explicit image.

What Dickens knew was that the dramatic ends up in theatres but
does not begin there. The lowly Trabb's boy has it all at his
finger-tips. We all have it in some degree; for as surely as we
can all speak and move we can also imitate speech and movement. We
can call upon this ability as a means of communicating and as a
means of knowing. Representation of action and speech through the
use of our own bodies and speech is the birthplace of drama.

How does this process work out in more detail? I have tried to
set it out diagrammatically (see Figs 1 and 2, p.153), taking the
risk inherent in all attempts to schematize - neatly - complex,
untidy human behaviour. To mitigate the hazard I shall attempt to
explain what began as a scribbled diagram on a scrap of paper in
those drama classes.

Since I see dramatic behaviour as being interwoven with all human
behaviour, I begin with an interrelated triad.

That is an absurdly simple way of inserting everything to begin
with. It says no more than that we experience the world and come to
develop our consciousness by acting in and upon it and that through
speech we articulate our consciousness and organize it new ways;
through communication we act in a new way.

Our observable actions are very complex for they consist not only
of those which enable us to wield our bodies in order to move or
come to rest but also to use them to act upon things with intent -
to do. In addition there is a whole language of meaningful
gestures, some expressive (the arms thrown up in horror or welcome),
controlling gestures (beckoning, waving for attention) some of them
highly codified (the conductor, policeman, umpire). Finally there
are all those involuntary actions which we learn to read and use
(drumming with the fingers, nodding and shaking the head), through
which we interpret mood, attitude and response. We watch others
closely when we wish to penetrate their innermost thoughts. To be
guarded or inscrutable we attempt to reduce the gestural clues we
give others so that, just as speech-flow silences are meaningful, so
the absence of gesture may become a gesture. Clearly there are
enormous inter-cultural differences - a great source of misunder-
standings and jokes.

A person digging or threading a needle or cutting down a tree is
not simply experiencing the world but acting upon it, changing it.
Indeed, for Piaget (1969) this is the fountain-head of our intelligence: 'The essential functions of intelligence consist in understanding and inventing, in other words building up structures by
structuring reality ... knowledge is derived from action ... to
know an object is to act upon it and transform it.' Language inter-

penetrates with action so that often one is meaningless without the other. Language to function at all must be a shared system: most of our messages must get through for most of the time. But groups differ from each other in many ways and different occasions provoke different kinds of language. Each individual's language has its unique qualities. All this we observe too. That is another long story but for present purposes I only wish to insist that we are talking, walking, doing animals. I want to consider these 'articulate mammals' at the stage when they act very competently, can use language to interact, to express ideas, feelings and attitudes, and also to form ideas about ideas, feelings and attitudes. Speech and action, I repeat, are intimately interrelated. Gesture and body language and instrumental activity are often so intimately orchestrated into the speech score that they must be considered as essential components embedded into it rather than embellishments. We may talk then of action-with-speech, bearing in mind (since I shall be getting back to dramatic action) that action can occur without speech and speech without action. You may do the washing up in miserable silence or may talk while doing it - about the washing up or anything else under the sun. Similarly speech can occur without action in monologue or dialogue (the telephone conversation).

Now I can return to my main theme. Developmentally it begins with the representation of speech and action in play. It is often difficult to distinguish at the early stages from imitation. A small girl who often says very distinctly, 'I will not have it!' exactly reproducing her mother's speech is not necessarily playing but rather trying out in the appropriate contexts a piece of ready-made language. She may learn later that it is not considered to be children's language except when playing. Once dramatic play is fully established it is usually quickly recognizable. The 'rules' prescribe, as they continue to do in adult life, that we must accept the actor-speaker is representing through the action-with-speech of another, or even of himself at another time - past or future, true or fictional. We have to construe the here-and-now event as both happening and not happening. It is the imposition of design on events which makes the difference. The onlooker must pick up the signals in order to interpret aright. Sometimes they are explicit and obvious, signalled by narrative conventions, special tones of voice or even 'props'. (5) Children withdraw to engage in dramatic play suspending the activities of life to do so. But they also do intermittently what we do as adults, so that dramatic representation is more ubiquitous than clearly marked-off episodes would suggest. What since classical times has been called direct speech (Oratio Recta) that is, the citation of the actual words, real or supposed, of another, contains within it, however, faintly, the features of enactment rather than mimetic reproduction. Consider the ways in which different speakers might say: 'So quite suddenly he said to me, "Do you like classical music?"' Volosinov's recently resurrected work (1929, trans. 1973) long ago drew attention to the significance of the use of direct speech and offers a brilliant analysis of its use in literature. He suggests that in double-voiced speech the voice of the other, the quoted one, is inevitably passive and therefore open to manipulation by the quoter. Thus his own intentions are superimposed upon it and its original goals are

transformed into new ones. We could say that exactly the same
applies to doubly-articulated action, in which we act the actions
of another in order to present them recognizably and at the same
time transform them. In both of these, double-voiced speech and
doubly-articulated action, it is the tension between the two components which gives us meaning.

Once we enter the world of representation in the form of enactment we can make some further discriminations or subdivisions;
these I call re-enactment, pre-enactment, and the enactment of
fictions. In speech or writing by reshaping experience through
imagination we can create what is not, what has not been and will
never be or what might have been or might be. What we can speak of
and write of we can perform, using as our sources and resources our
direct experience or more indirectly using the symbols provided by
our culture (witches, Superman, Dr Who, cowboys). Re-enactment is
the presentation (highly selected, edited and patterned) of what has
happened, like this:

> So I started nudging him. 'I think there's something creepy
> about this place,' and he said, 'Don't be daft. You're always
> imagining things.' So I started tugging his arm. Then this big
> fella comes up and says, 'Remember me?' etc., etc.

Pre-enactment is the rehearsal of how things might happen. It may
be a complete fantasy or the prelude to an ordeal or confrontation.
We need to peer into the fog of the future. Like this:

> He'll come round this evening all bluster and noise. 'Did you
> put the hose on our cat?' wagging his podgy finger in my face.
> 'Ah, Mr Penny,' I'll say, very polite, 'nice of you to call
> again. I know what you'd enjoy. Come have a look at my
> fuchsias. Sorry, I forgot. They're not there anymore.' You
> know him. He'll start mumbling. 'She didn't say nothing about
> ...', etc., etc.

The dramatic is always lurking just below the surface of the flow of
interaction ready to surface for a moment or longer. We can see
this readily if we attend to the flickers of mimicry, borrowed
gestures, voices, accents. The more relaxed and informal the situation, the less cautious and self-regarding the participants, the
more readily the dramatic breaks through, for like all expressiveness it withers with inhibition and coldness.

If the various forms of dramatic activity are ubiquitous, long
before they put on grease-paint and find their way into theatres,
they permeate our consciousness even more imperiously. When we do
not need them for communication we learn to internalize them. We
can produce our little dramas in our heads. Vygotsky's charting of
the process of the development of inner-speech (1962) needs to be
extended to embrace this other kind of inner-representation. Piaget
had proposed that egocentric speech (speech without an audience or
interlocutor) in young children disappeared because their language
became completely socialized. Vygotsky demonstrated that it did not
vanish but was internalized. The radical reduction of egocentric
speech occurs at about 7 years of age when it becomes internalized

as verbal thought. Dramatic play dwindles at the same time. Inner-speech, internalized action and imagery merge and the imagination can dramatize for our purposes the explorations of our minds. Inner-speech does not consist solely of interior monologue in which we listen to our voices. It can consist of the voices of others. The others and their actions can be represented by inner-imagery. But internalization takes for audience the self and does not have to be shaped and edited so that others can share our understanding. Inner-drama, like inner-speech, is not shaped by the pressures of an immediate audience. There is gain and loss. We gain in freedom, including freedom from taboo, and lose in reality-controlled discipline. In externalized drama we are obliged to deliver our thinking to others through yet another set of personae.

The ideas I have sketched up to this point could be further elaborated and refined. I have been concerned only to show how dramatic activity occurs as part of communication and thought, that it is part of the general process of representation. Like talk itself it is in such general, daily use that mostly it goes unremarked as something unusual. Everyone does it, most of us do it well and some are highly talented. One culture or subculture may foster it more than another. It is available as a means of knowing and explaining our world. Wherever there is vitality, spontaneity and intimacy it will out.

Institutionalized drama (theatre) may become stylized and intensely conventionalized but it draws its strength from popular performance just as all literary art is inconceivable without speech. Indeed we might say that organized drama is to spontaneous enactment what written language is to speech. Therefore, we should ask ourselves, 'If drama occurs without any designated apparatus, why do we need to introduce it, to develop all the paraphernalia of theatre? Does some new transforming element enter in which cannot be present in the spontaneous, fitful, unpredictable dramas of common interaction?' I have already suggested the answer which I can put another way. As spontaneous expressive language can become poetry so spontaneous expressive dramatic language can become a form of art. When the dramatic impulse becomes highly ordered and controlled it becomes theatre. But a theatre is a kind of social institution and is historically evolved. It will, therefore, develop its own conventions and stylized resources for delivering a meaningful virtual experience. In the course of its development it will often become sharply differentiated from its origins.

Dramatic activity thus becomes elevated by the creation of an intense focused moment of interpretation and understanding and presupposes an audience which has willingly, eagerly submitted itself to this experience. Perhaps the most significant shift is the creation of a text which is in our theatres the supreme form of control of the actor and the performance. In spontaneous drama we 'become' somebody else. With text the actor becomes somebody else's somebody else, somebody else's way of knowing through the dramatized word. The audience must carry out in a highly attentive and, in a sense, collective manner, an effort of understanding, of knowing what the antics signify. That capacity, perceiving how this thing means, is firmly founded on their daily experience of tendering and receiving dramatic meaning. This will remain true of theatrical

forms as diverse as Peking Opera, Malayan shadow puppets, Punch and
Judy, mystery plays, Kathakouli dance and European ballet. The
distance between these forms and everyman in his dramatic mode may
be similar to the difference between gossip and 'War and Peace'. It
is huge but bridged. To put it differently, we trace the progress
through gradations of conscious control, degrees of performance and
staging. The great Russian puppet-master who directed the most
elaborate and refined puppet theatre used to put a ball on each of
his forefingers and develop little dramas between the two 'people'
he had created. He would insist that all that was significant in
puppetry was there. The rest was elaboration. He was just as insistent that the fingers were activating the performer's built-in
dramatic sense of human action.

But I have jumped a step. All spontaneous drama is a collaboration between performer and onlooker who may easily switch roles.
However, they may also combine in the sense that the onlooker takes
on the game and the whole interchange is an enactment. Children's
dramatic play is an absorbed collaboration of this kind.

This is spontaneous group enactment in which emergent meaning
must be negotiated, in the main through the drama itself, although
at moments of breakdown children will readily switch to the other
reality in order to sort things out.

    X: Pretend you're sick
    Y: O.K.
    X: (speaks into phone) Hey Dr Wren, do you got any medicine?
    Y: Yes, I have some medicine.
    X: (to Y) No, you aren't the doctor, remember?
    Y: O.K.

(Garvey, 1976)

For the most part that early dramatic play disappears though not
entirely. I am not sure why this is so. Is it that children share
each other's construction of the world more completely and com-
pellingly than adults? That seems unlikely. More plausible is that
we are socialized into a particular view of adult dignity and com-
posure. We must not be caught off our guard. Spontaneity and
yielding to impulse has to be tamed or at least channelled. We
discriminate more and more firmly between play and work and regular-
ize play, allotting to it a safe place. Whatever the reason, it is
certainly rare for a group of adults to engage in collective group
spontaneous drama. It does happen of course. Charades are (or
were?) just that, and occasionally amongst groups of intimates the
invention catches fire. The probability is that the occasion has to
be licensed by intimacy, informality and a sense of holiday from the
work-a-day world. Drink helps. An instrumental purpose may be
glimpsed in serious and businesslike enactments such as the practice
which has grown up in some schools of rehearsing pupils for inter-
views for jobs and places at college, or in 'gaming' and simulation
exercises.

The growth of improvised drama in schools derives its strength
from the fact that it makes room for this missing link in the chain.
It offers to pupils the possibility of turning the individual and
sporadic into the collective and it provides a permanent regular

space for it. Even more, it can propose areas of attention that the
pupils themselves would not propose. There's the rub. For in much
improvised drama intentions are imposed on pupils that are alien to
them. The dilemma is familiar enough: compare the constrained
speech and abortive discussions of many classrooms with the speech
of pupils outside school. Speech outside the classroom does not
have to grope for motivation, nor does spontaneous drama. On the
other hand, since the customary communicative style of the classroom
does not invite interchanges which are like those of informal daily
conversation, improvised drama can be a huge liberation. If I am
right and the dramatic mode even in its slightest and most ephemeral
form is a way of communicating and understanding, then group drama
is a means of moving towards collective wisdom. Every participant's
insights complement and develop everyone else's and, potentially at
least, an understanding can emerge which belonged to no one at the
outset. This is what we hope will emerge from discussion, but so
often it does not. The analytic mode we prize and which takes so
long to emerge can be short cut by selective representation in which
all the analytic processes are out of sight. At the end of my attempts to look past the bleak little dramatic exercises being amia-
bly and perfunctorily performed in the classrooms by those children
under marching orders, I felt that if we could not do better than
that we should leave human dramatic 'language' to do its own work
or perhaps make classrooms places where it would easily emerge at
the right moment from a story, perhaps, or a disagreement. Fortu-
nately, there are drama teachers who do better than that, who,
building on the dramatic resources developed outside their classes,
take their pupils towards a co-operative enlargement of their dramatic vocabulary and towards a collective act of giving form to experience. I was more concerned, however, to explore the ways in
which drama can enter into all learning by, at one and the same
time, communicating experience and giving the communicator a deeper
understanding of experience. For, as Vygotsky said of play, spontaneous drama is imagination in action.
    We are, I hope, coming to realize that human beings have rich and
varied strategies for learning and communicating. We should be
cheered and delighted by the possibility of understanding a common
possession with so much potentiality. Accordingly, we should not
only honour it but also give it more sustained attention. The great
sociolinguist Labov (1972) almost stumbled upon his discovery that
vernacular speakers translating personal experience into dramatic
form can evaluate behaviour in a controlled and concentrated way.
At the end of his paper, which is analytical and statistical, his
admiration breaks through:

> When these devices [i.e. complex linguistic devices] are concen-
> trated and embedded deeply in the dramatic action, they can
> succeed in making the point. Many of the narratives cited here
> rise to a very high level of competence ... they will command the
> total attention of an audience in a remarkable way, creating a
> deep and attentive silence that is never found in academic or
> political discussion.

There is still much to discover about how spontaneous drama is con-

structed, how it works and the functions it fulfils. I have tried
to suggest why such further explorations could be rewarding.

ON THE EVERYDAY THEATRE

Actors
You who perform plays in great houses
Under false suns and before silent faces
Look sometimes at
The theatre whose stage is the street.
The everyday theatre
Common, unrewarded with honour,
But of this earth, living,
Made from the traffic of men together.
The theatre whose stage is the street.
Here the woman from next door -
Gives us the landlord.
Imitating his stream of words,
How well she shows him up
Trying to keep the conversation off
The burst water pipe.
Young men mime to giggling girls
In parks at dusk
How girls resist yet while resisting
Beckon to them with their breasts.
And there the drunk
Playing the pulpit parson
Refers the less fortunate among us
To the golden fields of paradise.
Earnest and gay the theatre of the street
Has uses
And dignity.
Not like parrot or ape
Do these men imitate for imitation's sake,
Unconcerned with what they show
Save that they themselves are imitating well.
They have their purposes in mind.
And in this, great actors that you are,
Masters of imitation,
Do not lag behind.
However polished your art
Do not step too far
From the everyday theatre,
The theatre whose state is the street.
Look - the man at the corner re-enacting
The accident.
Thus he gives the driver at his wheel
To the crowd for trial.
Thus the victim, who seems old,
Of each he only gives so much
That the accident he understood
Yet each lives before your eyes
And each presents in a manner

To suggest the accident avoidable.
So the event is understood
And yet can still astound:
The moves of both could have been different.
Now he shows how both could have moved
To circumvent the accident.
This witness is free from superstition.
Never to the stars
Does he abandon his mortals
But only to their own mistakes.
Notice too
How serious and careful his imitation.
He knows that much depends on his precision:
Whether the innocent is ruined,
Whether the injured one receives his compensation.
See him now do what he has already done
Over again.
He hesitates,
Calls on his memory's aid,
Doubts if his imitation is truly good,
Stops to demand correction for this detail or that.
Observe with reverence.
And observe with astonishment:
This imitator never loses himself in his imitation.
Never does he lend himself whole
To the person he plays.
He remains, disengaged, the one who shows.
The man he represents has not confided in him.
Nor does he share
The feelings or views of this man.
He knows but little of him.
His imitation does not engender
A third
Composed in roughly equal parts
of him and the other,
A third in whom but one heart beats
And one brain thinks.
His senses collected he, the performer,
stands and gives us
The man next door,
A stranger.
In your theatres
You would take us in
With your magical transformation
Somewhere between
Dressing room and stage:
An actor leaves his room
A king enters the play,
And at this I've seen the stage hands
Laugh out loud with their bottles of beer.
Our performer there on the corner
Spins no such spell.
He's no sleep-walker you may not address,
Nor high priest at service.

Interrupt as you will.
Calmly he will reply
And when you have had your say
Continue his performance.
Don't declare this man is not an artist.
By creating this distinction between the world and yourselves
You banish yourselves from the world.
If you declare:
He is no artist,
He may reply:
You are not men.
A worse reproach by far.
Declare instead:
He is an artist because a man.
What he does we may do
With more perfection
Thus gaining honour.
Yet we practise
What is universal,
Human,
To be seen every hour in the teeming streets,
Almost as popular as eating and breathing.

Thus all your acting
Leads back to daily life.
Our masks, you should say,
Are nothing special
If they remain mere masks.
Over there the seller of scarves
Dons the masher's hat
Dangles a cane
Pastes on a lady-killing moustache
and behind his stall
Cake-walks up and down
To prove how hat, moustache and scarf
Indeed change men
Most favourably.
They, like us, you should say,
Have their verses.
The newspaper sellers cry their headlines
With a rhythm to heighten
Effect and make their own refrains
Easier to sustain.
We learn, you should say,
The words of others
But likewise too salesmen and lovers learn.
And how often
The sayings of people
are repeated.
Thus common the quotation, the verse and the mask
Yet uncommon a mask seen large
Uncommon a beautifully said verse
And uncommon the intelligent quotation.

But let us understand each other.
You may perform better than he
Whose stage is the street.
Still your achievement will be less
If your theatre is less
Meaningful than his,
If it touches less
Deeply the lives of those who watch,
If its reasons
are less,
Or its usefulness.

Bertold Brecht

NOTES

1 It occurs to me that having put quotation marks round the phrase
   I have in effect dramatized the students, embedding their collective voice in my own thus giving it a meaning it would not
   otherwise have. I hope this becomes clearer in the rest of the
   chapter.
2 For a remarkable example see Rosen (1974), a Yorkshire woman's
   spontaneous narrative which also contains a sustained dramatic
   dialogue.
3 What makes the distinction more difficult than that is a shadowy
   area which we might call rehearsal. An adolescent, for example,
   needs to learn how to enter a room full of adults as an adult.
   There is much to be learned from people at the early stages of
   learning to use a new dialect. They legitimately protect themselves by dramatizing their first attempts. The big jump is to
   try to talk like a native, naturally, as we say.
4 Any novelist might be cited. Just recently at the urging of a
   colleague, Jane Miller, I read James Hogg's 'Confessions of a
   Justified Sinner'. The authorial voice is in measured, formal
   eighteenth-century prose: Hogg has some of his characters speak
   in a Scottish vernacular. At one point it erupts into the text
   like a Highland fling into a minuet.
5 Bruner et al. (1976) reports, 'it turns out that play is universally accompanied in subhuman primates by a recognizable form
   of metasignalling, a "play face", first carefully studied by the
   Dutch primatologist van Hooff. It signifies ... "this is play".
   It is a powerful signal - redundant in its features, which include a particular kind of open-mouthed gesture, a slack but
   exaggerated gait, and a marked "galumphing" in movement ...'.

REFERENCES

Argyle, M. (1967), 'The Psychology of Interpersonal Behaviour',
Penguin, Harmondsworth.
Birdwhistell, R.L. (1952), 'Introduction to Kinesics', University of
Louisville Press, Louisville.
Boomer, G. and Spender, D. (1976), 'The Spitting Image', Rigby,
Norwood, S.A.

Bruner, J.S., Jolly, A. and Sylva, K. (1976), 'Play', Penguin, Harmondsworth.
Cassirer, E. (1953), 'The Philosophy of Symbolic Forms', vol.1, Language, Yale University Press, New Haven, Connecticut.
Cazden, C. (1976), Play with Language and Metalinguistic Awareness, in Bruner et al., 1976.
Chomsky, N. (1959), Review of Skinner's 'Verbal Behaviour', in 'Language', 35, pp.26-58.
Chukovsky, K. (1968), 'From Two to Five', University of California Press, California.
Garvey, C. (1976), Some Properties of Social Play, in Bruner et al., 1976.
Goffman, E. (1959), 'Presentation of Self in Everyday Life', Doubleday, New York.
Hall, E.T. (1959), 'The Silent Language', Doubleday, New York.
Labov, W. (1972), 'Language in the Inner City', University of Pennsylvania Press, Pennsylvania.
Piaget, J. (1951), 'Play, Dreams and Imitation in Childhood', Routledge & Kegan Paul, London.
Piaget, J. (1969), 'The Science of Education and the Psychology of the Child', Longman, London.
Rosen, H. (1972), 'Language and Class: a Critical Look at the Theories of Basil Bernstein', Falling Wall Press, Bristol.
Rosen, H. (ed.) (1974), 'Language and Class Workshop', 1 and 2, privately printed.
Volosinov, V.N. (1973), 'Marxism and the Philosophy of Language', Seminar Press, New York.
Vygotsky, L.S. (1962), 'Thought and Language', Massachusetts Institute of Technology.
Weir, R. (1962), 'Language in the Crib', Mouton, New York.

Chapter 9

LEARNING IN PSYCHOTHERAPY
David Smail

In psychotherapy, as in almost every other area of organized human
endeavour, science and (in particular) technology are looked to to
provide, potentially at least, relatively painless mechanical solutions to the kinds of psychological problems which patients may
present. Ideally, it seems that the therapist should be a technical
expert trained in scientifically established procedures for alleviating distress. For most people - certainly for most potential
patients if not for all psychotherapists themselves - what lends
credibility to the activity of a psychotherapist is the stamp of
approval conferred upon it by what might broadly be conceived of
as 'science'.

Even though his modern detractors would laugh the idea to scorn,
Freud certainly believed that psychoanalysis stood squarely within
the scientific tradition, and took this as a major justification for
its continuation and expansion. At the other end of the psychotherapeutic spectrum, modern behaviour therapists are frequently
prone to assert the superiority of their methods over those of rival
systems on the grounds that only they can claim the support of a
scientific, quantified analysis of their effectiveness. Even those
psychotherapeutic systems which repudiate what they see as the
stranglehold of orthodox scientific values usually end up by appealing to some kind of technological benefit to their clients
(ease, speed, cheapness of treatment, etc.). It is interesting, in
the context of this volume, that the approaches in psychotherapy
which most explicitly take learning as a central theoretical preoccupation are at the same time those which are most vociferously
insistent on the adequacy of their scientific credentials - I am of
course discussing those approaches which derive from behaviourism in
one or another of its forms.

Before developing the theme of learning in psychotherapy, I
should like to consider a little further what seems to be meant by
the term 'scientific'; in so doing I shall rely on arguments that
I have developed in rather greater detail elsewhere (Smail, 1978).

Historically, presumably, the scientific attitude arose out of a
curiosity about the nature of the world which could no longer be
fettered by the scholastic dogmas of orthodox theology, and cou-
rageous men asserted what they could no longer deny as the evidence

of their senses, at great personal risk. The early history of science is thus imbued with a sense of discovery and intellectual adventurousness, of passionate, personal commitment to views which could quite literally prove life-threatening. But, because of what Polanyi (1958) has called 'a passion for achieving absolutely impersonal knowledge', it did not take long for scientists and philosophers to introduce, and attempt to enforce in science just that rigid dogmatism to which it was originally opposed. In order to render scientific knowledge impersonal and 'objective' (and hence, as far as possible, 'certain') scientists became obsessed with what seem like theological arguments aimed at establishing what qualifies an activity to be counted as 'scientific' or 'unscientific'. Science thus becomes identified with its methods: if you follow a set of impersonal rules of a kind approved by the scientific orthodoxy (if, that is, your methodology is acceptable) you may be accorded the status of being a scientist. If you don't, you may be condemned as 'unscientific' and excommunicated from the scientific establishment. In this way, scientific methodology is turned into an objective institution independent of the persons who apply it - a collection of articles of faith, but from which the faith itself has been removed because, as everyone knows, science is not concerned with values or beliefs, but deals in the objective revelation of factual truth. There is thus little difference between the orthodox scientist's confidence in his methodological principles and that of some fundamentalist religions in the infallible revelations of the Bible.

For me, Michael Polanyi has done more than anyone to expose the fallacy of this kind of scientism (Polanyi, 1958), and to demonstrate that, like any other branch of human culture, science is inescapably saturated with human values and depends for its existence utterly on the (very probably tacit) personal acquiescence of individual scientists in those values. Science is what scientists, as people, do and believe in, and there can be no objective guarantee of scientific infallibility.

What is particularly interesting (and nowhere is it more apparent than in psychology) is what Polanyi calls the process of 'moral inversion' whereby scientific values become hidden behind an assertion of objective validity. Thus the very disinterested objectivity of science is asserted with a ferocious, but disguised, moralism which, because it is not recognized, cannot easily be checked. It is perhaps true that many scientists and philosophers of science are today less naive in this respect than was the case a few years ago, but nevertheless, in the mainstream of psychology certainly, the condemnation of being 'unscientific' is still one to make the potential heretic fear and tremble for his academic or professional life: the established guardians of pure, 'value-free' science are awesome in their disapproval.

The fact that this moralism is unrecognized and unchecked has some interesting consequences for contemporary culture, and, as our particular concern, for the conduct of psychotherapy. The main consequence is that confidence (belief) in the powers of science and technology is underpinned, in the popular as sometimes in the professional mind, by a faith as fervent, as uninformed and as irrational as that which maintains the most bizarre magical or re-

ligious systems. There are even parallels with such systems in the
forms in which this faith is maintained, or, at least, betrays
itself.

As a general instance of this take, for the sake of argument, the
television programme 'Tomorrow's World'. (For those readers fortunate enough to be unfamiliar with it, this is a weekly revelation of
the wonders of modern science and technology which are about to
revolutionalize our lives.) These marvels are paraded before us
with a sense of mystery and awe. The magical light of the laser
beam causes unfathomable machinery to move mysteriously; computers
whirr and hum in the performance of unimaginable feats; complex and
difficult problems are solved by forces we can neither see nor
divine. We can only watch and wonder as these modern miracles are
revealed to us. And yet, of course, we cannot understand the mysterious workings of these awesome phenomena. They have to be interpreted to us, with a kind of dramatic urgency, by the modern
priests of this technological religion: young men (and the occasional woman) who have apparently studied the languages of science
and who know which switch must dextrously be flicked in order to
animate the gleaming banks of machinery and bring about their jaw-
dropping achievements. Much as priests may give explanations of the
religious mysteries we cannot understand, using the knowledge vouch-
safed to them through their special relationship with God, so these
journalists, faces aglow with zeal (like any good curate), will
invoke the physico-chemical theology which explains the wonders we
behold. To the average viewer, of course, these 'explanations' mean
nothing; they must be taken on trust as verities revealed to but
few. (If there are any real scientists in the audience, they are
probably limp with either derision or despair.)

What chance does the comically-robed priest, mumbling his impre-
cations and juggling with his censers and bottles of holy water,
have in the face of this competition? How much better could he do
if he had a computer installed behind his altar cloth in order to
stun his congregation at appropriate moments with amazing electronic
effects? And yet the real priest's job seems no different from that
of the inverted priest of technology. Both are promulgating an
ideology, hoping to convince us of a particular view of the world
and to suggest what our moral role in it should be.

The message of the religion of technology is that we should be
passive consumers of the products of expertise and mechanical invention. If we acquiesce in the mysteries of Science, our needs
will be met, our interests defended, and we shall be cured of all
ills. Thus have we injected science and technology with all our
religious longings and hopes, and abandoned our personal nature,
with all its painful moral implications and uncertainty in order to
live by the 'objective' decisions of the world of machines. (In
fact, of course, we have even gone as far as to credit machines with
our own personhood - quite serious scientists debate whether computers can 'think'. One can go even further than this - serious
scientists, sometimes the same ones, have also taken machines as
models whereby we might understand human behaviour.) We cast ourselves on the mercy of a just, merciful and bountiful Mechanism in
which we can trust because It is objective, unlike vengeful and
unpredictable old Jehova.

But, of course, we depersonalize ourselves at great risk. Our
institutions run riot and our machines threaten to destroy us (we
even populate the heavens with them with that very purpose in mind)
because we no longer trust ourselves to enact our moral decisions.
As Ivan Illich (1975) suggests, we are in the grip of a greedy dream
in which we trade our humanity for a technological promise of a life
from which pain and suffering, and possibly even death itself, can
be removed.

And so it is also with our personal moral and emotional dilemmas:
we hand over responsibility for them to experts, in the belief that
they will operate technically upon us to resolve them. When one
thinks about it, it really does seem an extraordinary indication of
human weakness that we should have invented 'psychologists', and a
poignant example of our desperation to abdicate the responsibility
for understanding, nurturing and accepting ourselves. At one level,
perhaps, people tend to know this - hence the popular (and healthy)
derision in which head-shrinkers of all kinds are held. There is
something patently absurd about one order of being claiming to be
an expert about the same order of being. If psychology is successful in the way I should want it to be, it will destroy itself
through becoming superfluous. However, we are a long way from that
at present.

Our mechanistic faith has put us out of touch with the sources of
our own social and emotional distress - perhaps, indeed, has been
invented precisely to obscure these sources from us. For, whether
we abandon ourselves to God or to Science, the motive is presumably
the same: to rid ourselves of a terrible responsibility for the
fallibility, pain and risk of living. The very fragility of the
mechanistic structures we erect testifies to the desperation of our
undertaking. For example, despite shoring psychiatry up with all
the paraphernalia of medical technology and 'scientific' methodology, it is a quite extraordinarily ramshackle construction. Its
methods are at best crudely empirical, its effects questionable, its
theories, where they exist, naive and chaotic, its ethical philosophy so obscure and unelaborated as to be unidentifiable. These and
related observations have of course been well put by writers such as
R.D.Laing and Thomas Szasz. And yet, of course, psychiatry is one
of our major medical institutions, consuming millions of pounds and
supporting vast pharmaceutical interests. Despite the fact that its
simplistic precepts fly in the face of almost everything that a
rational and reflective person, in his heart, knows about himself
and others, psychiatry has been sanctified by the stamp of mechanism; it has been dressed up in technological garb so that it may
the more plausibly disguise from us the real causes of our unhappi-
ness. If, as I should want to suggest, it is a central part of the
truly scientific attitude to take one's experience seriously, then
psychiatry is little more than a primitive form of magic. Rather
than seeing that misery and madness arise for the most part out of
the ways we act towards each other, we prefer to turn to the refined
alchemy of medicine for reassurance that really all this is nothing
to do with us, but only our wayward, and in principle adjustable,
biochemistry.

The psychotherapies, or at least some of them, have of course not
been quite as crass as this, and, given an interest in rationality

and the evidence of one's own experience, one may be thankful that
most psychotherapeutic theories do see human distress as arising out
of human commerce with the world and the other human beings in it.
But, as I suggested at the beginning of this chapter, even in the
psychotherapies we still do not escape the postulation of mechanisms. Whether a patient is a victim of an unconscious conflict or
of an unfortunate set of 'reinforcement contingencies', he is immediately rendered the passive owner of a mechanical fault. This
kind of conceptualization engenders in the patient, understandably
enough, an expectation that the fault will need correcting by a
suitably-qualified expert, into whose hands he may with confidence
place himself. Faced with such passivity, however, the expert
himself, i.e. the therapist, finds that he can accomplish nothing.
In order to change, the patient has to do something; he has to
become an agent. Although most psychotherapists have a partial
understanding of this paradox, and at least manage to cope with it
to some extent in their daily work, failure to recognize its fundamental significance (that it totally undermines any possibility of
casting psychotherapy in mechanistic terms) has proved frustrating
to the fruitful development of theory in psychotherapy. In order to
take seriously what one finds in the psychotherapeutic situation one
would have to abandon some of the central dogmas of mechanism, and
thus risk academic and professional purgatory.

Above all, psychotherapy is a personal meeting in which the
activity of both therapist and patient is crucial. The patient
brings to the therapeutic situation a problem (even if he couches it
in terms of 'symptoms') which he has up to that point been unable to
solve. It will be his task during the course of therapy to learn to
solve it; what he will not find is that the therapist can solve it
for him.

Mainstream psychology conceives of learning in terms of a mechanistic technology that is, aptly enough, usually labelled as
'training'. As a good example of this, take the following publish-
er's blurb, recently received, about a 'Trainer's Manual and
Workbook' entitled 'Parenting Skills':

A complete programme for parent training workshops. The
programme is arranged in modules to facilitate the achievement
of effective skills and objectives in child rearing. In a group
setting the parents and their trainer can explore the most
skillful (sic) means of evaluating the child-parent relationship,
management of children's behaviour, circumstances that increase
or decrease behaviour, and selecting behaviour patterns that
should be changed, managing personal feelings in situations that
require impartial actions, parent-parent and parent-child interactions.

The aim of projects such as this is, obviously enough, the mechanization of human activity, and the language and concepts used, such
as they are, are becoming increasingly familiar in the psychotherapeutic, as well as related fields. The individual's personal
struggle at, as it were, the forefront of his activity, in his relationship with his environment and the people in it, becomes
distanced from him through the intervention of an expert who has

the technical knowledge to provide him with the skills that will
enable him to cope; he can become programmed, like a computer, to
deal with problems that, it is implied, are not problems at all, but
arise out of a deficit in skill. In other words, the promise is
held out that difficulties in living, like any others, can be solved
through technical intervention.

As in other areas, what nourishes this dream is a blind faith in
mechanism rather than any rational appraisal of evidence. In the
psychotherapy literature, for example, research workers tend to
ignore their own findings because they don't accord with their
mechanistic assumptions. As far as it tries to isolate 'variables'
and validate techniques, the psychotherapy literature, like that of
psychology in general, abounds with contradictions which themselves
become obscured in endless squabbles about methodology. Despite
this, however, some regularity emerges in that many studies point to
the importance for therapeutic success (problematic though that
concept may be) of the quality of the personal relationship between
therapist and patient (for discussion of such findings see, for
example, Frank, 1973; Smail, 1978). And yet most such studies, and
most of the commentaries on them, are either curiously dismissive of
this observation, or else try to mechanize it in some way. Frank,
for instance, feels that because psychotherapy seems to involve
'non-specific', personal qualities such as responsibility, courage
and influence, it must as an enterprise be relegated to the field of
the 'healing arts', cast, that is, out into the darkness beyond the
light of scientific understanding (because, presumably, science
necessarily can only deal with mechanisms). As a more specific
example, Sloane et al. (1975), in what is in fact a very thorough
study of the comparative effectiveness of psychotherapy and behaviour therapy, more or less dismiss the finding - one of the
clearest of the study - that patients experience their therapists'
personal qualities as being particularly important, because experience is not objective.

Furthermore, research in psychotherapy tends to destroy the significance of findings concerning the personal nature of the therapeutic relationship precisely through attempting to mechanize them.
For example, therapists of the Rogerian school observed that, as
indeed Rogers himself suggested, understanding (empathy) is an important feature of therapy. It therefore seemed reasonable to them
to develop measures of 'therapist empathy', such as rating scales,
which would identify those therapists who had it and those who did
not. One of the obvious mechanistic aims of such a programme is, of
course, to find ways eventually of training therapists to acquire
optimum levels of empathy. But what such an approach overlooks is
that understanding is a relational quality which arises between
persons, not something you can have, or learn to acquire, to some
kind of constant degree. It is not surprising, then, that in the
Sloane et al. study measures of therapist characteristics of this
kind failed to produce significant results, even though patients
felt subjectively that the characteristics themselves were important. Because of reigning dogma, credence is of course given to
the 'objective' rather than the subjective findings, and so what
might well in fact be a valid observation is necessarily invalidated
through mechanism, and disappears.

No part of this kind of exercise seems to me to have anything to do with science, if by being scientific we mean taking the experience of psychotherapy seriously. Rather, the experience of psychotherapy is ignored in order to propitiate the gods of mechanism.

If the experience of psychotherapy is taken seriously, it may be seen, as I have already suggested, as a process of personal learning. Learning, I should want to argue, is for the most part something someone does (though not necessarily wills), an active process in which, through his relations with others and with the world, he changes himself. In psychotherapy, the patient changes himself, at least partly through his relation with the therapist. There are three aspects of this process which I should like now to discuss: negotiation, action and relation.

NEGOTIATION

The patient comes to the therapist with at least some ideas about what is the matter with him. He may have a problem - in relation to others, himself, or both - or he may be suffering from 'symptoms'. Either way, he has built a network of meaning around his complaint. The complaint, of course, can vary greatly in the degree of its elaboration. At one end of the scale a patient may tell a relatively uncomplicated tale of feeling unaccountably dizzy and sick when travelling on public transport; at the other, he may relate a detailed story about failing relationships and loss of self-esteem which he accounts for through a thoughtful analysis of his early childhood experiences.

Now the expert mechanist may feel it enough to accept the patient's complaint at face value and, as it were, consult his therapist's workshop manual (assuming it is sufficiently comprehensive) to find out what to do next in cases of this kind. However, the non-mechanistic therapist is likely to be more cautious about accepting or endorsing the patient's view of himself. First of all, he will want to be sure that he knows what the patient means, and second, he may feel that the patient is deceiving himself about the nature and significance of his problems. Should this be the case, his task will be to negotiate with the patient an account of his predicament which both find satisfactory; for, if their communication is to be in any way effective, their meanings will have to be shared (for a social psychological treatment of this process, see Harré and Secord, 1972).

Two key concepts that are likely to arise in one form or another during the process of negotiation are self-deception and responsibility.

As has been well recognized in, for example, psychoanalysis and existential philosophy, there is no particular reason to suppose that an individual is any better judge of the meaning of his own activity than he is for that of others. It is true, of course, that we have privileged access to our own feelings, but what we make of them, what we tell ourselves (and others) about them is open to as much bias and error (perhaps more) as are our interpretations of the behaviour and motives of others. Space will not allow the development of this argument here (see Fingarette, 1969; Smail,

1978), but it must surely be clear to all but those who wish to be
deliberately obscurantist that the need for the preservation of
self-esteem alone accounts for many lies we (very possibly unknowingly) tell ourselves. In the ordinary course of daily living
most of us do not pause all that often to consider the whys and
wherefores of our activity - we simply act. If we do happen to stop
to think about our reasons for acting in such-and-such a manner,
they have to be constructed from our observation of our own activity, and in fact these constructions are often revised, possibly more
than once, in the course of time.

Having listened to his patient, the therapist, then, may come to
feel that the former's account of his difficulties is inaccurate in
some important respects. He may feel, for example, that a patient's
dizziness and nausea on leaving her home are not (as she is likely
at first to think) phenomena that arise 'out of the blue', but
constitute the somatic manifestations of an anxiety which she has
good reasons for feeling - she may perhaps be afraid of the social
encounters that going out makes possible, and yet not wish (in a
sense) to recognize her fear because of the injury such recognition
would do to her self-esteem. Baldly stating to her this kind of
interpretation of her symptoms would be unlikely to be of help since
it would mean her having to abandon too quickly for comfort her
established networks of meaning. Through his relationship with her,
the therapist has to negotiate new meanings which both can share and
which allow the patient to develop good reasons for changing. However, before somebody can change himself, he has to recognize also
that his activity is something he does; he has, in other words, to
accept responsibility for it.

Most psychotherapies recognize the importance of patients acknowledging ownership of, or taking responsibility for their own
conduct, but over and over again adequate consideration of the
issues has been hindered by the prevailing mechanistic dogma's insistence on some more or less rigid form of determinism. This situation is not helped by the frequent concern of patients themselves
to reject the idea that their 'illness' could have anything to do
with their own agency. For this, of course, they can scarcely be
blamed, since they are encouraged by almost every aspect of contemporary culture to see themselves as 'dysfunctional' machines.

The therapist's difficulty is to negotiate a view of responsibility which does not imply blame or imputations of guilt or way-
wardness. It seems to me that the concepts that are available in
our everyday language to explicate the notions of responsibility,
deliberation, blame, accountability, etc., are extremely inadequate,
and we are usually left with little more than appeals to the crude
mechanism of cause and effect, or else to blunt moral condemnation
or approval. A more detailed attempt at analysing these issues is
once again outside the scope of the present chapter, but perhaps I
could suggest a way in which it might be possible to conceptualize
responsibility in the sense I wish to use it. Basically, this is
simply to see the person as agent rather than as victim (of circumstance). This is not to say that circumstances cannot exert powerful effects on the individual, nor to suggest that he is necessarily
to blame for those of his actions which offend others, but merely to
make clear that his reasons for acting are his reasons, good or bad,

and nobody else's (this position is considerably elaborated in
Smail, 1978). When the person sees that he had - from his point of
view at least - good reasons for acting, say, neurotically, it
becomes possible for him to adopt new ones. Reasons, furthermore,
do not have to be consciously deliberated, formed, as it were, in
advance of action (though I know this is how we often see them), but
form an integral part of action. Indeed, one's reasons may be read
off from one's actions: only understood, that is, after the event.
There is of course nothing new in such conceptualizations; they are
also to be found in phenomenological and existential philosophy
(e.g. Sartre, 1969; Merleau-Ponty, 1962), and similar positions
have been outlined by modern British philosophical psychologists
(e.g. Gauld and Shotter, 1977). Through his negotiative relation
with the therapist, then, the person learns about the reasons for
his actions, and develops the possibility of acquiring new ones.

ACTION

In order to change, the person has to do something. Change does not
take place through somehow juggling the contents of one's head, but
through placing oneself bodily in a new relationship with the world.
Particularly in the case of someone who has developed complex
strategies for dealing with emotional threat or distress, to change
such strategies demands considerable courage. This is something I
shall return to in the next section, but for the moment I should
like to consider some of the more conceptual difficulties associated
with the idea of adopting new activity.
    The main problem seems to me to lie in the everyday philosophical
assumption to which most of us subscribe, that action is more or
less inextricably linked to reflection; that, for example, before
we do something, we decide to do it, or attempt to calculate its
consequences. I think it possible that sometimes we do make decisions or calculations in this rather cerebral way, but more often
we don't. Like reasons, decisions are on the whole an integral part
of our actions, to be read off from them as they take place. Similarly, our calculations, which of course are closely linked to
reasons, cannot be understood but as a part of our acting. Calculations, moreover, so often prove to be wrong that they would
scarcely provide an adequate ground for action. Rather, it seems
to me, action necessitates a certain kind of commitment, carried
out in the context of faith.
    Lest it seem that these somewhat abstruse speculations are far
removed from the subject of psychotherapy, I should like to stress
that it is precisely in the area of so-called 'neurotic' behaviour
that they seem most cogent. Philosophical discussion of these
issues with patients has often, in my experience, been particularly
effective in helping them to change.
    What seemed to me a very clear, if because very naive, de-
scriptions of committed action was given to me by a boy in early
adolescence who was talking about the feelings involved in, for the
first time, asking a girl who was important to him to dance. 'It's
a funny feeling: you don't know whether you're going to do it, but
suddenly this feeling comes up inside you, and you just sort of find

yourself walking towards them.' Not all occasions, of course, are
as important to us as this one was to him, but it may be that if we
do not recognize his formulation as descriptive of our own more
mundane activity, this is largely because our awareness has been
dulled by long practice.

Many patients (and, of course, not only patients) find themselves, on the other hand, contemplating action, brooding on the
necessity for a prior decision to be made. A young woman described
how she wanted to go out to socialize in the evenings, but couldn't
decide to open the front door. She had, of course, no commitment to
going out, and no faith that anything would be achieved by doing so.
So she interposed between herself and the action a decision that
only served to paralyse her. Similarly, a recently divorced middle-
aged man teeters on the brink of a new relationship with a woman he
does not entirely trust. He is unable to commit himself, but
instead performs endless calculations about the consequences of the
various possibilities open to him ('what if this, what if that').
Acting in the face of threat seems in the end to be something that
people can only do when they give themselves over, in faith, to
commitment. They place themselves in a new relationship to the
world, taking the consequences on trust. In psychotherapy, this
seems to come about when the person recognizes, through his relation
to the therapist, that there is nothing else he can do. Action
demands commitment, faith, and risk.

Whether the risk was worth taking or not can only be learned once
the person has taken up his new stance in the world, and discovered
its consequences. Patients, of course, often have very exaggerated
fears of what may befall them if they change. Left on their own,
they might be paralysed for ever by the enormity of the decisions
they see facing them. What may help them to change is the therapist's feeling that their fears are indeed exaggerated, and his
reassurance and encouragement. Once the change has been made, the
action taken, the patient finds out for himself that it wasn't as
bad as he expected. One of the advantages (of which, practically,
there are several, but conceptually few) of behavioural therapy is
that patients are placed in new relationships to the world, rather
than simply left to ruminate about decisions.

RELATION

The medium of therapeutic learning is the patient's relationship
with his therapist. Early in the history of modern psychotherapy,
C.G.Jung was one of the few therapists who had the courage to point
to the personal nature of this relationship:

> twist and turn the matter as we may, the relation between doctor
> and patient remains a personal one within the impersonal
> framework of professional treatment. By no device can the
> treatment be anything but the product of mutual influence, in
> which the whole being of the doctor as well as that of his
> patient plays its part (Jung, 1954).

A statement such as this takes courage if only because it threatens

the professional, 'expert' status of the therapist. If, for
example, the therapist's relation to his patients is personal, how
can he justify accepting money in return for professional services?
How can he guarantee the validity and effectiveness of his expertise? Most therapists have failed to grasp this nettle with any
firmness, and have instead attempted one way or another to establish
the technical nature of the therapist's role, or, as Jung put it, to
surround themselves 'with a smokescreen of fatherly and professional
authority'.

The early psychoanalysts were emphatic that the therapist should
remain 'neutral' in the therapeutic relationship, restricting himself to the technical task of 'interpreting the transference'. This
kind of stance could not last long in the face of evidence that
neutrality is not something that can be established or imposed uni-
laterally, and that therapists' attempts to be neutral are likely to
be seen by patients as coldness and distance, if not a kind of hostility. Furthermore, research work by Carl Rogers and his associ-
ates suggested that the effective ingredients of therapy were
precisely the personal qualities of therapists, in particular their
warmth, empathy and genuineness towards their clients. However, as
I have already pointed out in relation to empathy, it was not long
before these qualities were once again mechanized, and modern therapists tend to refer to them as aspects of their 'therapeutic skills'
- stock responses that can be switched on or off as the occasion
demands. Even the 'growth movement' in psychotherapy, despite its
avowal of humanistic values and its contempt for orthodox psychology
and psychiatry, has a way of trivializing and mechanizing fundamental aspects of human relations by rendering them technical (a
blistering attack on such approaches, well worth reading, can be
found in Koch, 1971).

The only alternative to this kind of approach, it seems to me, is
to take seriously the personal nature of the therapeutic relationship. Not all psychotherapists have shied away from so doing.
Peter Lomas (1973) courageously identifies love, stripped of all
technical artifice, as the most powerful therapeutic force; Dorothy
Rowe (1978) reveals the healing quality of her gently critical
caring for her clients. It is notable how such therapists do not,
as some others have done, become lost in a welter of sentimentality
or a tangle of mutual dependencies with their clients. What makes
this possible (and psychotherapy a unique form of relationship),
perhaps, is precisely the impersonal framework in which, as Jung
pointed out, it is set. Relationships as intense as those often
involved in psychotherapy would be hard (even if perhaps not impossible) to contain if they were not set in a context in which it
is clear that the therapist's involvement is limited to more or less
set times and places, and so on.

Whatever a person does, it is in relation to, under the gaze of,
others. Loving acceptance validates and makes whole; its withdrawal is annihilating. How uncomfortable it is even to refer to
such topics in the cold context of a technical profession of psychotherapy, and how easy to render them trivial in the process of doing
so!

Apart from caring, there are other characteristics of the therapeutic relationship that make it possible for the patient to learn.

On the whole the best model of therapeutic learning (and perhaps most other kinds of learning as well) seems to me to be that of master and apprentice. The relation of patient to therapist is thus similar to that of apprentice to master. But by no means one-sidedly: if the therapist is to understand his patient, he must also be prepared to make himself the patient's apprentice in coming to appreciate his view of his world. What the master knows in this kind of situation is how to provide the apprentice with the kind of experience which will enable him to learn. Thus, in the therapist's case, he will encourage the patient to take up a certain kind of stance in relation to his environment which will allow the latter, bodily, to experience it in new ways. As, again, Lomas has noted, this is not unlike the relation of patient to child (and it would not seem unreasonable to characterize the child as an apprentice adult).

This implies, of course, that if the therapist is to be a useful master he must have an accurate appreciation of the experience his patient/apprentice needs, and must as a person be in possession of that experience himself. It also implies that his apprentice may eventually surpass him in the very skills and qualities he helped him to acquire.

I have chosen the master/apprentice model because it seems to me to be one which acknowledges that although, inevitably, some people are more capable or knowledgeable than others, knowledge and capability are acquisitions open to anybody and are not just the property of 'experts'. Initially, the master is able to do things which the apprentice is not, but, finally, the apprentice may be able to do them better. Moreover, the master does not pass on his ability: his knowledge consists rather in helping the apprentice's ability to be drawn out. He suggests to the apprentice a certain stance in the world that will afford the latter the experience necessary to discover what he can do. If he is to be successful, the master must also be ready to learn from his apprentice, and continually to modify his approach to the apprentice's special characteristics. This is not the formal superiority of the professional expert, but the facilitation of a process in which skills and abilities may evolve to ever higher levels in those who are permitted to develop them. I do not wish to suggest by this that psychotherapists are or should be people who have mastered the conflicts and difficulties of living - life cannot be arranged through any amount of skill to be painless - but rather that they know some of the ways in which pain may be faced, and have met some of the situations that generate it. Certainly, it helps if the therapist can recognize in his own experience the difficulties of which his patients talk; if he cannot, he must do his best to apprentice himself to his patients in order to learn their difficulties for himself.

In this way, the therapist cannot change the patient through the application of technical rules read off from some kind of diagnostic manual, but, through negotiation, develops with him a shared context of personal meaning which enables him to encourage the patient to take up a new stance in the world - a stance, furthermore, which, because of his own personal experience, the therapist confidently expects to be fruitful. Like a good master, he knows what to expect, even if the patient does not.

There can be no technical guarantee of a therapist's effectiveness. However unusual it may be for someone to set himself up as
an expert professional on the grounds of little more than his
qualities as a person, it seems that we must acknowledge that this
is the case with psychotherapy. However, there should of course be
safeguards: it seems reasonable to expect, for instance, that
therapists should be exposed to the kinds of experience which will
allow them to develop and refine their personal qualities and to
acquire the kind of intellectual appreciation of their calling which
enables them to examine and make explicit what they are doing. It
is presumably also important for them to be subject to the (negotiative) scrutiny of their colleagues.

What I have tried to suggest in this chapter, then, is that the
nature of psychotherapy is such that we can only be radically un-
compromising in our rejection of a mechanistic explanation of its
functioning. Psychotherapy is fundamentally a personal activity for
both therapist and patient, and can be developed and discussed conceptually only through use of a language which takes account of
this. Concepts such as negotiation, action, relation, self-deception, responsibility, courage, etc., may of course not prove to
be the most useful in enabling us to develop our appreciation of
psychotherapy as a process of personal learning, but at least, I
should wish to argue, they do not frustrate it. For this reason
alone, I would consider them more scientific than many of their
competitors.

REFERENCES

Fingarette, H. (1969), 'Self-Deception', Routledge & Kegan Paul,
London.
Frank, J.D. (1973), 'Persuasion and Healing', Johns Hopkins
University Press, Baltimore.
Gauld, A. and Shotter, J. (1977), 'Human Action and its Psycho-
logical Investigation', Routledge & Kegan Paul, London.
Harré, R. and Secord, P.F. (1972), 'The Explanation of Social
Behaviour', Blackwell, Oxford.
Illich, I. (1975), 'Medical Nemesis', Calder & Boyars, London.
Jung, C.G. (1954), 'The Practice of Psychotherapy', Collected Works
vol.XVI, Routledge & Kegan Paul, London.
Koch, S. (1971), The Image of Man Implicit in Encounter-Group
Theory, in 'Journal of Humanistic Psychology', 11, p.109.
Lomas, P. (1973), 'True and False Experience', Allen Lane, London.
Merleau-Ponty, M. (1962), 'Phenomenology of Perception', Routledge
& Kegan Paul, London.
Polanyi, M. (1958), 'Personal Knowledge', Routledge & Kegan Paul,
London.
Rowe, D. (1978), 'The Experience of Depression', Wiley, Chichester.
Sartre, J.-P. (1969), 'Being and Nothingness', Methuen, London.
Sloane, R.B., Staples, F.R., Cristoll, A.H., Yorkston, N.J. and
Whipple, K. (1975), 'Psychotherapy versus Behavior Therapy', Harvard
University Press, Cambridge, Mass.
Smail, D.J. (1978), 'Psychotherapy: A Personal Approach', Dent,
London.

INDEX

action: dramatic, 152-69;
    learning as, 176,182;
    logic of, 148; need for,
    178-9; Piaget on, 159,169;
    and play, 160-2; reasons
    for, 74-6; and speech,
    159-60
actual self, perceived, 3-4
adolescence: and adults, 168;
    in Africa, 100; and
    feelings, 178; friendships,
    79,89; identification in,
    79; and reading, 56-7
adults, 163,168
Africa, 94-108,140-1
agency, in family, 9
aggression, 30,84
alcoholism, 3
alienation, 41; see also
    failure; maladjustment
Almquist, E., 92
Angrist, S., 92
Argyle, M., 155,169
Ariès, P., 29,32
Arnold, K., 82-3,91
assessment, teaching for, 39-44
attitudes: to knowledge, 9;
    to women, 69-93
attribution theory, 137

babies, 8,15; see also children
Bakan, D., 9,15,30,32,88,92
Barthies, R., 62
Baur, M., 19,21,23
behaviour: disruptive, 26-7,32;
    good, 23-33; sex-typed,

85-90; variations, 77-80;
    see also discipline;
    psychology
behaviourism, 7,135,139
beliefs, 141
Berger, P., 7,15
betrayal, 122
Birdwhistell, R., 155,169
body language, 152,155,158-9
bookishness, 49,58; see also
    reading; literacy
boys, 87-90; see also children;
    masculinity
brainwashing, 11
Brecht, B., 157-8
Breen, D., 78,92
Britton, J., 60
Broverman, I. and D., 93,143,150
Bruner, J., 154,168-9
Bullock, Sir A., 52

Canada, higher education in,
    109-10
Carlson, R., 88,92
careers, women's, 73
case studies, see psychotherapy
Cassirer, E., 152,155-7,169
Cazden, C., 154,169
change, 124-5,141
children: as mini-adults, 85;
    and peers, 23,26,31;
    unhappy, 26-9; and women's
    roles, 85-90; see also
    babies; boys; family;
    girls; pupil
Chodorow, N., 86-92 passim

183